HOUNDS

HUNTING BY SCENT

BLOODHOUND.
Excellent nose but not shaped for speed.
Champion Ledburn *Beau Brummel.*

FELL HOUND OF CUMBERLAND.
Symmetrically made for rough country. *Kiskin,*
champion Eskdale and Ennerdale Hunt Show.

PENNSYLVANIA HOUND.
Excellent nose and cry.

BIG STRIDE.
S. L. Wooldridge's famous field trial Walker
hound.

SIR EDWARD CURRE'S CROSS-BRED
WELSH BITCH, *Hefty.*
Imported and photographed by the author, 1922.
These hounds have excellent nose and cry.

ROUGH-COATED WELSH.
Excellent nose and cry. *Conqueror,* res.
champion Welsh National Hound Show.

TAUNTON VALE HARRIER.
An active small hound. Photo by author, 1922.

FRENCH STAGHOUND.
Notable for size.

HOUNDS
HUNTING BY SCENT

David Hancock

The Crowood Press

Previous Books by the Author
Dogs As Companions – 1981
Old Working Dogs – 1984 (reprinted 1998 and 2011)
The Heritage of the Dog – 1990
The Bullmastiff: A Breeder's Guide Vol 1 – 1996
The Bullmastiff: A Breeder's Guide Vol 2 – 1997
Old Farm Dogs – 1999
The Mastiffs: The Big Game Hunters – 2000–06 (six editions)
The Bullmastiff: A Breeder's Guide – 2006 (one volume hardback edition)
The World of the Lurcher – 2010
Sporting Terriers: Their Form, Their Function and Their Future – 2011
Sighthounds: Their Form, Their Function and Their Future – 2012
Gundogs – Their Past, Their Performance and Their Prospects – 2013

First published in 2014 by
The Crowood Press Ltd
Ramsbury, Marlborough
Wiltshire SN8 2HR

www.crowood.com

British Library Cataloguing-in-Publication Data
A catalogue record for this book is available from the British Library.

ISBN 978 1 84797 601 7

Page 1: Late 18th-century hunting scene – *Sporting Magazine* frontispiece.
Page 2: Types of modern hound from *Hounds and Hunting through the Ages* by Joseph B. Thomas MFH, 1928.
Page 3: German scent hound.
Page 5: The Hunts of Maximilian, 1520.

Typeset and designed by D & N Publishing, Baydon, Wiltshire
Printed and bound in Malaysia by Times Offset Sdn Bhd

CONTENTS

DEDICATION

This book is dedicated to the seekers of excellence in our native hound breeds, and, in the packs, to devoted huntsmen like Will Goodall and Joe Bowman and influential Masters such as Sir Edward Curre and Sir Ian Heathcoat-Amory, whose devotion and commitment has allowed us to enjoy and admire the remarkably gifted and distinctive breeds of hounds that hunt by scent in so many different countries around the world. We owe them an immense debt of gratitude for their inspired work over several centuries. May we honour their memory by producing hounds that they themselves would have been proud of; these remarkable dogs are under unprecedented threat in an increasingly urban world. We need to meet that threat by breeding high-quality hounds – perhaps for different purposes than past sportsmen had ever intended but providing a spiritual outlet for the outstanding hounds they bequeathed to us. In conserving such superb canine athletes we pay respect to our sporting forefathers and their immense achievement in developing them for our enjoyment today.

Valued Hunt Servants: Anthony Chapman (Windermere Harriers) and Joe Bowman (Ullswater Foxhounds). (Photo: Richard Chapman 1932).

Sir Ian Heathcoat Amory with the Tiverton Hounds (Lionel Edwards, 1929).

ABOVE: *Will Goodall of the Pytchley, with the Earl and Countess Spencer (John Charlton. 1930).*

RIGHT: *Sir William Curre with his famous hounds (Lionel Edwards, 1929).*

PREFACE

Who is not stirred by the sheer dash, unrestrained joy and committed enthusiasm of a pack of hounds in full cry! It's part of our sporting heritage; it's in *our* blood as well as theirs. This book is a celebration of the scenthound, whether British, French, American or a lesser-known breed from the Baltic or the Balkans. These remarkably talented hounds were specifically bred over many centuries to have quite remarkable scenting power, often at some speed. We need to respect their heritage and breed them in a way that is honest towards their past and not in pursuit of some contemporary whim. This means being faithful to their breed history and not ignoring it out of modern haste and arrogance. If we are not aware of how they came into being, exactly what they were designed for and precisely how they functioned in the field, how can we breed them true?

Those who use dogs – sportsmen, hunters, shepherds and ranchers – demand dogs with a capability. The hunting world both here and overseas has long sought field excellence ahead of any cosmetic value or respect for registries. The maintenance of a stud-book has for them been important as a breeding record, not the dogmatic insistence on a closed gene-pool, come what may. Writing in *Hounds* magazine in 2004, Charles Fielding, an acknowledged expert on hound breeding, used these words: 'Fortunately hounds are bred from in the winter when their working abilities are foremost in the mind, but woe betide anyone who tries to breed for looks alone.' It is hard to imagine any breed registered with the Kennel Club (KC) following such a philosophy. Breed purity and cosmetic appeal has in so many breeds held sway over soundness, health, historic type and ability to fulfil the breed's original purpose, aspects covered here. This book is not a manual covering breeding, nutrition, care and maintenance, but an examination of the origin of the hound breeds, their function as sporting dogs, their current flaws and their future in an increasingly non-sporting world.

Generally speaking, in the world of dogs, kennel clubs keep the breeds going and sportsmen keep the functions alive. Our KC does stage field trials, working tests, agility and obedience events but it's sportsmen who *use* hounds, gundogs and terriers as sporting assistants. They rely on the KC to bring structure and

The Chase *by Walter Hunt, 1912.*

This is the Dachsbracke – the German Badger Hound.

German hunter with his Schweisshund, 1890.

discipline to the breeding and trialling of dogs. But some canine body really should sort out nomenclature and Group allocation in breeds of dog, as this affects not just the quality of Group judging knowledge in the show ring but also their future design. The Dachshund, for example, is recognized by our KC as a hound, perhaps because the word 'hund' was interpreted as hound, whereas it actually means dog.

The Dachshund is no 'running dog', very much an earth-dog, and is not covered by this book. The Dachs-**bracke**, the German badger-**hound**, is included.

In the medieval hunt, terms used then were also loosely applied, with perhaps the best explanation being in the Appendix to the Baillie-Grohman's editing of *The Master of Game*, the Duke of York's translation of Gaston de Foix's *Livre de Chasse* of

Wild Boar Hunt *by R.J. Savery (1576–1639); bandogge on left.*

TOP: *Young man with his Zwicdarm or strong-headed sighthound/ par force hound: A. Moro's* Le Nain du Cardinal Granville.

BOTTOM: *Seventeenth-century hunting scene –* The Hunting Party *by Jan Fyt (1609–61).*

1387. Hunting mastiffs were alauntes; brachets or bercelets were hunting dogs that accompanied those who shot their furred game (rather like the Bavarian Mountain Hounds of today, with their valued tracking skills) but could also mean small bitch hounds; lymers or limiers were leashed scenthounds, used rather as 'tufters' are used in the Staghound packs; raches were the smaller, mainly white packhounds but could also refer to bitch hounds; bandogges were the ferocious 'seizers', slipped at the kill, to save the more valued running hounds; greyhounds were the Grehounds or levriers, not the modern breed of Greyhound, with the fierce and shaggy Irish and Scottish Deerhounds called the *'levrier d'attache'* or 'held-dog' and the smaller, smooth-coated hound, the *'petit levrier pour lievre'* or small harehound. A brace, or more usually a brace and a half, was held by a fewterer. Heyrers were the tricolour Harriers of today; gazehounds, not used in couples, were used in packs 'at force'.

The word 'forest' once referred to any area of ground used for hunting, not a sizeable wood. The word 'deer' was used to denote any animal, hence the German word 'tier' for animal. Researchers using medieval sources need to be aware of such past meanings. In his exhaustive *Lexicon of the Medieval German Hunt* (1965), David Dalby lists the various terms for hunting dogs used then. The word *wint* was used to denote both the purpose-bred Greyhound and the heavier *veltre* or *zwic-darm*, which was a blend of hound – Mastiff and Greyhound – resembling the bull lurchers of today.

The German boarhound or Great Dane (known there as the Deutsche Dogge or German Mastiff – the Danish Mastiff is the Broholmer) will always be a hound, despite its Group allocation by kennel clubs. The Dalmatian may well be the medieval 'dama-chien' or deer-dog and a genuine hound (*see* later section on Staghounds). The Mastiff was once prized as a heavy hound – the famed Englische Dogge. The ancestors of the Bulldog were also used in the hunting field – the *'bullenbeissers'* of central Europe. But then the Hound Group has long been basically ill-composed; there were always four types of hound, never just scenthounds and sighthounds. As discussed later, a more accurate composition would be a four-way split identifying: hounds that hunt by speed (sighthounds), those that hunt by

Fourth-century votive relief, Crannon, Greece; Molossian Dog depicted on right.

stamina (scenthounds), those that hunt 'at force' (par force hounds, like the Great Dane and the Rhodesian Ridgeback) and the heavy hounds, including the holding dogs, perpetuated today by some of the mastiff breeds. The international kennel club, the Federation Cynologique Internationale (FCI), now acknowledges 'dogues', dogges or mastiffs, separately from 'molossers'. The molossian dog is well recorded by the ancient Greeks, who described two forms: the huge shepherd's dog or flock guardian, usually white, and a giant hound.

In a later chapter, I devote space to the evolution of both the Rhodesian Ridgeback and the Dogo Argentino, two breeds created, unusually, in recorded history and therefore authentically exemplifying the way breed design was shaped by function. Does it really matter, getting a breed's history or its original function wrong? I believe it does and that a verified provenance can have value for the dogs of today. The breeds of hounds that hunt by scent, using stamina to run down their quarry, have served man for over ten millennia, filling his pot, providing sport and supporting man, in what he has always been, a hunter. We must now keep faith, both with our ancestors, who left these superb canine athletes in our care, and with our hounds, by breeding them to *function*, not just for cosmetic appeal. This book is a plea for just that.

The illustrations in this book, apart from exemplifying the text, tell a story too; as Aubrey Noakes wrote in his *Sportsmen in a Landscape*:

The English aristocracy and landed gentry from the

seventeenth to the nineteenth century enjoyed great privileges and wealth, yet most of them preferred country life and sport to a town existence. This preference is reflected in the pictures they commissioned. Thus English sporting pictures are not only to be cherished as memorials of old sporting occasions, but should be regarded as useful guides to an understanding of our social past.

The Lost Hounds, *depicted in 1810.*

ACKNOWLEDGEMENTS

The author is grateful to the staff at Sotheby's Picture Library, Christie's Images Ltd., Bonhams, Arthur Ackermann Ltd, David Messum Galleries, Richard Green & Co., Rountree Fine Art, The Bridgeman Art Library, The Nature Picture Library, The National Art Library, The Wallace Collection, R Cox & Co., Lane Fine Art, The Kennel Club, The American Kennel Club, The National Trust, The Royal Collection – Photographic Services and private collectors, (especially the late Mevr AH (Ploon) de Raad of Zijderveld, Holland, who gave free use of her extensive photographic archive of sporting paintings), for their gracious and generous permissions to reproduce some of the illustrations used in this book.

AUTHOR'S NOTE

A number of the illustrations in this book lack pictorial quality but are included because uniquely they either contribute historically to or best exemplify the meaning of the text. Old depictions do not always lend themselves to reproduction in today's higher quality print and publishing format. Those that are included have significance beyond their graphic limitations and I ask for the reader's understanding over this.

Where quotes are used, they are used verbatim, despite any vagaries in spelling, irregular use of capital letters or departures from contemporary grammar. For me, it is important that their exact form, as presented by the author originally, is displayed, as this can help to capture the mood of those times.

Return from the hunt: German nobleman with tracking hound, 1874.

German hunter with tracking hound c.1890.

HOUNDS AND THE HUNTING HABIT

A vast collection of hound lore has accumulated over the centuries, some authentic and much legendary and false, but it is true to say that few animals have given so much sport and pleasure to men and women as the branch of the canine world known as hounds…Hounds are a familiar sight in the English countryside and there are few people, countryman or townsman alike, whose hearts do not beat faster when they hear the cry and see a fast hunting pack streaming over plough and field on a good scenting day… For centuries, hounds have been stitched into the tapestry of British sporting history…

C.G.E. Wimhurst, *The Book of the Hound* (1964)

Anyone contemplating the writing of a book entitled *Hounds of the World* has a job on their hands if the title is truly to reflect the text. Wherever man existed he utilized hunting dogs; the immense spread of hound breeds in the inhabited world and the sheer multi-plicity of local types indicates their value to man. We in Britain are rightly proud of our packhound breeds and very aware of the merit of the French breeds. But we have long been almost dismissive of the lesser-known scenthounds from more distant smaller countries or remote areas of bigger countries. The recognition of breeds is a haphazard matter in any country; our Foxhound has more varieties than the Belgian Shepherd Dog or the Dachshund, without earning a name for each of them. Our Harrier too has its Studbook and West Country varieties. In France, where they even named their crossbred hounds as distinct breeds – like the Anglo-Poitevin or the Anglo-Gascon-Saintongeois, the Foxhound crosses with native hounds – this would have soon been resolved. In the Balkans and Eastern Europe they are only just recognizing some of their native hound breeds – realizing the importance of their sporting heritage – and this is covered in Chapter 3.

In Hot Pursuit, Foxhunting, *1890.*

Three French hounds: (from left to right) Anglo-Poitevin, Saintongeois; Chien Courant de l'Ariege; and Race de Virelade.

A Group of Gascon-Saintongeois cross Foxhound hybrids.

Varying Recognition

Here, our KC recognizes fewer than twenty different breeds in its Hound Group that are not sighthounds, choosing to exclude our own Harrier (which it once recognized) and the German Boarhound or Great Dane (whose omission is covered in a later chapter), but including six breeds of Dachshund, whose principal function was that of an earth dog or terrier, and is therefore not covered in this book (but covered in depth in my *Sporting Terriers*, Crowood, 2011). The FCI recognizes nearly fifty in its Group 6 (Scenthounds), including our Harrier, but not the Dachshund, or the Basenji (as we do in our Hound Group), and puts the Spitz hounds into a Nordic Type section. The FCI does, however, rightly in my view, consider the Dalmatian to be a hound. They recognize the Bloodhound as the Saint Hubert Hound. We put the Dalmatian (and two Japanese hunting dogs, the Akita and the Shiba Inu) into the Utility Group. This mismatch causes problems for judges, whose expertise may not embrace the breeds they encounter abroad. It is not exactly helpful either for breeders of Great Danes and Dalmatians: should their dogs be hound-like or indeed be designed for any one single hunting field function?

Dalmatian greets Great Dane – two lost hound breeds (photo: David Lindsey).

Dachsbracke (on left) and Schweisshund in late nineteenth-century German stag hunt.

Imprecise Division

I argue on succeeding pages that the division of hounds into two categories: scent and sighthounds, is too arbitrary. All hounds hunt by sight and scent; the scenthounds succeed in the hunt because of their stamina, the sighthounds because of their speed. But

where do the 'par force' hounds fit into this? They hunted, and in some countries still do, 'at force' using scent and sight, being represented today by breeds like the Great Dane, the Rhodesian Ridgeback, the Dogo Argentino (all of which are later covered in more detail, because their evolution was recorded) and the Black Mouth Cur. And what about the hunting mastiffs used to close with big game and then 'hold' it, represented today by the mastiff breeds?

Rhodesian Ridgeback displaying its distinctive ridge.

Black Mouth Cur – famous treeing breed.

They were the heavy hounds but languish in the KC's Working Group. They are covered by this book, however, and their role explained.

The national kennel clubs of the world are guilty of neglecting the rich heritage behind their native breeds of dog. It may be timely for the Masters of packhounds to do more to educate the public at large about Britain's scenthound heritage and spread the word beyond hunt followers. This book is intended to stimulate a wider interest in the world of the scenthound. It is a much wider world than our show rings and hound shows indicate. The scenthounds of the world are remarkable animals; their heritage is one to be celebrated.

Hunting Style

Function and therefore type in hounds is directly related to hunting styles. In his mighty tome *An Encyclopaedia of Rural Sports* of 1870, Delabere Blaine summed up hunting in Britain down the ages:

> The records of the British chase, previous to the Roman invasion are few and uncertain… The invasion of the Romans did not probably restrict the venatorial pursuits of the Britons… The Saxons, in common with all the northern intruders, were much more attached to hunting than the Romans… Early in the fourteenth century hunting was becoming an organized as well as a popular pursuit…the fox also became an object of the sportsman's search in the succeeding centuries… Of hunting generally it may be remarked, that it became truly an organized pursuit during the last century only, since which time considerable alterations have occurred in the practice of it. Indeed, the opinions and habits of the sportsmen themselves, the horses they ride, and the dogs they employ, have all been for some years past undergoing a gradual change.

If one word had to be chosen to typify the hunting habit in Britain it would have to be 'change', constant change. This has meant the hounds adapting too.

In his book *Monarchy and the Chase* of 1944, 'Sabretache' wrote:

> All these Norman kings, whatever their misdeeds in other regions, were unquestionably imbued with a genuine love of hunting, the conqueror being both knowledgeable, and, at the same time, the best veneur, and, likewise, the man who did a very great deal to improve the breed of the indigenous horse. He knew what to do and he did it. Though the Conqueror did not initiate hunting in England, to his credit it must be recorded that he added a few weighty stones to the foundations laid by the Saxons.

What disparate influences: ancient British, Roman, Saxon, Norman styles, and each of them affected by social attitudes as well. Hunting styles change and with them the hounds change as well; the quarry of course played a key part in their development too.

Noble Patronage

> If any huntsman had been bold enough to suggest to William the Conqueror that stag hunting was on the way out and that the noble staghound would be forced to give way to a hound bred to hunt the fox, it is possible he would have been executed on the spot… And it would have sounded like nonsense because, in 1066, and for many centuries afterwards, the fox was vermin and every effort was made to stamp out the species. They were driven into nets, clubbed to death, trapped, and any method was considered good provided it ended in the death of a fox. The stag and the hare reigned supreme although, it must be admitted, it was the practice of many hunts to chase anything that turned up.
>
> C.G.E. Wimhurst, *The Book of the Hound* (1964)

> The eighteenth century was the golden age of field sports in Britain. Shooting over pointers, which were also expected to retrieve the game shot, hunting with the new breeds of foxhounds, coursing, or hare or otter hunting were the regular sports of the countryside… Buck hunting was also growing less common and red deer, as noted, was only extensively hunted in the West Country.
>
> Michael Brander, *Hunting and Shooting* (1971)

These two quotes summarize very neatly the way in which hunting habits – and therefore the hounds in support, can change century by century, and, as the twenty-first century is already indicating, external pressures on hunting can have highly significant, but hopefully not permanent, effects. In Victorian times, the nobility and landed gentry had a huge influence on dogs, sporting breeds especially. In his *Monarchy and the Chase* of 1944, 'Sabretache' wrote:

> If Victoria the Good had been a hunting lady, she would have at once realized the fact that when she came to the throne her country was little short of a hunting paradise. Hounds had improved out of all knowledge; the well-bred hunter was in similar pro-fusion…

There were 200 packs of Foxhounds, with the Duke of Beaufort, Earl Bathurst, the Earls of Lonsdale, of Derby and of Darlington, Viscount Portman and Lords Donerail, Portsmouth, Fitzhardinge, Coventry and Bentinck taking a keen interest. Lord Bagot showed Bloodhounds and Lord Wolverton ran a pack of them in Dorset, later sold to Lord Carrington in Buckinghamshire. The Marquis of Anglesea kept Harriers and Sir John Heathcote-Amory favoured Staghounds. The Duke of Atholl maintained a pack of Otterhounds, as did the Marquis of Conyngham in Ireland.

TOP RIGHT: The Beaufort Hounds *by Alfred Wheeler (1851–1932).*

MIDDLE: Two 1905 Peterborough champion Foxhounds: Earl Bathurst's Damsel and Harper of the Fitzwilliam.

The Portman Kennels *by Lionel Edwards, 1933.*

But this was a time of social change, with newly wealthy sportsmen entering the hunting field as well as the country sports world more generally. Many were livestock breeders too.

Enlightened Breeding

The early years of the twentieth century saw the West Country continuing to favour its Staghounds and Harriers, the Basset Hound becoming the choice of some hare-hunters and significant changes in Foxhound breeding; the importance of an infusion of Welsh Hound and Fell Hound blood into many packs, as well as the value of the Belvoir stallion hounds, was recognized. More importantly, the emphasis on drive, nose, cry and pace led to the development of more athletic, lighter, less-boney hounds.

The main instigator of this was Sir Edward Curre at the Chepstow Hunt. By the end of the Great War he had already had some twenty years of combining the merits of top quality English bitches with proven Welsh stallion hounds, usually in a white or light jacket. He inspired others like Sir Ian Amory of the Tiverton and Isaac Bell of the South and West Wilts and influenced the Heythrop, North Cotswold and Cattistock packs. Out went the massively timbered so-called 'bovines' and less favoured were the clas-

TOP LEFT: *The Earl of Lonsdale in Kennels.*

MIDDLE: *The Marquis of Conyngham's Otterhounds, 1936.*

LEFT: The Earl of Darlington's Kennels *by Henry Chalon, 1813.*

ABOVE LEFT: The Pride of the Belvoir *by John Emms, 1841–1912.*

ABOVE RIGHT Fell-type bitch in the Ullswater, 1932.

RIGHT: Welsh Hounds by Arthur Wardle, 1897.

sic tricoloured Belvoir markings. By the 1930s, the 'Peterborough type' had been superseded by the lighter-boned, pacier hounds with better stamina. The importance of the 'female line' in breeding was recognized, overcoming the slavish adherence to the 'sire-dominated' thinking of the previous century. The Harrier packs maintained their more balanced approach to hound breeding.

Riding to or Hunting with

It could be said that after the First World War, hunting the fox with hounds moved on to become riding to hounds. The distinguished American Master of Foxhounds (MFH), Joseph B. Thomas, describes this well in his important book, *Hounds and Hunting Through the Ages*, published in New York in 1937:

The Curre white hounds by T. Ivester Lloyd, 1937.

In Britain hunting to ride is now all the vogue as opposed to riding to hunt: quick bursts lifting hounds to holloas and over numerous foxes have played havoc with veritable hunting in the old sense… The deliberately dishonest huntsman is inexcusable, he ruins hounds and he deceives his followers. Cheering hounds to a false line, laying drags, dropping foxes at the end of a drag line, making his field believe hounds are hunting a fox when they are in reality hunting the huntsman, expressed mildly some of his whiles… In England, where a huntsman's tips depend largely on his reputation as a 'smart' huntsman giving the riding contingent many short quick gallops, it is also a great temptation for a huntsman to be euphemistically speaking a faker.

These are strong words, but need noting. For me the 'thrill' of the chase lies in watching hounds at work, not horses jumping, much as I enjoy steeplechases and point to points. The joy of seeing supremely fit, strongly motivated hounds surely lifts the spirits of every dog-lover.

Persistent Faults

A hound show like those at Peterborough, Harrogate, Ardingly, Rydal, Honiton or Builth Wells should be

a joy to visit if you admire fit dogs, dogs in tip-top condition. At a number of recent hound shows I have been disappointed to see some of the long acknowledged scenthound flaws creeping back in: fleshy feet, bunched toes, toeing-in, over-boning at the knee and forelegs arrow-straight when viewed from the side, allowing no 'give' in the pasterns. Towards the end of the nineteenth century, the Foxhound fraternity lost its collective head, prizing massive bone, knuckling over at the knee, bunched toes and toeing-in, during what the well-known hound writer Daphne Moore, in her *Foxhounds* of 1981, referred to as the 'shorthorn' era. If experienced huntsmen can lose their way so catastrophically, it is hardly surprising if breeders of breeds recognized by the KC – who do not 'work' their animals – get lost sometimes. The draught-dog bone strangely desired in the Mastiff, the muzzle-less Bulldog and the long list of terrier breeds with upright shoulders, despite the wording of their breed standard, exemplify how breeders and fanciers, and clearly not just show ones, can lose their way. Dogs, hounds especially, are functional creatures, subject to our whims. If those possessing those whims lose sight of function then a dark shadow looms over a breed.

At KC-licensed shows, the lack of fitness amongst most of the exhibits is a cause of concern. Judges, in their critiques, mention poor movement in breed

RIGHT: *Puckeridge Foxhounds Colonist and Cardinal, 1902 by G. Paice.*

BELOW RIGHT: *Judging at the Peterborough Show, 1890.*

after breed; a fit dog will *always* move better than an unfit one. Old-timers knew this and resorted to road-work, not just to tighten up the feet but to improve movement. Packhounds at hound shows are always supremely fit and it is such a source of pleasure to see such animals on the move: effortless power, utter harmony, perfect balance, rippling muscles, coats with a real bloom. The condition and physical soundness of the hounds of the pack are timely reminders to *all* hound owners that their dogs need to be regarded as canine athletes not ornamental possessions, deprived of exercise, of spiritual nutriment and of 'instinct-outlets'; hounds need to be indulged but not spoiled, their latent longings respected. Hunting may be at the mercy of contemporary thinking, but the needs of the hounds are eternal. Hunting, as a sport, may have become contentious; the fundamental needs of the hounds may require redirecting, but their skills are precious and really have to be conserved.

Misplaced Compassion

After the all-time high of hunting in the 1930s, the Second World War, as had the First, devastated the hunting field, the packs especially. The requirement for maximum food production, extensive afforestation and wide-reaching social change altered not just the hunting

country but public attitudes to the sport. Significantly, the leading animal charity, the RSPCA, despite having been founded by the keen foxhunter Richard Martin, mounted a much more militant opposition to all hunting with dogs. The anti-hunting pressure-group, the League Against Cruel Sports (LACS), managed to capture the new generation of young activists, as well as considerable funding. The defection from LACS of three leaders: Richard Course, Jim Barrington and Graham Sirl, when they realized that a hunting ban would not prevent the death or suffering of foxes and might well increase suffering and death rates, has been strangely overlooked by both loud-voiced politicians and the lazier mainstream media outlets.

In contemporary Britain, consensual moral vanity has invaded the sphere of individual conscience and instigated major change, certainly creating changes in hunting habits, and not entirely to the benefit of the quarry. Nowadays the word hunting has come to mean foxhunting, which in itself has wider-ranging perils. The mean-spirited Hunting Act of 2004 was aimed at 'men in pink' and admitted to be, by more honest politicians, an act of class warfare rather than an animal welfare move. How many of them know of the fifty-year-old Banwen Miners Hunt? The fact that this Act has achieved what Danish kings, Norman knights and urban-dwelling wealthy reformists failed to do over a whole millennium – the denial of a working man his freedom to hunt – seems to have escaped contemporary socialist thinking. There is rich irony in the fact that communist gurus such as Lenin and

Engels were keen hunters, the latter riding to hounds with the Cheshire hunt. If animals have 'rights', do hounds not have a 'right' to hunt naturally?

There is sadness in seeing foxes, maimed by an inaccurate shot, struggling to survive in remoter country areas; if foxes have to be controlled then surely the most humane method of dispatching them should be pursued. The bare fact that this is best achieved by the lead Foxhound and not a riskier shotgun blast seems to have little appeal for today's welfarists. Personal prejudice should never override honest humanity. Foxhunting is casually described as a country sport, but at its very least, it is in reality a form of humane enlightened pest control that has both shaped our countryside and created a rural pastime that enjoys a dedicated following. Hare-shoots can be like a slaughterhouse; hare-hunting allows escape. Even those with hostile views on hunting can wax lyrical about a pack of hounds simply

Hare hounds fail to spot the hare, 1897.

Counting the bag after a hare shoot, 1947.

flowing over the countryside. Hunting has long been best regulated by those who respect their quarry and have an interest in their perpetuation. For a thousand years hounds were considered the best tool to control recognized quarry; they still are! This book campaigns for hounds, whether here or abroad, in packs or in domestic kennels, to be *used*!

> One of the best features of hunting is that it gives all classes a chance of meeting on terms of equality. In the hunting field all men are equal with the exception of the master and the huntsman – they should be absolute autocrats. The peer must take a back seat if the butcher with a bold heart can pound him over a big fence.
>
> Otho Paget, *Hunting* (1900)

It is very important that foxhounds catch enough foxes to justify their existence. Farmers and shooting people expect it and it is up to the hunt to keep the balance of the right number for their country, other-wise every 'Tom, Dick or Harry' starts having a go, often with cruel results. In a hill country it is essential to catch every fox possible, leaving only the minimum for the continuance of the species. Harehounds have no such duty and a large tally is meaningless.

'Hareless', writing in *Hounds* magazine (December 1989)

> Critics say that hunting cannot possibly be a form of pest control as they kill so few compared with other methods. This is to fundamentally misunderstand hunting and wildlife management. Wildlife management is not about numbers killed, but the health and size of the population left alive. A hunt is perfectly suited to achieving this, being a combination of sport, wildlife management and pest control and not just any one of those things.
>
> Jim Barrington, Countryside Alliance animal welfare consultant, writing on political website www.politics.co.uk (January 2013)

CHAPTER 1

THE SCENTHOUND PROVENANCE

It is easy to visualize the gradual domestication of the dog. It is likely that the forerunners of the modern hunting dog were slinking, furtive creatures, allies in hunting, like the jackal following the lion pack, for what they might gain as a result. While hanging about the cave mouth ready to seize any scrap of meat or bones available, they would also give warning of any intruder. Gradually, as man established his ascendancy, so the dog became at least semi-domesticated. As the young of each played and tumbled together in the dust outside the cave, so that essential bond between hunter and hunting dog was formed.

Michael Brander, *Hunting and Shooting* (1971)

Origins and Ancestry

I believe that in the domestication of the dog, the hounds came first, not of course looking like contemporary breeds of hound in conformation, but first in functional use for man. The seventeenth-century French naturalist, Buffon, I know, for one, argued that the sheepdogs came before them but I can find no logic in that. To use sheepdogs primitive man had first to become a farmer of sorts yet man was a hunter-gatherer long, long before he became a farmer, although I acknowledge that in some places sheep were domesticated before dogs. The sheep-

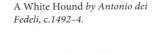

A White Hound *by Antonio dei Fedeli, c.1492–4.*

OPPOSITE PAGE

TOP RIGHT: *Strongly made Hound, Graeco-Egyptian bronze, third century* BC.

BOTTOM: *The Boar Hunt by Johann Ridinger, 1729. The 'seizers' rush to the boar.*

dog's instinct for rounding up numbers of sheep or singling one out for attention almost certainly developed from the hunting style of primitive wild dog and is still practised in the wild today.

Before man kept animals of his own, he needed to fill his pot with the meat of wild animals and what better ally than a tamed wild dog acting as a hound. Such a canine ally could assist man to locate game in the first place, be used to drive the game towards precipices, pits or human hunters with their primitive weapons, such as spears. Subsequently these domesticated dogs were to be trained to drive selected game into specially constructed enclosures or into cleverly positioned nets. In due course very fast game was hunted using very fast dogs, big game was hunted with big dogs or hunting mastiffs and feathered game hunted using dogs that could either silently (like a setter) or noisily (like a bark-pointer) indicate the location of the quarry. In time the tracking dogs became specialist hounds, able to hunt boar or hare, wild asses or deer, bison or elk. In Europe, the names of the early breeds in the hunting field indicate their function: *Bufalbeisser* (buffalo-biter), *Bärenbeisser* (bear-biter) and *Bullenbeisser* (wild bull-biter).

Danziger Bährenbeißer

Niederländischer Bollbeisser.

TOP LEFT: *The Danzig 'bear-biter' or holding dog used on bear.*

TOP RIGHT: *The Netherlands bull-biter or Dutch holding dog, used as a 'pinner' of bulls.*

LEFT: *Stag hunting using nets and hounds by Johann Ridinger, 1729.*

The Ancient World

Much is made by breed historians of the hounds of Egypt, Greece and Rome, and certainly the Celts, the Greeks and the Romans greatly prized their hunting dogs and left descriptions of them. Hounds were extremely valuable as pot-fillers and were therefore extensively traded, but there is ample evidence of hound-like dogs long before these times. In the mesolithic period, 9,000 years ago, one or two species of larger animal provided the main source of meat in the human diet. In Europe these were red deer and wild boar, in north America the bison and in western Asia the gazelle and wild goat. One survey (Jarman, 1972) carried out in 165 sites of late palaeolithic and mesolithic age throughout Europe revealed the meat sources of the hunter-gatherers: 95 per cent of the sites indicated the presence of red deer, 60 per cent showed roe deer, 10 per cent revealed elk and chamois and a few had bison and reindeer, and 20 per cent of the sites indicated the presence of dog. One of the earliest records of dog remains comes from the palaeolithic cave of Palegawra in what is now Iraq, some 12,000 years old. Canid remains found at Vlasac in Romania date from c.5400–4600BC and the other remains there indicate no other domesticated animals.

Running mastiff depicted in Roman artefact from first–third century AD.

BELOW RIGHT: *Assyrian Hunting Dog in painted clay, found at Kultepe.*

Well before 2000BC there were huge hefty hunting dogs throughout western Asia and a variety of hunting dogs in ancient Egypt, their white antelope dog resembling our modern harriers in conformation. The Sage Kings of the Yellow River valley in China, the Dravidians of the Indus valley in India and the Sumerians in the valleys of the Tigris and the Euphrates were, especially by European standards of that time, sophisticated hunters. Discoveries from near Ergani in Turkey dated from 9500BC and from east Idaho in the United States dated from 9500–9000BC prove the existence of tracking dogs in cave settlements. Ivory carvings from Thebes, dating from 4400–4000BC, depict fast running hounds. The Phoenicians had hounds hunting both by speed and by stamina using scent. In Babylon powerful short-faced hounds were used to hunt wild asses and lions. The Assyrian kings, assisted by their keepers of hounds, hunted lions, wild bull and elephant. From 2500BC onwards hunting with hounds was a favourite entertainment for noblemen in the Nile delta.

One scribe of the 19th Dynasty described a pack of hounds, 200 of one type, 400 of another, stating that 'The red-tailed dog goes at night into the stalls of the hills. He is better than the long-faced dog, and he makes no delay in hunting…' In the Rig-Veda, an ancient Sanskrit record of Hindu mythology, we can find hound-like dogs described as 'broad of nostril and insatiable…' In time the specialist hounds developed physically to suit their function, the 'long-faced' dogs needing a slashing capability in their jaws backed by excellent longsighted vision. The 'broad-nostrilled', wider-skulled, looser-lipped dogs needed plenty of room for scenting capacity in both nose and lips where scent was tasted. As hounds became linked with human preferences in method of hunting and choice of quarry, so the breeds developed. Flavius Arrianus (Arrian), in the second century AD, described two Celtic breeds: the Segusiae (named after a tribe from a province which included what is now Lyons) with excellent noses, good cry but a tendency to dwell on the scent; and the Vertragi (literally 'lots of foot'), rough-haired, greyhound-like dogs.

Prototypal Hounds

Claims have been made for the Segusiae being the prototype of our modern scenthounds – Bloodhounds, Foxhounds, Bassets and Harriers. But Arrian found nothing remarkable or noteworthy about them, merely explaining that they hunted in the same way as Cretan and Carian hounds. Xenophon records seeing hounds in Asia Minor. I suspect that the Greeks and Romans found the Celtic greyhound not a new breed but a variety of one of the oldest types in existence. In time the Greeks became aware of the hounds from the Rhineland called Sycambrians, the Pannonian hounds from what is now northern Yugoslavia and the Sarmatian hounds from southern Russia. From the north of the Himalayas came a ferocious breed of hounds known as Seres after the people of that name. From further south came the red-brindle 'Indian' hounds, recommended by Xenophon for hunting deer and wild boar. From Persia in the first century BC came the Elymaean hounds (more precisely from the Gulf area), the fierce Carmanians, the savage mastiff-like Hyrcaneans (from the area where Tehran now is and probably more like today's broad-mouthed breeds

than any Molossian) and the fighting hounds, the Medians. In Asia Minor were the Carians (from the area where the hound-like Anatolian shepherd dogs of today come from), esteemed by Arrian as tracking hounds, with good nose, pace and cry. The much bigger variety of the Carian, the Magnesian, was a shield-bearer in war. And from the south of this region came the Lycaonian hounds, highly regarded for their admirable temperament.

Links with Wolves

In North Africa, Aristotle tells us that the Egyptians favoured the smaller sighthound type, comparable with the so-called Pharaoh hound and Whippet of today. The Libyans had good hounds and the Cyrenean hounds were allegedly crossed with wolves, with lurcher-like all-purpose hunting dogs known to exist in central and southern Africa. In ancient Greece, Epirus in the extreme northwest, produced the Acarnanians, which unusually for those times ran mute; the Athamanians; the Chaonians (from which came the legendary Laelaps); and the longer-eared Molossian hound. Since the cynologist Otto Keller produced his personal theory linking the latter with the big mountain dogs of Tibet and then with the Tibetan wolf, mastiff and Great Dane researchers have had a field day. The Molossians of ancient Greece were in fact usually sheepdogs, sometimes shaggy-coated and often white. Xenophon referred to the Locrians as the powerful short-faced boar-hunting hounds.

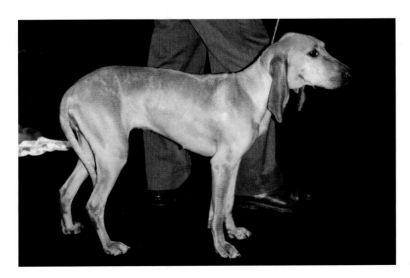

Italian Segugio at English dog show, 1992.

For me, the most important Greek hound was the Laconian, sometimes called the Spartan hound. This hound was good enough to be held in high esteem for many centuries, hence the Shakespearean reference – although the description there is not accurate. We have on record a great deal of information on the Laconian hound, a Harrier-sized scenthound with small prick ears, free from throatiness or dewlap. It was more tucked-up than our scenthounds of today but not as much as the modern sighthounds; the contemporary Italian breed, the Segugio, ears apart, being the nearest modern equivalent. Tan and white or black and tan, bold and confident, built like a steeplechaser, their fame spread wide and their blood was extensively utilized. Xenophon's chief delight was hunting hare with them.

Equally important, however, is the Cretan hound, a superb tracker in the mountains, with one variety – the 'outrunners' – running free, under the control of the huntsman's voice only, the first to do so in Europe until the end of the sixteenth century. The Cretan was subsequently crossed with the Laconian to produce the Metagon, so highly praised by Gratius but strangely by no other. It could be that the stamina-packed Laconian of the Greeks was crossed with the skilled trackers, the Segusiae of the Celts, to found the subsequent scenthound types further north, the Norman hounds, St Huberts, the great white hounds of France and the grey hounds of Louis XV.

ABOVE RIGHT: Kritikos Lagonikos or Cretan Hound of today.

Chien de Normandie, 1897.

White Hound of France, manner of Desportes, early eighteenth century.

BELOW LEFT: *The Hunt of Louis XV, 1740.*

BELOW: Louis XV Out Hunting Stag in the Forest, *by Jean-Baptiste Oudry, 1730.*

OPPOSITE PAGE
TOP RIGHT: *Deer tracker/herd-keeper, Vienna, 1870.*

BOTTOM: *Par force hunt of the fifteenth century, Florentine School, Toulouse Museum.*

Specialized Use

In time specialized functions led to specialist breeds; the Franks, for example, developing specialist hunting dogs to support their expert *bersarii* (for large game), *veltrarii* (for greyhounds), *beverarici* (for beavers and otters), falconers and wolf-hunters. In wolf-hunting, scenthounds and sighthounds were used in mutual support. Leashed scenthounds or limiers were usually employed to put the whole pack on the correct line, rather as 'tufters' do in stag-hunting to this day. Hunting with hounds became the obsession of noblemen all over the world, fortified by the medieval superstition that the strength and guile of animals passed on to man when he ate their flesh. Par force hunting, relying on the strength of hounds, may have been replaced by 'hunting cunning', which relies on the unravelling of confused scent by skilful hounds and big game hunting with giant hounds may have lapsed. But the pursuit of game by man with hounds spans 11,000 years and from such a heritage is likely to survive modern pressures just as the hounds themselves have adapted to each century. As perhaps the greatest hound breeder of modern times, the much-respected Isaac 'Ikey' Bell, Master, first of the Galway Blazers, then of the Kilkenny and later of the South and West Wilts, once wrote on behalf of Foxhounds:

And don't think: 'Man's a hunter!'
It's strictly a hound's game.
Hunters we are by birthright;
You are but one in name.

Even though he lived by hunting, primitive man worshipped animals. In modern man also, the desire to hunt is paradoxically compatible with love of wild life. Hunting is a highly satisfying occupation for many persons because it calls into play a multiplicity of physical and mental attributes that appear to be woven into the human fabric… Certain aspects of a hunter's life are probably more in keeping with man's basic temperament and biological nature than urban life as presently practiced.

Rene Dubois, *So Human an Animal: How We Are Shaped by Surroundings and Events* (1968)

Hunting by Scent

As fuming vapours rise,
And hang upon the gently-purling brook,
There, by the encumbent atmosphere compress'd,
The panting chase grows warmer as he flies,
And thro' the network of the skin perspires;
Leaves a long – steaming – trail behind; which by
The cooler air condens'd, remains, unless
By some rude storm dispers'd, or rarefied
By the meridian sun's heat,
To every shrub the warm effluvia cling…'

Commenting on those words by poet William Somervile, Peter Beckford wrote in his 1781 *Thoughts on Hunting*:

I cannot agree with Mr Somerville, in thinking that scent depends on the air only: it depends also on the soil. Without doubt, the best scent is that which is occasioned by the effluvia, as he calls it, or particles of scent, which are constantly perspiring from the game as it runs, and are strongest and most favourable to

The joy of the pursuit – The Pack Splits *by Thomas Blinks, 1898.*

the hound, when kept by the gravity of the air to the height of his breast…

It's the seeking of 'best scent' by the group of dogs covered by this book that makes them stand out; they are simply scent-driven. And we, like them, are intrigued by its mystique.

Scent Sources

As D. Caroline Coile PhD, in an article in *Dogs in Canada* of November, 1996, pointed out, the scenting powers of dog have long attracted the attention of the scientists; and stating that Droscher in 1971 found that a barefooted man leaves roughly four billionths of a gram of 'odorous sweat substance' with each step he takes. H.M. Budgett in his *Hunting by Scent* of 1933 found that water formed 99 per cent of such a gram in the first place. In locating this minute sweat sample, the tracking dog has to overlook the accompanying, conflicting and much more powerful surrounding smells – animal, vegetable and mineral – and most men on the run wear shoes! Caroline Coile also reported that the experiments of the Russian psychiatrists Klosovsky and Kosmarskaya on puppies led them to believe that the senses of smell and taste were so interconnected that they were virtually acting as one, and, could in general, act interchangeably.

It is now accepted that pad pressure, causing herbage (live plants) to be bruised or broken by quarry, releases sap, as well as breaking soil 'skins' created by surface drying or through excess moisture 'holding up', which leaves substantial scent. This is in contrast to the undisturbed surfaces around the pad-fall of the quarry. The released sap has a distinct odour for the hound, with pad pressure too allowing greater evaporation from the disturbed surface. Of all the scent sources, ranging from anal gland discharge, urine splash, animal blood from scratches to drops of saliva, body scent followed by bruised herbage and broken soil skins, make up the main contributors. Very dry or very wet conditions affect the surface of the soil and contribute too to scenting success – or failure!

On the question of hounds hunting more than one quarry, as opposed to pursuing one scent only, the great hound expert Sir Newton Rycroft, in his *Hounds, Hunting and Country* (2001), argued that hounds will always have a favourite quarry, which

Inspired by scent – On the Scent by George Wright (1860–1942).

may not be the huntsman's favourite quarry at any given moment. He recalled Ivester Lloyd's words on how in the old days the Welsh Foxhounds of the Ynysfor used to hunt fox, otter, hare and pine marten. But Rycroft himself preferred to use French hounds of wolf-hunting ancestry, believing that their skilful nose on the cold drag of a wolf would assist their descendants on a fox which had a long start before them, as can occur in Forest hunting. He pointed out, however, with characteristic good sense, that 'I cannot see what it profits a hound or pack of hounds to have inherited good noses if their huntsman has not the time, patience nor the sensitivity to allow them to develop these good noses to the full.' Scenting skills need support! In Bloodhound trials it has been noted that the most successful hounds are those handled with the greatest rapport. The breed is also prized because of its 'freedom from change' capability; in other words, the Bloodhound relentlessly pursues *one* trail and does not get sidetracked, as the phrase appropriately goes. This breed seems to use its *brains* as well as its nose when unravelling scent.

Nose Consciousness

In his informative *Gundog Sense and Sensibility* (1982), Wilson Stephens writes:

To gundogs, with centuries of nose-consciousness bred into it, noses are for serious business, eyes merely come in useful occasionally. I have never needed to teach a dog to use its nose but, more often than not, have needed to inculcate the habit of using the eyes – notably, of course to mark the fall of game.

The Bloodhound – ace tracker, with understanding handler.

Bloodhound in use in the Great War to locate casualties.

Newton Rycroft writing on this in *Hounds* magazine in December 1995, states that:

> As regards nose, it is not too difficult for a huntsman to assess the noses of individual hounds, but I think it must be more difficult for him to assess the general excellence or otherwise of their collective ability as a pack. After all, his nose is not much use to a huntsman except to carry his spectacles should he wear any. He can say 'Looks like a scent today' but his Labrador, whom he left behind at home, might be much more explicit.

Tracking talent is an immense hound virtue, both to the pack and to a handler.

In an informative article in the magazine *Dogs in Canada* in October 1983, Maryellen Rieschick pointed out the loss of scent in house dogs, going from a warm room out into a freezing day and finding no scent at all. She also wrote:

> A dog learns to track people in the right direction, instead of following a trail backwards, in three ways. First, the dog learns that the lighter scent produced

On the Scent, Foxhounds unravelling scent, nineteenth century.

from the ball of the foot indicates the direction of travel. Because the weight of a person's body is placed on the heel of the foot when he steps forward, it causes the heel to have a much heavier concentration of scent than the ball of the foot. A second way… is that individual scent ingredients will evaporate at different rates of speed…a dog can register 'scent images' as they change in concentration, and therefore make out the direction of the track he is following. A third method is…a steadily increasing concentration of scent…

A dog reacts to the scent strength received by each nostril, hence the wavy line followed by tracking hounds, as the right nostril, then the left, perceives the best scent.

I have noticed when using dogs on a trail that the dog's head is carried higher during morning tracking, perhaps because the air is rising, bringing the scent with it. It is also noticeable that scenting ability varies from individual to individual dog within a pack, within a breed. The speed of a hound on a trail varies similarly, with accuracy not always sacrificed for pace. I suspect too that it is the determination and sheer persistence of the Bloodhound that makes it so effective at following cold trails, just as much as its scenting powers. Using Labradors as tracker dogs in the Malayan emergency showed me that scenting prowess isn't enough by itself; you need a fanatical obsessive like a Bloodhound for really testing trails. The variety of trails used with hound sports indicates their versatility; they can follow, not just animal scent but a drag or artificial trail, or hunt the clean boot, the trail left along a pre-arranged route by human quarry.

Specialization from Sensitivity

A dog's sense of smell is many hundred times as powerful as ours. The reason for this lies in the fact that the areas inside a dog's nose that detect smells are roughly fourteen times larger than the equivalent areas in man. But a detector needs to be matched by a comparable performance in a receiver; the part of the dog's brain dealing with smell is proportionately larger and better developed than the human equivalent. One estimate gives a figure of forty times as many brain cells connected with the detection and perception of smell in the dog as in the human brain.

The sheer sensitivity of the nose of dog allows it to specialize in hunting deer or fox, otter or hare, man or truffles, and to locate avalanche victims, drugs, the wounded on the battlefield, explosives, temporary graves, dry rot, melanomas, the onset of epilepsy… even 'moonshine' in America.

A German trainer of dogs for the police and then the army, Konrad Most, conducted experiments in the 1920s to determine whether dogs were using ground scents or individual scents on the trail. In one such test the tracklayer walked on foot for a while and was then carried roughly three feet above the ground for the remainder of the trail, on a suspended cable. Four highly experienced tracker dogs then attempted to track this trail. All four quite separately failed to track their quarry past the point where he left the ground. This, and other tests, supported the theory that dogs follow a scent based on disturbed ground scents.

Different scents too initiate different responses in individual dogs, not surprisingly. The ability to detect pheromones (chemicals produced by an individual that signal members of the same species) varies markedly too from one animal to another. Sportsmen have sometimes reported on hares being capable of 'shutting off the scent' when in immediate danger from pursuing hounds. Some French hunters believe that the scent of rutting stags is 'distasteful' to hounds and that their scent differs when they have lost their horns. Hounds hunting in water or on river banks have revealed that otter scent is water-soluble and gets washed away whereas mink scent is not water-soluble and must be tracked in a different way.

Tracking Prowess

The tracking ability of the dog has been used to show that identical twins produce an identical odour. A dog can follow the trail of either twin after smelling an article belonging to one of them, although cases have been recorded of a gifted dog actually differentiating between the two. This tracking ability can be impaired by temperature change, rain, humidity, frost, wind, competing odours and the sheer passage of time. But no human or machine produced by man would get on such a trail in the first place. This tracking skill backed by dog's response to training is a valuable element in the unique man-dog partnership. Pigs employed to locate truffles usually eat them!

Eager Basset Hounds in hot pursuit by T. Ivester Lloyd, 1934.

Yet to limit scenting powers just to the nose is not entirely correct. In his informative *The Mind of the Dog* (1958), R.H. Smythe observed:

Now, odours, scents or smells represent the delights of paradise to every dog...it is well known that delicate smells make the mouth water. Saliva dissolves the scent-bearing vapours and so the dog not only smells them but also tastes them. It is believed that hounds use both smell and taste, especially when the scent becomes strong, and it is believed by many that when hounds 'give tongue' they are actually savouring the delightful odour as it dissolves in their saliva.

In pursuit of this belief our ancestors utilized the 'shallow flew'd hound' to hunt by sight and scent, in that order, as a 'fleethound' and the 'deep-mouthed hound' as a specialist scenthound.

Link with Skull Shape

There is a link too between well-developed sinuses and the ability to track. The best trailers have the skull conformation to allow good sinus development, adequate width of nostril and good length of foreface so that there is sufficient surface between the nostrils to house the smell-sensitive lining membrane.

Scenthounds, gundogs and other hunting dogs depend on the shape of their skulls for their acute smell-discrimination. In pedigree breeds, the wording of the description of the skull in the breed standard can therefore directly influence the scenting prowess of the dog. The narrower skull of the terrier leads it to prefer to hunt by sight, show less interest in following a trail of scent yet, through selective breeding, show enormous interest in scent coming from below ground. In his book *Hunting* of 1900, Otho Paget links hound intelligence with scenting ability, stating that the remarkable ability to follow weak scent on roads possessed by some hounds was rooted in their memory and reasoning powers, and warning that, 'One of the greatest objections against breeding hounds too close is that their brain-power becomes reduced.'

Hunting by Scent and Sight: the Par Force Hounds

This book concentrates on the scenthounds but the par force hounds, hunting using scent and sight, at pace, included the holding dogs, the strong-headed, broad-mouthed, modified brachycephalic type, used at the kill in medieval hunting and as capture-dogs since, the world over. These dogs have been used as hunting mastiffs or matins for over a thousand years. There are in addition, however, what might be called 'running mastiffs', huge par force hounds which hunted using sight and scent, more often on boar. Their surviving examples are breeds like the Great Dane, the Dogo Argentino, the Rhodesian Ridgeback, the Broholmer of Denmark and the Catahoula Leopard Dog. These were hounds of the chase, too valuable to be sacrificed at the kill, not trained or bred to be recklessly brave and prized for their looks more than any holding dog breed. They all excelled at following a scent at great speed and deserve our admiration.

No scientist has ever been able to explain satisfactorily the mysteries of scent in the hunting field. Scent is variously affected by the direction of the wind, heavy rain, freezing fog, high humidity, different crops, baking heat and the ground temperature, but no one has confidently stipulated the conditions needed for good scenting. Alington, in his essays with Routledge, entitled *The Mysteries of Scent* of 1932, observed that 'scent is almost certain to be good between 3.30 and 4.30 after a warm October day, when the thermometer suddenly drops to near freezing point.' He then hastened to add: 'Under no other conditions would the writer care to back his opinion that scent will be good'! Not a lot of value there then! No wonder the scientists stay away.

In conclusion then: speed, dash, stoutness, and nose are the four things to go for and insist upon in the modern staghound. I know that I have not assigned the same importance to nose in what I have said as to the other qualities – perhaps I have not attached enough. But still, for the 'sweet' scented deer give me stoutness and speed first… I have come across some observations of Mr Smith's, which are so wise that they shall finish it up for me. After laying stress upon the supreme importance of nose and stoutness, he says: 'The two qualities often go together; for it is the stoutness which makes a hound willing to try to hunt and make use of his nose, which a slack hound would not try to do.'

Lord Ribblesdale, The Queen's Hounds and Stag-
hunting Recollections (1897)

It is also found, particularly with the aromatic vapours from animals, i.e. scent, that the rate of diffusion is slowed down in a humid atmosphere and quickened in a dry one. The fraction of saturation of the atmosphere with water vapour at a given temperature is termed the humidity or relative humidity of the atmosphere and it has been observed by scientifically minded hunters in the USA…that good scenting conditions were invariably found when the humidity as registered by hygrometers, was over 60 and vice versa when under 60. It must, however, be stated as a matter of experience that humidity can be regarded as only one of the many factors affecting scenting conditions.

Dr D. Jobson-Scott, Beagling for Beginners (1933)

In the old days it was looked upon as a maxim that a southerly wind and a cloudy sky prognosticated a good hunting day. Of course, this wind and sky told of the falling mercury, and betokened rain, but it also told of calm and heavy atmosphere; a semi-satisfied

The Par Force Hunt – *a stag hunt with strong-headed hunting mastiffs by Johann Ridinger, 1729.*

one, not hungry, not unduly absorbent, hence not likely to affect so much the vapour given off by the run fox. A satisfied atmosphere which may be kind and palatable, so to say, to the nose-nerves of the hound.'

'Yoi-Over', *From Hold Hard! Hounds, Please!* (1924)

The connecting link of venery is that which holds the pack to the quarry – scent. The basic, if obvious, fact that there would be no foxhunting were it not that the fox leaves a scent-trail and that hounds are able to hunt the air that has come into contact with the scent particles is not always given the emphasis it deserves. Day by day it is upon scent conditions that sport depends, and in the long run it is according to the extent that scent is masked by man-made smells that the future of foxhunting partly depends.

J.N.P. Watson, *The Book of Foxhunting* (1977)

Nose is hardly the first consideration with a staghunter. The scent of a deer lies so high and sweet, that most days there is enough scent to carry them all along with their sterns as tobacco pipes – a rare thing with foxhounds. Nor do the Queen's Hounds profess, like the St Huberts, to take a line along the bottom of

a stream, that is, under water, as tunefully as along its soggy margin. A well-watered road is more likely to be the scene of any signal exploit in the neighbourhood…

Lord Ribblesdale, *The Queen's Hounds and Staghunting Recollections* (1897)

That no uncertainty in the world is greater than that of scent is the conclusion I have arrived at after close observation extending over more than forty years; and I should be sorry to take it upon myself to lay down any rule with regard to it, knowing, as I do, that it has always been a puzzle to the best recognized authorities in many generations. Mr Jorrocks remarks that scent is a 'weary, incomprehensible, incontrollable phenomenon, constant only by its inconstancy…'

Earl of Suffolk, *The Encyclopaedia of Sport* (1897)

How perfect is the hound at smelling, who never leaves or forsakes his first scent, but follows it through so many changes and varieties of other scents, even over, and in, the water, and into the earth! What music doth a pack of dogs then make to any man, whose heart and ears are so happy as to be set to the tune of such instruments!… For my hounds, I know

Otterhounds pursuing a warm scent by John Noble, 1889.

the language of them, and they know the language and meaning of one another, as perfectly as we know the voices of those with whom we discourse daily.

Izaak Walton, *The Compleat Angler* (1653)

Hunting as a Pack – Creating a Team

The hound should be intelligent and sensible; that is to say he should hunt calmly and methodically with the sole object of contributing to the pack his share of skill and work… All first class hounds begin with more initiative, more keenness and more faults but when experience has calmed their first fire and has given them skill and knowledge they have crossed the barrier of ordinariness in front of which so many beginners remain.

Comte Elie de Vezins, *Hounds for a Pack* (1882)

The collection of hunting dogs covered by this book are not just driven by scent but uniquely can operate in some numbers together as one team, work in support of each other to one common goal, the successful pursuit of ground game. Sighthounds work best in a brace or a brace and a half. Gundogs work individually. Terriers are not always good at sharing a task. Pastoral dogs can combine in company with their fellows but not in group activity. Sled dogs work as a team but not as a pack. Creating a pack of hounds is a skill. It's a combination of shrewd breeding, well-judged entering and patient education when young, but all rooted in instinctive inherited behaviour.

Hounds hunting *as a pack* have not always been fully covered by writers – or even kennel clubs – although in 1882 Comte Elie de Vezins, quoted above, produced a masterly account of how individual hound abilities could be coordinated to produce one unified result. Artists down the centuries have often portrayed hounds in unlikely identical postures in their efforts to dramatize the unified chase of the pack. Kennel clubs divide the hound breeds very arbitrarily into scent or sighthounds, leaving no sub-division for 'par force' hounds, which hunted 'at force' using scent and sight, or for the heavy hounds which pulled down big game. The latter did not hunt as a pack and are covered in a later section. Nowadays we think of a pack of hounds as a uniform body, but in the medieval hunting field, the pack embraced many diverse elements.

ABOVE: *Awaiting release* – Hounds in Kennels *by W.H. Trood, 1893.*

RIGHT: *Released joy* – Going out for the Hunt *by Fannie Moody (1885–97).*

Par force hunting was eventually replaced in Britain by 'hunting cunning' in which the unravelling of scent became more important than the steeplechase of the former style. But 'fleet hounds' were preferred in the north of England, where par force hunting lasted longer. Contemporary breeds like the Great Dane, the Rhodesian Ridgeback and the Dogo Argentino are classic par force hounds, perhaps better termed 'running mastiffs'. It could be that the Dalmatian was once one too, its name possibly coming from 'dama-chien' or deer dog. The heavy hounds were the hunting mastiffs, used as 'seizers' to pull down big game, as Snyders, Rubens, Ridinger and Riedel depicted in their sporting art. But for many the principal occupation of the scenthound was *in the pack*.

Respecting Hounds

Whatever twenty-first-century thinking may bring to hunting with dogs, historians have demonstrated man's long need for dogs as pot-fillers in primitive times, his regard for hunting as a noble pursuit and the fascination it held for mankind all over the world. The Ancient Greeks would not have been impressed by a 'civilization' that frowns on hare-hunting whilst tolerating harehounds being imprisoned in cages for 'scientific experiments'. They respected both the hound and its quarry – and revered the hunter. No educated person would regard the Ancient Greeks as uncivilized. For them, the hounds and the hunters worked together – as a pack.

In his *Hounds and Hunting in Ancient Greece* (1964), Denison Bingham Hull wrote:

> It was the very danger of the boar hunt that made it fascinating to the Greeks; victory was essential, for there was no safety except through conquest. It was that urge to display courage that made the boar hunt the highest manifestation of the chase for the hunter; that urge to show that he too was made of the same stuff as the heroes of the Iliad and the Odyssey, his forefathers, that compelled a man to take the risks and face the danger.

I would place the courage of the hounds ahead of that of the human hunters. But man and hound acted as a team; the hunter could not manage without the hound, and the hounds needed to work with each other.

Recognizing Role

Because of Buchanan-Jardine's book *Hounds of the World* (1937) and the late George Johnston excellent *Hounds of France* (1979), we know a great deal about French hounds. But regrettably our knowledge of Baltic, Balkan, Swiss, Dutch and German, even American hounds, is far from complete. The most impressive entries that I saw at the World Dog Show in Helsinki a decade ago were the Finnish Hounds, handsome and functional. Some of them could have passed muster as one of our Foxhounds. Not surprisingly the hounds that hunt in packs, mainly by stamina, look very similar in whichever country they developed. It is worth noting that the Bassets and Bloodhounds that still hunt in packs lack the exaggerations of the show ring specimens.

Not every scenthound type or breed has the *packhound* instinct. In their enlightening book *The Coon Hunter's Handbook* (1952), Whitney and Underwood record:

> In the early days of America, the black and tan was the individual hunter that ran his own fox and cared nothing about packing, as the true English foxhound does. A pack of black and tans is almost useless for riding to, because of their individual temperaments. Each will let the other hounds run their foxes while he runs his own.

A pack has to be built on instinctive corporate endeavours, but in Germany and Switzerland, for example, hunters need hounds to work individually – usually to the gun. It would be interesting to put such hounds together, as a pack, to see if individual skills could still be incorporated into a unified application. The wider hound diaspora is covered later.

Each one of these scenthound breeds has the classic build for such a role – they truly look like canine athletes and resemble one another. In many countries fielding hounds in packs, the Masters have striven to achieve a level pack, in which the pack 'signature' – height at shoulder and coat colour usually – identifies the pack itself. All these hound features need conserving if we are to retain their separate identity, instinctive skills and sporting prowess.

A feature of any conservation lies in their recognition, breed by breed. Just as the KC has recognised the Beagle, the Basset Hound, the Otterhound and

ABOVE: *Bavarian hunters and hounds, 1895.*

LEFT: *Czech hunter with a tracking hound, 1900.*

the Foxhound as breeds, we need to safeguard our Harriers too. On the Swiss model, described later, allowing two sizes in each hound breed, the Foxhounds and Harriers of the packs would make up more than just two breeds. The black and tan Dumfriesshire Foxhounds (now lost to us), the rough-coated Welsh Hounds and the West Country Harriers would be considered to be distinct breeds. The Staghound of today is really just a Foxhound with a different function; we lost our huge Devonshire Staghounds a long time ago. The old 'Talbot Tan' hound however still crops up in litters. It is significant that Edward, second Duke of York, in his *The Master of Game* (1406) gave his view that: 'The best hue of running hounds is called brown tan. I prefer them to all others…' Together with Fell Hounds (as distinct from Trail Hounds), which once benefited from Pointer blood, and the English Basset, which has been revitalised with Harrier blood, this is a rich heritage of hounds hunting in packs to be lost.

The 'Talbot Tan' cropping up in this Sligo Farmers' Foxhound. (Photo: B. Dolan)

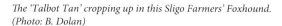

Foxhunting in the North *by Richard Ansdell, 1845, depicting James Machell with his hounds at Windermere.*

BELOW LEFT: Fell Hound Mountain *by Murray Urquhart, 1922.*

Use of Outside Blood

The blood of the Fell Hound and that of the Welsh Hound has been utilized by Foxhound breeders in building a pack. In *The Foxhound* magazine of November 1910, the Fell Hound and its country was described:

> The foxes are for the most part found on the ledges of the mountains whose sides vary from 45 degrees to 70 degrees, and are sometimes even more steeply inclined; with a surface formed of rock or loose shale, they graduate into slippery grass slopes at the base.

Hounds therefore hunt the 'drag' slowly up until they find. For this country the hound which has proved the most useful is one of light frame all round, hare-footed entirely, exceptionally well let-down and developed in hind quarters, with good neck and shoulders and loin, ribs carried well back, long in pastern, and withal shallow in make. Great scenting powers and endless endurance are needful, with a considerable amount of pace.

It is easy to see why some MFHs would wish to strengthen their own pack by introducing such valuable assets, but some disliked the tendency, valuable in the Fells, for such hounds to give tongue too freely.

Welsh Hound Blood

Writing on this hound in his *Hounds of the World* of 1937, Buchanan-Jardine stated:

> Pure strains of Welsh blood show certain very marked characteristics in the hunting field. First of all, the best of them have really excellent noses and abundance of patience to use them in puzzling out the coldest possible line: this quality can be of great value where hounds hunt the overnight drag of their fox up to his kennel before finding him, as is done sometimes in hill countries where foxes are scarce; it can also prove of use in sticking to a cold line if the hunted fox is a bit ahead.

This facet, along with their rough, weather-proof coats and more musical voices, led to their being a prized breeding source for some English packs – yet not to everyone's taste. After some rather silly exchanges in sporting magazines of that time, Sir Edward Curre wrote in to state (quoted in Lionel Edwards' *Famous Foxhunters*, 1932):

> I deplore this wordy warfare as to Welsh versus English hounds. It seems to me the subscribers to the various packs are the people to complain how you breed your hounds. Sir Villiers Foster, Mr George Evans, Mr Isaac Bell, Mr Henry Lowndes, Mr Dalgety and others have tried the cross of Welsh, and I believe it improves work, especially in bad scenting countries.

His words have weight.

Their versatility was prized too; the Welsh Hounds of the Ynysfor were used on fox, otter, hare and pine marten. The work of the Welsh Hound Association in compiling and publishing a studbook and registering Welsh Hounds that must reach a certain standard, whilst establishing a record of the breeding of these hounds, is quite admirable. The Association aims to preserve the key characteristics of the breed so that a national breed can be maintained on accepted lines. The Penrhiwfer Foxhounds exemplify the small packs belonging to this Association; a private pack, established thirty years ago, hunting the Rhondda

Valley and now the recently disbanded country of the Pentyrch, it is made up of around twenty couple of mainly pure Welsh Hounds, hunting twice weekly. Much of their breeding goes back to the old Pentyrch blood, famed for great voice, huge drive and deep scenting ability, allied to correct conformation for such a hound.

Corporate Needs

Understanding the corporate needs of a hunting pack means being aware, not just of any shortcomings but knowing where and how to seek the remedy or improvement. A pack that hunts as a unit takes years to build and even longer to develop into a genuine team. As Joseph B. Thomas wrote in *Hounds and Hunting* in 1937: 'To say just how to hunt a pack of hounds

ABOVE RIGHT: Welsh Hounds of 1904.

The Belvoir *by Cuthbert Bradley, 1911.*

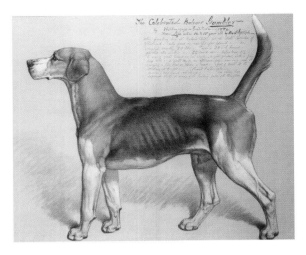

The famous Foxhound Belvoir Gambler by Basil Nightingale, 1884.

limited. Show breeders have no requirement, beyond their own conscience, to perpetuate truly functional hounds or ones able to hunt as a pack.

Top-Quality Packs

Throughout this book, I mention outstanding packs in each of the native scenthound breeds, and behind each one are remarkable hunt servants. Just one example is Frank Gillard, huntsman to the 6th and 7th Dukes of Rutland at the end of the nineteenth century. In his book, *English Fox Hunting – A History* (1976), Raymond Carr wrote of him:

> His reputation rested on his pack; the Belvoir hounds were noted for their even appearance and their bright tan, their sheer beauty…their blood was diffused in every fashionable pack in England. A pack like the Belvoir was the reward for superb kennel management and impeccable selection in breeding over a century. The Belvoir kennels were 'a national institution'.

A comparable story could be told of every famous pack; the dedication, knowledge and long-term planning of such devoted hunt servants produced renowned packs of hounds across England and Wales, with perhaps the phrase 'impeccable selection in breeding' being the common factor. Selection of stock is forever the deciding element in breeding top quality animals.

is an impossible task. All one can do is to lay down certain principles, and then allow intelligence, temperament, experience and observation to do the rest. One must never think that he knows more than a good hound…' Thomas was an outstanding MFH and a noted creator of top-quality packs. In such men you see the crucial difference between the breeding strategies of sportsmen and show breeders; the former seek performance and physical qualities based on that; the latter seek anatomical excellence based on a word picture but restricted to pure stock, however flawed or

The Dumfriesshire Foxhounds in full cry by Lionel Edwards.

Whipcord – a Foxhound with some Welsh blood by T. Ivester Lloyd, 1936.

Triomphe, a Gascon-Saintongeois hound, close to pure Gascon type.

I have quoted Buchanan-Jardine in many aspects of hound breeding and hunting throughout this book, but his achievement with the development of the Dumfriesshire Foxhounds from 1921 onwards as an outstanding pack was rooted in his immense knowledge of the various hounds of Britain and France, and, especially, his great skill in blending disparate blood. He combined the blood of the Welsh Hound (through Whipcord), that of the Bloodhound (through Ledburn Boswell) and that of the French Gascon-Saintongeois (through Triomphe) to produce quite outstanding hounds like Harlequin. He then introduced top-quality English blood, in black and tan coats, from the like of Silverton Woodman and Croome Clansman. Later he used doghounds from the College Valley and Tynedale in the production of tall, handsome virile hounds with great voice and superb hunting ability. The Second World War interrupted his plans, then in the early 2000s, following the Hunting Act, the pack was split up and sold off to eager hound breeders in France and America. A valuable if doomed story of pack-creation.

The Classical Period

Perhaps it is wishful thinking to expect all breeds hunting in packs to survive. It is possible to find in

Greek and Latin literature some sixty-five breed types by name, although some are merely synonyms. The Greeks had hound breeders who insisted on the importance of pure bloodlines. But not all their hounds

Harlequin, three parts Foxhound, one part Bloodhound by T. Ivester Lloyd, 1936.

were Greek in origin, for the Greeks were a maritime people, with knowledge of the whole Mediterranean littoral and the Black Sea. Pollux and Oppian referred to a breed called the Iberian, associating it with the Spanish peninsula, not the Iberia of the Caucasus. In Italy there was the Ausonian, discovered by Greeks living in Naples, the Salentine and the Umbrian, able to run down game, as a pack, but not kill it.

In time the Greeks became aware of the hounds from the Rhineland called Sycambrians, the Pannonian hounds of northern Serbia and the Sarmatian hounds from southern Russia. Russian hounds were almost swamped by blood from our Foxhound until Count Kisenski drew up a standard for the national hound in 1890, based on the famous Belousov pack, which originated in Tartary. There is probably truth in Betteloni's opinion of 1800: '...mastiffs from Tartary, molossians from Epirus, hounds from Flanders...' The Greeks described hunting mastiffs as 'Indian dogs', coming from Hyrcania by the Caspian Sea. They knew the importance of hounds hunting in unison, not just in support of each other, but in support of a different complementary hound role.

Arrian was aware of the rough-haired Celtic hounds, perpetuated today in the griffon breeds. Not surprisingly, France has lost some ancient hound breeds, the strapping Normandie, Virelade and Montemboeuf types, with the latter two perpetuated in the striking Gascon-Saintongeois. From Persia the Greeks imported the Elymaean hounds, the fierce Carmanians and the battle dogs of the Medes. From Asia Minor came the Carians, esteemed by Arrian as trackers with nose, pace and cry. As well as the somewhat overplayed Molossian hounds, Epirus produced the Acarnanian Hound, which, unusually in those times, ran mute. Arrian recorded the value of the pack.

The most important Greek hound was the Laconian, sometimes called the Spartan and referred to by Shakespeare. Just as interesting was the Cretan hound, which produced a variety called the 'outrunners', running free, under voice control only – the first to do so in Europe until the end of the sixteenth century. The distinct breeds developed as hounds became specialist packs: the Locrians as powerful short-faced boarhounds, the Laconians as lighter harehounds, for example. Function led to design and

we forget this at our peril. We also err in thinking of packhounds as all thundering along with common skills; a pack is essentially a *team*.

Complementary Skills

Some Foxhounds developed a skill for tracking on roads; one sporting magazine describing a particular hound as 'a warranted macadamiser'. Lord Henry Bentinck kept a detailed hound book, detailing each hound's special gifts; against 'Regulus 1861' he noted 'Regulus for roads'. Over a century ago, in France, Comte Elie de Vezins set out the blend of skills needed to compose a pack. He built his pack around a leader or *chien de tête*, possessing great scenting skill and pace, a natural leader, supported by three types of *chiens de centre*. The latter were made up of *chiens de centre pur*, happy to follow and verify the leader; the *chiens de centre avance*, to back the leader vigorously and keep the pack up with him; and the *chiens seconds*, one or two hounds which press the leader, replacing him if he tires. He also mentions the *chien de chemin*, like Regulus, and the 'skirter' that always looks for short cuts – brainier, perhaps, but not a team player. He acknowledged the value of individuality, provided it supported the work of the pack.

In his informative booklet *Memories of My Life at the College Valley* (2012), the acknowledged master huntsman and hound breeder Martin Letts writes:

> The skill of the breeder is to cement the hunting abilities of his hounds (abilities that are exposed by regular and frequent work) by intelligently selecting the sire and the dam... Animals, especially those in tight communities like a pack, recognize success and dominance, and they respond speedily to it by following others' examples, especially when encouraged by their huntsman... I advance the opinion that often a huntsman's attention is too focused on the hounds at the head of the pack... However the hound that excels in every aspect of the chase – the finder, the accurate hunter, the one that reinstates the hunt – and displays these attributes consistently on nearly every day in the season is the dog or bitch most worthy of breeding.

The interdependence of packhounds acting together will forever be an aspect for the most careful consideration.

Acting as a Pack

The French, who hunt in woods a great deal, and the Americans, who often hunt at night, value the 'music' of their hounds much more highly than we do. When hounds are hunting as a pack, their voices in unison seem to convey precise messages to each other and to the accompanying field. Pack confidence appears to improve when the hounds are 'speaking', with the 'cry' of the pack conveying to the huntsmen the nature and stage of the chase. Mute packs have been known to leave hounds behind at checks; a pack working as a team gives incentive to the less committed, and voice is just one method of doing this. The vital point is for the hound to give voice honestly and not for the wrong reasons, leading to misled fields in pursuit. In his book *The Sporting Dog*, published in America in 1904, Joseph Graham summarized the key elements in pack-forming:

> …the master first seeks uniformity of look and pace. Uniformity of look includes color, size, shape, expression, coat and the typical points of ear and brush… In work, a perfect pack not only presents quality of pace but similarity of style. The master tolerates no flyers in front, no stragglers behind. The overfast as well as the overslow must be drafted out and sent away from the kennel. Whatever the duration of the run, the hounds must not string out.

These expectations do not exactly reward initiative and individuality in hounds, but emphasize the unison and uniformity behind a true pack, acting together to one purpose.

At a hunting forum held in the United States in 1971, attended by the leading MFHs of several countries, T.F. Ryan, Master and Huntsman of the famous Irish Scarteen pack, stated:

> …if you study hounds, as we all do, you see a tremendous difference in them on different days. I don't know whether it applies to foxhounds as well as my own breed, the Kerry Beagle, but it is terribly obvious at home that on a good scenting day the hounds, not only are they like an orchestra, but they are beamed-in on the one wave length with themselves and their huntsman, and they are working so completely as a team that it is an absolute treat to hunt them and see them work.

Those sentiments ably describe the pack spirit that embraces the hounds and the humans in one unified common endeavour.

Scale of Hunting

It is forgivable to underestimate the sheer scale of hunting in bygone England. In his *The Noble Science – A Few General Ideas on Fox-Hunting* (1911), Delme Radcliffe records that:

> In a speech, April 1911, the Earl of Lonsdale, master of the Cottesmore, said: 'There are 229 packs of hounds in the United Kingdom, and that means over 9,000 couples of hounds…in season 1910–11, the Earl of Harrington's six-days-a-week pack, with eighty couples was the largest…' When the Father of the Science, the great Meynell, first went into Leicestershire, he never took out fewer than one hundred couples of hounds… One hundred couples were drawn for the hunting pack (leaving, I should imagine, but a small residue for the solace of the feeder at home)…

(Can you imagine 200 terriers out hunting together!) He was referring to Foxhound packs only; the challenge of producing a coordinated, mutually supporting pack, with such numbers deployed in the hunting field, must have been quite awesome, especially if hunting took place on six days a week. In contrast the Farndale, a trencher-fed pack of just eight couples, hunted the Yorkshire Moorlands to great effect on the predatory fox population.

Until recently, we have had around 300 quarry packs, mainly Foxhound but ranging from Beagle and Harrier packs to Fell and Mink packs. That's over 20,000 hounds, able to work in unison, many with extraordinary scenting skills. We have rarely made use of these talents away from the hunting field. But we know of dog's ability to indicate buried bodies, hidden mines, dry rot in buildings, concealed drugs, the onset of epilepsy and the presence of melanomas. These hounds also have the health and virility much needed in some KC-registered hound breeds. It would be a supreme irony if the best-bred, healthiest dogs in Britain were subject to a massive cull as a result of a campaign from an animal welfare society formed for the prevention of cruelty to such creatures! The Ancient Greeks gave us the word 'hubris' meaning excessive moral pride in humans or defiance of the gods, leading to nemesis. It appears to be contagious; but no dog has ever caught it!

A good pack moves as a solid cohort and not as a mob of straggling bow-wows. Nothing is more beautiful than to watch a really even pack swinging in its tracks. It is almost like a flight of starlings wheeling on the wing, with not a single careless straggler to spoil the perfect symmetry of the movement. A good pack, too, should carry what is called 'a good head', i.e. there should be no lateral straggling and no tailing out behind. In order to insure such cohesion of movement a pack, in addition to being well-trained and in perfect condition, must be 'level' or 'even'… Levelness in a pack should include size, shape, speed and physical features generally, but a certain amount of consideration may also be given to the formation of the head and the character of the countenance and even to colouring.

Dr D. Jobson-Scott, *Beagling for Beginners* (1933)

…the highest virtue in a foxhound is not merely the exquisiteness of his nose, but in his being true to the line his game has gone, and a stout runner to the end of the chase. But he must not only thus signalise himself in chase, he must also be a patient hunter with a cold scent, and also with the pack at fault… The prevailing faults of hounds, too often innate, can only be cured by education. The greatest of all are, skirting, or not being true on the line, and throwing the tongue improperly…

Nimrod, *The Life of a Sportsman* (1903)

ABOVE LEFT: The Farndale, a trencher-fed pack of eight couples, on the Yorkshire Moors, 1920.

The Percy bitches, by Henry F. Lucas-Lucas, 1900 – a level even pack.

Constructing the Hound – Stamina for the Chase

The hound, to be well-made and beautiful, should have the head well-made and longer than it is broad; the forehead wide; the eye large and bright; the nostrils well-opened and moist rather than dry; the ear low, narrow, hanging down and curled inwards and longer than the nose by only two inches. The body of a size and length proportionate to the limbs so that without being too long it may be more slender than stocky; the shoulders neither too wide nor too narrow; the back broad, high and arched; the haunches high and wide; the stern broad near the back but terminating like that of a rat and loosely curved in a half-circle; the thighs well tucked up and well muscled; the leg vigorous, the foot lean and the nails thick and short. The height of hounds for the hare and the roe is from 21 to 23 inches; that of hounds for the stag from 25 to 28 inches; and that of hounds for the boar and wolf from 23 to 25 inches.

Comte Elie de Vezins, *Hounds for a Pack* (1882)

Shouldering the Blame

If in any KC-registered hound breed there are too few fanciers, or even judges, conversant with sound construction and correct movement, then a visit to a hound show such as Peterborough, Honiton and Ardingly would be of enormous benefit. Over the last half-century, I have found that KC-registered breed club members rarely step outside their self-prescribed world; they usually lack vision and are on the whole, inward-looking and rarely innovative, their officials preferring to repeat the past rather than look to the future of their breed. Guidance on the physical appearance of the hound breeds registered with the KC relies far too much on the interpretation placed on the words in the official breed standard or word picture of a breed; this phraseology has in recent years been improved but still lacks clarity in far too many respects. For example, the wording of breed standards on shoulders is usually quite good; the understanding of those well-chosen words however is less good. Expressions like 'lay of shoulder', 'well-laid shoulders' and 'sloping shoulders' are used by many without any clear concept of their implications, and, more importantly, the *reason* for their inclusion.

ABOVE: *'Shoulders neither too wide nor too narrow…' Foxhound at the Honiton Show, 1999.*

BELOW: *'…well-made and beautiful…' Today's Foxhound.*

Tom Horner, the great terrier breeder and all-round judge, wrote authoritatively on this very point. His words have value for hound devotees. He worked in J.V. Rank's Ouborough Great Dane kennels in 1933, preparing the twenty dogs there for exhibition, all of which excelled in movement. Such men gained enormous experience; Rank's great rival, George Stewart, had a Great Dane kennel housing between 100 and 300 dogs at any one time.

In his informative book *All About The Bull Terrier* (1973), Horner wrote:

> …to secure the very important good lay back of shoulders, it is necessary for the dorsal bones to be of good length. Well laid back shoulders are highly desirable for a number of reasons, a well laid shoulder has a firmer attachment to the chest wall than an upright one, it is also likely to be matched by a good length of upper arm, which, in turn, will mean that the elbow will be placed well back from the forechest, and the foreleg will have freedom to reach out well in movement.

The stilted abbreviated front movement of so many of the smaller breeds illustrates the limitation imposed on a dog's forward movement by a lack of slope in the shoulders and a lack of length in the upper arm. But this restricted, handicapped forward action is actually praised by some ignorant TV commentators at Crufts – choosing to call it 'typical'!

For me, the first point of real quality in a dog lies in clean sloping shoulders. Well-placed shoulders give a perfect base for a proud head carriage. They provide too the balance between the length of the neck and the length of the back, preventing those disagreeable dips in topline which mar the whole appearance of a dog. I learned, over the years, to start any judgement of the shoulders by considering the position of the elbow. If the elbow is too far forward, then the dog is pulling itself along rather than pushing, capitalizing on the drive from the hocks and thighs, through the loins. The great Foxhound expert, Capt. Ronnie Wallace, in his video *Hound Standards* (Countryside Audio and Visual, 1999), states that the shoulders are controlled by the elbow. He knows his subject; he bred superbly constructed hounds. The main difference in construction between an English Basset and a KC show-ring Basset Hound is the position of the elbow.

It is only when the scapula and the humerus are of the right length *and* correctly placed that a dog can achieve the desired length of stride and freedom in his front action. Sighthounds can have their upper arms 20 per cent longer than their scapulae. In smaller breeds they tend to be equal in length. Dogs that step short in front are nearly always handicapped by upright shoulders and short, steep upper arms. A dog of quality must have sloping shoulders and compatible upper arms to produce a good length of neck, a firm topline without dips, the right length of back and free movement on the forehand. The upper arm determines, with its length, the placement of the elbow on the chest wall. Many dogs that are loose at elbow are tight at the shoulder joint and the forelegs tend to be thrown sideways in a circular movement. If the dog is tight at elbow the whole leg inclines outwards, causing the dog to 'paddle'.

In their commendable emphasis on superlative shoulders, Foxhound men have sometimes undervalued other parts of a hound's anatomy, which is not always wise. A *sound physique* is surely the key element in any hound's make-up, with every part of it contributing to a successful hunting dog. In his editorial notes to Beckford's celebrated *Thoughts on Hunting* (a later edition), Otho Paget wrote that, 'Backs and loins should always be there, but a good shoulder is a necessity.' (I would have thought that a good loin was as important and is so often an undervalued part of the hound's anatomy. I therefore devote more words to this below.) As Richard Clapham points out in his *Foxes, Foxhounds and Fox-hunting* (1936): 'Show judges are apt to pay more attention to the fore-end of a hound than his hind-quarters, but this is a great mistake, for it should be remembered that pace and jumping ability are derived solely from the hind-quarters.' In many modern hound breeds a far greater degree of angulation in the hindlimbs is being sought.

Show-Ring Misconceptions

In every animal walking on four legs the force derived from pressing the hindfoot into the ground has to be transmitted to the pelvis at the acetabulum, and onwards to the spine by way of the sacrum. In overangulated dogs the locomotive power is directed to an inappropriate part of the acetabulum. In addition, so as to retain the required degree of rigidity of the joint

Staghounds on the flags.

West Country Harriers being judged.

between the tibia and the femur, other muscles have to come into use. In the over-angulated hindlimb, the tibia meets the bottom end of the femur at such an angle that *direct* drive cannot ensue. The femur can only transmit the drive to the acetabulum *after* the rectus femoris muscle has contracted, enabling the femur to assume a degree of joint rigidity when connecting with the tibia. This means that the femur rotates anticlockwise whereas nature intended it to move clockwise.

Excessive angulation in the hindquarters, with an elongated tibia, may, to some, give a more pleasing outline to the exhibit when 'stacked' in the ring. But in the long term it can only lead to anatomical and locomotive disaster. Such angulation destroys the ability of the dog's forelimbs and hindlimbs to cooperate in harmony in propelling the body. Yet I have heard it argued by breed specialists at seminars that it will increase the power of propulsion operating through the hindlimbs and on through the spine. If it did, the racing Greyhound fraternity would have pursued it with great vigour. I have heard a dog show judge praise an over-angulated dog because it 'stood over a lot of ground'! So does a stretch limousine, but it requires a purpose-built construction to permit the luxury.

Discomforting Leg Construction
The Basset Hound, like the Dachshund, is an example of an achondroplasic animal; achondroplasia is not a disease but an inherited condition in which the long bones of the leg do not attain normal length, disproportionate dwarfism in effect. Scientists tell us that the achondroplasic short-leg gene affects heavy bone more than fine bone and that it will therefore be more difficult to obtain a short-legged dog with straight legs if the bone is heavy than if it is light. It is not surprising therefore that the straight-legged English Basset of the hunting field has appreciably lighter bone than the crooked-legged standard show-type Basset. In their book, *Medical and Genetic Aspects of Purebred Dogs* (1994), Clark and Stainer reported that:

> The Basset Hound is placed in the chondrodystrophoid group of dogs. The conformation of the breeds in this category leads to many inherent problems. The most common problem in the Basset is the high incidence of shoulder and foreleg lameness. There appears to be a high incidence of osteochondritis dessicans. Deformities of the distal radius, ulna and carpal joint are frequently seen.

Basset Hounds with excessively short crooked legs *suffer*; a sporting breed should not be bred to suit our whims but always to honour past function.

Learning about Loins
It is not unusual for those involved in dogs to be fairly hazy about the loin. I can recall standing ringside at a hound show, alongside a former MRH and a distinguished judge, and listening to his observations, especially those based on his confusing the hounds' flanks with their loins! A much-respected lurcher breeder once told me that for years he had thought that the loin was another word for the groin. I once

sat through a two-hour lecture on locomotion in the dog, given by a lecturer from a vet school, and realized that the loin had not been mentioned once. He did refer to muscles like the rectus abdominis, the principal flexor of the spine, the great oblique, which arches the back, flexes the spine or inclines it laterally, and the lumbo-dorsal/thoracolumbar fascia, where the loin is situated.

This distinguished scientist was so used to lecturing to students, undergraduates with a good knowledge of anatomy, that he had forgotten the importance of respectful simplification to an audience that may have lacked specialist knowledge but contained people just as intelligent, and certainly more perceptive, than he. What he lacked the empathy to explain was that the loins comprise the lumbar area, extending from the end of the rib cage to the start of the pelvis, forming the upper section of the couplings region. The coupling comprises the whole muscular band joining the chest and hindquarters, not just in the loin area. The loins overlie the lumbar vertebrae, can differ in length, flexibility and capability, according to the length of these bones and their substance, as well as to the width of their prominence on each side. This accounts for breed differences, originating in function. Not surprisingly, the loins of a Foxhound are not the same as those in a terrier.

Judge Awareness

No breed wants sagging loins, giving a drooping backline at the coupling. But requirements vary in breeds from slightly tucked loins, arched loins and a need to be 'light in loins'. Judges of every breed need to be aware of the loin. Good length of loin can make a dog look more rectangular than square, when the actual distance from the sternum to the point of buttock is in reality not much greater than the height at the withers. A short-loined exhibit can so often be more eye-catching, especially if it displays a long neck and upright shoulders, but it is not a sound animal.

The long dorsal muscle, which extends the spine or bends it to one side, is especially noticeable in the loins, where each vertebral bone carries the weight of the body in front of it, together with the weight of its own body mass. Towards the sacrum, each vertebra is accepting greater total weight than the one before it – the vertebrae get bigger, moving rearwards, throughout the lumbar region. It is not difficult to

appreciate therefore the importance to a substantial breed, like the Bloodhound, as well as the fast, lithe leaping dog, of the loin. Breeders of Foxhounds have long been aware of this importance, but perhaps haven't always given it the attention it merits.

Hound breeders have long acknowledged the impact made by sagging loins on endurance, but also knew the limitations of the hound being *too* short-coupled. Generally speaking, over-shortness of body, as opposed to shortness of back, carries more disadvantages than a little extra length, which gives more flexibility and easier whelping. It is vitally important for judges to know how to spot the crucial difference between a long body and a long back; the two don't always coincide! In his valuable *Memories of My Life at the College Valley* of 2012, Martin Letts writes:

> Length between hip and hock is a pace indicator, just as an angled hock and muscle at the stifle as are indicators of power behind the saddle. I also look for width in the pelvis to allow natural thrust and to allow the hind limbs to pass to the outside of the front limbs at top pace…

It is always vital to look at the *whole* hound when considering sound construction, not one favoured feature, a bad mistake in late Victorian hound breeding.

Lacking Endurance

Knowledge of how a dog's anatomy *works*, rather than mystical powers, is why the so-called gift of 'an eye for a dog' puts one judge in a different class from another. A desirable arched loin can be confused with a roach or sway back. An exhibit may get away with a sagging loin in the show ring or even on the flags at a hound show; but it would never do so as a working or sporting dog. It would lack endurance and would suffer in old age. Yet it is, for me, comparatively rare to witness a judge in any ring in any breed test the scope, muscularity and hardness of the loin through a hands-on examination. For such a vital part of the dog's anatomy to go unjudged is a travesty. The lumbar vertebrae are quite literally the backbones of the loins, *lumbus* being Latin for loin. Any arch should be over the lumbar vertebrae and not further forward.

An obsession with shoulders can lead to the overlooking of failings elsewhere in the hound; the whole hound needs scrutiny, with total soundness being the key. In his own book *Hunting* of 1900, Otho Paget wrote:

> The merest novice amongst hounds will be struck at once on visiting Belvoir with the character and quality of the pack. At the first glance your eye fails to distinguish one hound from another: they are all of one type, yet each has an individuality of its own, which gradually comes to you as you look more closely. They have bone and strength, yet there is no lumber, and every movement denotes activity. Legs and feet are perfection; backs and loins appear made to carry muscle; and the thighs, over which the rippling sinews play, suggest a graceful strength. Generations of careful breeding have imparted to this pack a certain dignified air of calm superiority...

He was clearly assessing the hounds on their overall merit, rather than stressing one particular physical feature. And he didn't overlook the loin.

In an attempt to appreciate the value of the loin to the hound, I think of the hound as a four-wheel drive, rear-engined vehicle with its transmission in the loins. They are an absolutely key feature of the canine anatomy relating to movement. If we prize movement then we must understand the loins. But just try researching the subject even in weighty books on dogs, and even in those on packhounds. Anyone assessing a hound on the flags who doesn't check the strength of loin in each and every exhibit is simply not doing his job!

Taking the Strain
In his book *The Foxhound of the Future* of 1953, C.R. Acton makes a number of points for me:

> A hound usually shows more signs of wear and tear in its forelegs than in its hindlegs, and this is due to the fact that the former, being the nearer to the centre of gravity, bear the larger share of weight and act as the chief propellers of the body. The hindlegs themselves provide **drive** and the second part of the propelling movement for the jump... Whilst the forelegs touch the ground first on arriving from a jump and, consequently, take the concussion of the actual impact, the loins and quarters ease the strain, hence the necessity for strong loins and muscular quarters on hound or horse.

Rhodesian Ridgeback with well-developed loins.

I am dismayed when I see hound breed exhibits in KC show rings being proudly displayed by their owners quite evidently carrying weak under-muscled loins and under-developed quarters – and some of them win!

No Hoof – No Horse
'No hoof, no horse' is a time-honoured saying in equestrian circles but I've never heard a cry of 'No foot, no dog' in canine circles. And when I see judging at KC-licensed dog shows, I find it rare indeed to see a judge check a dog's feet. But which is more important, sound feet or set of tail? I suppose in an arena where dogs are valued solely for what they look like rather than what they can do, this is not surprising. Ignoring the soundness of your dogs' feet is, however, a recipe for disaster in breeding programmes. Unless sound feet are produced, especially in sporting breeds, then the future of the domestic dog as an active animal is threatened. In *The Foxhound of the Future* Acton wrote:

> There are still some kennels where the hounds stand on the sides of their feet and knuckle over at the knee, but most Masters to-day prefer the natural foot. The two extremes are the pre-war Belvoir foot and knee, and the Fell foot. They are usually referred to as 'cat foot' and 'hare foot' respectively, though both terms are stupid as each are essentially dogs' feet.

The most knowledgeable people on feet should be the Foxhound breeders. Whatever contemporary attitudes towards the sport of foxhunting, there is no doubt in my mind that the Foxhound is the best-bred dog in the country. In his book on the sport, referred to above, the renowned Lake District hound expert Richard Clapham wrote: 'No matter what other good qualities a hound may possess, if his feet cannot stand wear and tear…his usefulness in life is… at an end.' He went on to praise the hare-foot or to him natural foot, claiming that the cat-like or club-foot needs more attention in kennels. He describes the hare-foot as a fairly long, closely knit, shallow-padded foot, similar to that of the wolf, coyote and fox. But the breed standard of hounds like the Rhodesian Ridgeback and the Otterhound calls for a round, compact foot. The Basset Hound is required to have massive feet but be capable of great endurance in the field. Huge feet mean greater and longer contact with the ground and therefore more strain. No working hound benefits from massive feet.

Importance of Shape

The arguments over whether a round, compact foot is preferable to the oval hare-foot in scenthounds have gone on for two centuries. In his contribution to The Lonsdale Library's *Deer, Hare & Otter Hunting* of 1929, the Earl of Stradbroke, Master of the Henham Harriers, had this to say about feet and pasterns:

> I have found that the hounds that last the longest, and go out on the greatest number of days in the season, are the lighter built hounds, often, too, those with what we all try to breed out, 'hare-feet'!… I cannot help thinking that in advocating so strongly a short joint we go too far, and there should be a little more length, than is generally considered to be the per-

Coniston Fell Hound with perfect hare-feet.

Does the Basset Hound need 'massive feet'?

fection aimed at. Greater length gives the necessary elasticity to save a jar to the shoulder, when landing from a jump.

If, however, you look at the breed standards of the hound breeds, hunting by scent, recognized by the KC, you find considerable variation between them. According to the KC, a Beagle's feet must not be hare-footed; the Otterhound's and the Foxhound's feet have to be round; the Grand Bleu de Gascogne's feet have to be long and oval; the Norwegian Elkhound's feet have to be slightly oval; the Finnish Spitz's feet need to be round; the Basset Bleu de Gascogne's feet should be oval. No wonder the breeders of these breeds and those who judge them in the ring get confused by conflicting instructions.

Being Let Down

Stradbroke's point about saving 'a jar to the shoulder' is a fair one; ramrod straight front legs, as seen from the side, lack spring and force-absorption; too short a pastern in the front legs restricts that essential springiness. The breed standards also insist that such breeds are well let-down at hock, that is, have their hocks close to the ground. This is an often misunderstood term; in both racehorses and sporting dogs, the seeking of long cannon bones led to the use of this expression. It was never intended to promote short rear pasterns, but long muscles in what in humans is the calf, *leading to* a low-placed hock or heel. In a different sense sporting dogs are being 'let down' by such advice in both cases set out above; elasticity is essential in the hound's front legs and ample extension is vital in the hindlimbs. Over-compact feet, rounded and too tight, are in fact a handicap when the hound is striving to gain from ground pressure at pace, as users of the Fell Hound have long accepted. Some of the wording in the KC's breed standards is ill-advised and judges are slavishly obeying them when they should be challenging them.

Big Bones

'The search for large bone is going to bring with it an obvious increase in growth rate which in turn renders the dog more liable to such problems as OCD, UAP or FCP...' Those words by the late Dr Malcom Willis in his authoritative *Practical Genetics for Dog*

This Foxhound portrayal unwittingly reveals a hound over-boned and badly footed, only typifying bad breeding for a faulty design.

Breeders (1992) don't seem to impress dog breeders perhaps as much as they should. Some breeds are actually prized for the weight of their bone, with many judges seeking heavy bone in exhibits, if their critiques are anything to go by. A century ago, Foxhound breeders lost their way and sought hounds with heavy, dense, massive bone, claiming that this feature provided stamina. They themselves however, when riding to hounds, rode hunters not carthorses – and still managed to keep up! Their folly was subsequently exposed by a hound expert from America, the legendary 'Ikey' Bell. It wasn't until the late 1920s that the misguided passion for over-timbered legs, tightly bunched toes and absurdly compact feet was finally bred out in some packs of Foxhounds.

Breeders of horses know that 'good, flat bone' provides the quality, not massively thick bone. Breeders of Foxhounds have learned the importance of bone from past follies. The late Victorian/

Belvoir Belper 1903 – over-knuckled at the knee and massively timbered.

Edwardian Foxhound breeders, perhaps in a vain attempt to surpass the superlative light hounds of such as Lord Bentinck, unwisely opted for over-boned hounds. Daphne Moore, a Foxhound authority, in her book *Foxhounds*, described such hounds as 'built on massive lines, with great bone, barrel ribs, knuckling over knees, very short upright pasterns ending in a foot which was round, fleshy and often pigeon-toed.' I have previously pointed out how this was appropriately termed the 'short-horn' period in hound breeding and thankfully it was soon abandoned. It was abandoned because it handicapped the hounds. A heavy hound such as the Fila Brasileiro can so easily become just that, rivalling our Mastiff for immobility, needless bulk and bone problems. At World Dog Shows I see substantial but athletic specimens in this breed and they are so impressive.

Needless Weight

The accomplished hound breeder Buchanan-Jardine gave the view, in his book *Hounds of the World*, that, 'Great weight of bone is unnecessary and rather a hindrance than the reverse…' It is of course the muscles that control the bones, not the other way round;

Sanity restored! A fine Foxhound from the Crawley and Horsham, by Francis M. Hollams, 1949.

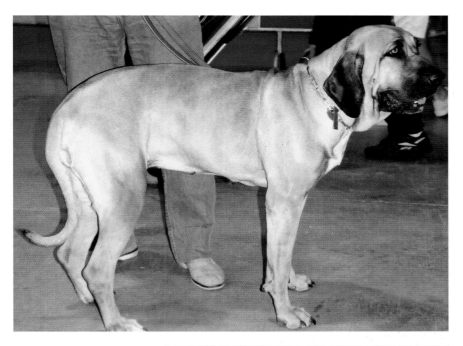

A powerful Fila Brasileiro – but not at all over-boned.

muscular development is far, far more important than the thickness of the bone. It is a lazy response to state that 'what applies to Foxhounds doesn't apply to my breed'. The lessons learnt by any breeder in any field are worth heeding. To prize a dog mainly because of its weight is astonishingly naive. To boast of an unsound dog's shoulder height and poundage is, to me, a sure sign of an insecure personality needing to have his ego boosted by the size of his dog. To be proud of a sound big dog is surely, in the larger breeds, every good breeder's aim.

Sadly, dog breeding in pure-bred dogs is conducted, not on lines of desired and measurable improvement but on repeating the past, despite advances in scientific knowledge and a pronounced loss of type in some breeds. When, as part of my professional responsibilities, I ran a rare breeds farm, I was able to benefit from a range of systems and recommended procedures, not utilized in adapted form by dog breeders. Even when breeding longhorn cattle, I never once heard the desirability of heavy bone mentioned in breeding programmes, and these were creatures weighing a ton and a half each. Strength and power in animals doesn't reside in bone size, as racehorses, antelopes and hyenas demonstrate only too vividly.

A pigeon-toed hound at the 1999 Honiton Hound Show.

Head study of a Bloodhound by Arthur Wardle, 1940.

The Eyes Have It

If you find joy in watching a galloping Harrier scanning the foreground or an Otterhound focussing on suspected scent floating its way before tensing up instinctively, you appreciate fully the close link between sight and scent in sporting breeds. These two particular senses have been highly developed in such breeds by man for centuries. Both senses mean more to dogs than to us; that alone is reason enough to prize them and strive to protect them. It is believed that dogs have 20/75 vision, meaning that they are able to see clearly an object from 20ft away that a human with normal vision would see at 75ft away. Cats have roughly 20/100 vision and horses 20/33, closer to ours. But dogs have vastly superior night vision and the detection of movement. They thrived as predators because of their combined better-developed senses of sight, hearing and smell. The low-light vision of dogs is greatly superior to ours too, facilitating hunting at night.

Dogs are more aware of events around them than human beings are. Their eyes are set on their heads at a 20-degree angle, whereas we have our eyes set looking straight ahead. Dogs have a much wider field of view than we do, around 250 degrees against our 180 degrees. Perception of depth depends on binocular vision, which is the visual area where the two eyes overlap. The greater the binocular field, then the greater the depth of perception in a species. We excel in depth perception, with a visual overlap of around 140 degrees; dogs have a visual overlap of around 80 degrees only. They need all the help they can get in depth perception. By limiting further their binocular vision we increase their burden more than we realise. This additionally imposed limitation is one dogs could do without. Sunken eyes in the Bloodhound and red raw eyes in the Basset Hound are unwanted features.

Ear Examinations

The length of a dog's head is an inherited characteristic that is almost as variable as the length of the dog's ears. Each breed has a relationship between the lengths of the dog's legs, its body, its head, its muzzle and its ears. Far better surely, in breed standards, to describe these proportions in relation to each other *and* the limits desired. In the standard of the Beagle, for example, the ears are required to extend to the nose tip. Overlong ears, getting longer with each generation, are of no benefit to the dog. Why not state that the Beagle's ears should extend to the nose but no further? Breeders and judges would then know that

Two show Basset Hounds at Bath Dog Show, 2009.

excessive ear length was frowned on in the standard. This was in fact the wording of the early breed standard and it was not wise to change it. It is just not good enough to state that a scenthound's ears should be 'long' or 'very long' or that they should extend at least to the hound's nose. Basset Hounds that step on their own ears are handicapped animals. There is a health handicap too in overlong ears. The thick, heavy, low-set ears cut off the circulation of air in the ear canal, thereby providing a breeding ground for bacteria and yeasts that cause chronic ear infections. A very hairy ear canal further restricts air circulation. Disappointingly, hair in the ear canal is not mentioned in any breed standard.

Head study of a Beagle – what ear length does this breed need?

Seeking the Superfluous

Writing three centuries ago, Alexander Pope penned these prescient, perceptive words:

Beauties in vain their pretty eyes may roll;
Charms strike the sight, but merit wins the soul.

Beauty does appeal to the eye and please the mind. But merit, real merit, that quality which justifies reward, does more – it lifts the spirit, satisfies the quest for high standards, truly 'wins the soul'. Beauty alone can never be enough, even at a dog show where physical perfection is aimed at, however impossible the task. When a handsome dog displays ugly movement it immediately ceases to be a beautiful dog to me. When a stunningly handsome dog reveals serious anatomical faults on closer inspection, the charms that struck the sight soon trouble the mind. When you know that a strikingly good-looking dog carries hereditary flaws that will be passed on to its offspring, the mind should rebel and the soul take control. The beauty of a show exhibit, stacked for the judge's admiration, can be very temporary. Its genes and their accompanying faults and flaws are permanent.

The Danger from Fads

Fads may be passing indulgences for fanciers but they so often do lasting harm to breeds. If they did harm to the breeders who inflict them, rather than to the wretched dogs that suffer them, fads would be more tolerable and certainly more short-lived. But what are the comments of veterinary surgeons who have to treat the ill-effects of misguided fads? In his informative book *The Anatomy of Dog Breeding* (1962) vet and exhibitor R.H. Smythe wrote:

In attempting to breed dogs which compare favourably with the standard laid down for any particular breed, we are guided by the aesthetic angle, and we completely disregard the fact that the majority of dogs are basically unsound or deformed, and that it

is this fact which makes them valuable. We shall earn no marks if we succeed in lengthening the limbs of a Scottish Terrier or tightening the skin of a Bloodhound. Their beauty lies in their imperfections and we must maintain these if the breed is to retain its popularity.

This is an extremely outspoken honest statement from a most knowledgeable and experienced sportsman and exhibitor. We tend to condone past fads but need to be watchful about newly fashionable ones, often promoted to suit the plans of one influential kennel.

Breeders of British breeds are sometimes accused abroad of seeking exaggeration, exaggeration to a degree which is harmful and untypical. Those perpetuating our native breeds *must* remember the function for which that particular breed was developed, whether that function has lapsed or not. Only then can real, genuine, historically correct type be preserved. Every breeder of one of our native breeds has a special duty to safeguard its future; we must never let breeders from foreign countries change type or dictate what our breeds should look like. In his informative book *The Theory and Practice of Breeding to Type* (1952), C.J. Davies concluded: '...animals nearest to the "correct type" are those best adapted for the work which they are supposed to perform.' It is so important to remember this when assessing a dog or planning a litter. Breeders and judges, think hard before you make decisions – the future of all our magnificent breeds of dog are in your hands.

The fads are to be ignored. So to ignore them may prevent one's winning with one's dogs under faddist judges while the fads endure but, in the long run, one will have better dogs and more success with them if one does not run after each showy and reasonless innovation that appears in one's breed. Such fads are liable to side-track the major purpose to breed logically constructed and well-balanced dogs.

Kyle Onstott, *The Art of Breeding Better Dogs* (1947)

CHAPTER 2

THE SPECIALISTS

The Foxhound

> What other breed of dog is there that could trot out a dozen or fourteen miles along the roads to a meet, then gallop about for five hours or so, often hard enough to tire out two thorough-bred horses in succession, all the time using his nose, intelligence and voice, then come home at night with his stern up, and do it regularly twice a week?…it is a great deal to expect of a dog.
>
> Sir John Buchanan-Jardine MFH, *Hounds of the World* (1937)

Absence of Standardization

If any breed of dog should be chosen to epitomize the English sporting dog then the Foxhound has to be a top choice. The Bulldog may serve to exemplify British stoicism, the Bull Terrier to illustrate sheer tenacity and perhaps the Jack Russell to typify English eccentricity. But the Foxhound, for breeding excellence, field performance and sporting aura – some might say handsomeness too – is way out in front as the sporting dog. It may be questionable to regard the Foxhound as a breed, with some packs having claims to a distinct type or variety under that name, as the Curre, the Belvoir and the Dumfriesshire packs long demonstrated. But the KC recognises the Foxhound as one breed, with one breed standard, and, as with every breed registered with them, will seek standardization and conformation to a set word picture. This is often in conflict with the sportsman's need to design a hound for the quarry it pursues and the country it hunts, with hunt preferences coming to the fore in time.

The North-South Divide

In his *Sporting Dogs* of 1945, Croxton Smith records:

> The Southern Hound type was preserved in the Hailsham Harriers in Sussex. In 1910 I got in touch

Lady Curre's Windsor of 1930.

with the Rev C Morgan-Kirby…who had collected a pack of what he believed to be old Southern
Hounds…he came to know Mr Peachey's Harriers…
it was claimed that the hounds had been in the family for 800 years and that until 1890 they were pure
Southern Hounds… Mr Morgan-Kirby wrote to me
that there were great differences between the Southern and Northern-Southern hound; the former was
short-legged, blunt-headed, heavy-bodied and had
not very long ears… What he called the Northern-
Southern were herring-gutted, with a high dome,
beautiful, lean-cut head, deep flews and long pendant
ears; they were also taller and shriller.

The classic Belvoir markings.

Old Southern Hounds by T. Ivester Lloyd, 1934.

Sir Edward Curre and his hounds, with a hunt terrier, 1921.

Morgan-Kirby later wrote that by 1910 it was impossible to get pure Southern Hounds, claiming their decline came from excessive inbreeding. Hounds that 'decline' are soon replaced by sportsmen, just as they would have been by primitive hunters.

In his excellent book *English Fox Hunting – A History* (1976), Raymond Carr summed up the evolution of the hound of today, writing:

> The basic strains of the English foxhound have been traditionally divided into northern and southern hounds. The northern hound or beagle was smaller than the southern hound, sharp-nosed, 'fleet', hunting 'more by the Eye than the Nose.' The southern hound (it probably came from Gascony in medieval times) was renowned for its steadiness, its resistance to riot, its capacity to work on a scent with patience; but it was heavy and slow… The two strains could still be distinguished as late as 1830 when Scrutator noted the distinction between the 'neat' Belvoir hounds and the heavier Cottesmore pack.

To this day, each pack reveals, from time to time, the ingredients from way back that influenced its type and form today.

Colour Differences

Hounds used on fox, like the Welsh, with its rough-haired 'griffon' coat, the Fell, with its lighter frame, those indicating the Curre influence at Chepstow, with that characteristic white coat, the Dumfriesshire, with its distinctive black and tan jacket (both now sadly lost to us as packs) and, say, the Belvoir with its classic tricolour markings, don't exactly fit in with one firmly worded blueprint. Although the KC standard for their breed does allow any recognized hound colour and markings, I doubt however whether they would be happy with merle, as found in the Dunker Hound of Norway; harlequin, as found in the Russian Hounds; or the red-tick and blue-tick coat colourations found in US hound breeds. All these breeds are recognized by overseas kennel clubs. Foxhound experts like Beckford, Osbaldeston, Paget, Bell, Higginson, Wallace and Rycroft have long expressed clear views on the coat colour and the conformation of the Foxhound.

Beckford gave the view that 'the colour I think of little moment'; Fox, for over forty years a huntsman and whipper-in, wrote in 1924, under his pseudonym 'Yoi-over', of: '…our native foxhounds…rich and varied colours, tan – deep and light – black and tan, and the white flicked and bitten; one was white and spotted like a Dalmatian carriage dog.' Rycroft has questioned whether the tan eyebrows on a black and tan hound indicate a throwback to the ancient St Hubert hound, going on to state that blue-mottle is often linked to a good nose. In his masterly *Hounds of the World* Buchanan-Jardine wrote:

Head study of Welsh Foxhound.

BELOW: *Dumfriesshire Foxhounds sketched by Comte Xavier de Poret.*

In the colour of foxhounds there are again different tastes. At one time, Belvoir tan hounds were the only ones in the fashion, and the less white they had on them the better coloured they were considered to be. Now there is a fashion among some Masters for very light-coloured hounds, sometimes almost white... I have known many good hounds marked with blue-mottled colour, and with tan ticks down their legs, perhaps throwing-back to the old Southern hound blood. Again, I have known many very good hounds with a lot of black about them, particularly about the head...it is really a great mistake to allow oneself to be prejudiced by mere colour when breeding hounds...

That judgement could be valuably extended to read 'when breeding dogs more generally'.

Breeding Model

The breeding of Foxhounds should act as a model for dog breeders everywhere. The whole aim is to produce a better-performing hound, with cosmetic points never ahead of field ability. The mania for pure-breeding has rarely afflicted sportsmen, hound breeders especially. Ronnie Wallace at the Heythrop used outcrosses that were American, West Country Harrier, Fell and Old English, but not Welsh, as

ABOVE LEFT: Tiverton Foxhound, in a black and buckskin coat.

Blue-ticked, wheel-backed hound.

is often the case in the pursuit of improved scenting and voice in some English packs. I recall talking about Foxhound breeding with a well-known MFH in the mid-1950s and hearing of his preference for using not an 'outsider' but the better brother or sister (in the field) of a Peterborough winner. For him, this provided performance *and* conformation.

The early years of the twentieth century saw significant changes in hound breeding; the benefit of an infusion of Welsh Hound and Fell Hound blood into many packs, as well as the added value of the Belvoir stallion hounds, was recognized. More importantly, the emphasis on drive, nose, cry and pace led to the development of more athletic, lighter, less bony hounds. The main instigator of this was Sir Edward Curre at the Chepstow Hunt. By the end of the Great War he had already had some twenty years of combining the merits of top-quality English bitches with proven Welsh stallion hounds, usually in a white or light jacket. He inspired others, like Sir Ian Amory of the Tiverton and Isaac Bell of the South and West Wilts, and influenced the Heythrop, North Cotswold and Cattistock packs. Out went the massively timbered 'shorthorns' and less favoured were the classic tricoloured Belvoir markings. By the 1930s, the 'Peterborough type' had been superseded by the lighter-boned, pacier hounds

ABOVE RIGHT: Eskdale and Ennerdale Fell Hounds, 1933.

Peterborough Show winners by A. Baker c.1890.

Typical of pre-1914 English Fox-hound

College Valley "Ranger" Inbred to "Morpeth Random" with some
Fell blood
An example of cross breeding on Mendelian principles

*Duke of Beaufort's winning doghound Fencer '32, at Peterborough
1936 (above); Belvoir Charter '13 (below).*

*College Valley 'Ranger' inbred to 'Morpeth Random' with some
Fell blood. An example of cross breeding on Mendelian principles.*

with better stamina. The College Valley pack, with its strong Fell Hound base, became renowned as the best fox-catching hounds for over half a century.

Writing in his *Hounds and Hunting Through the Ages* (1937), Joseph B. Thomas, himself a distinguished MFH, gave the view that '...a well made hound standing, say 23 inches, symmetrically put together anatomically, with sufficient bone on which to hang muscle, must have an advantage over a hound of equal height that carries weight of bone more than essential for strength.' An editorial in the prestigious sporting magazine *The Foxhound* of July 1911 stated: '...by concentrating attention on the qualifications in breeding hounds which produce perfection in conformation we have somewhat overlooked these important factors for

success in the hunting field...excessive development in one particular must act detrimentally upon the others.' This was in a discussion about the alleged loss of endurance, nose, tongue and pace in Foxhounds at that time. At that time too, the importance of the 'female line' in breeding was finally acknowledged, overcoming the slavish adherence to the 'sire-dominated' thinking of the previous century. Breeding hounds in the twentieth century became more and more an exercise in Mendel's principles than hitherto.

Hound Show Effect

Hound shows like the prestigious Peterborough event have long had considerable influence in the Foxhound world, though they have had their critics too. In *English Fox Hunting – A History* (1976), Raymond Carr writes:

> Some great breeders have doubted whether the characteristic Edwardian emphasis on appearance and size, fostered by Peterborough, produced the best kind of working hound… One side held that Peterborough shows were improving the standard of hounds all over the country by setting a high standard for every kennel. The other that the mania for Belvoir blood had produced 'lumbering caricatures of their ancestors'. Peterborough was 'a place of temptation'; masters took hounds almost entirely to gratify their hobby of breeding for shows…

There was once an old saying that 'More foxes are lost at Peterborough than anywhere else'. Today this sort of criticism is aimed at working terrier and lurcher shows too; man's desire to show off his stock is fine when the wallet and the ego, are held less important than the soundness of the exhibits.

Breeding for performance ahead of appearance and breed dogma means that the applied breeding criteria are definitive. If the hound doesn't measure up, it's not bred from, no matter how pretty it is. It produces healthier sounder hounds since the chase reveals every fault. Racing Greyhounds have succeeded in the show ring but it is less likely that a show Greyhound would win on the track. The socialization of Foxhounds by puppy-walkers allows hordes of delighted children to descend on them in the arena at country shows. This is an exercise that could not be similarly conducted using a couple of dozen unleashed dogs from quite a number of pedigree breeds. But however admirable their temperament, it's their anatomy which wins the most praise. In his book *Hounds* (1914), sportsman and veterinary surgeon Frank Townend Barton wrote:

> This brings the author to make a statement that very few will, on reflection, feel inclined to dispute the truth of. It is this: That the Foxhound is built upon lines displaying greater economy of material than that of any other variety of dog. Every ounce of bone and muscle is placed where it can be utilised to the best advantage.

That last phrase should be the diktat guiding all those who breed or judge hounds.

No Accidental Success

Admiration of Foxhounds led to there being more paintings of them and books on them than any other breed of dog. This level of excellence has not come about by accident. In his book *The Foxhound of the Future* (1953), C.R. Acton wrote:

Some of the Fernie Bitch Pack, 1927.

Though the science of genetics, itself, is new, the principles of heredity were in operation before Mendel's time. For years the breeding of fox-hounds by selection was based upon success, and the elimination of such methods as were unsuccessful. Such success was achieved by methods that were, unbeknown to the exponents, to a certain extent in accordance with the principles upon which the science of genetics is based. Hugo Meynell, Lord Henry Bentinck, Lord Willoughby de Broke, Lord Fitzhardinge were applied biologists, whether they realized the fact or not.

Every type or breed of hound *must* have the physique that permits it to *function as a hound*.

It is to such men that we owe the Foxhound of today, and, whatever its restricted use, it stands as a tribute to British livestock breeding down several centuries. In the first volume of *The Foxhound Studbook*, published in 1866, by Cornelius Tongue, it was stated that 'the successful breeder of hounds should follow the

Some of the Fernie Dog Pack, 1927.

The Fernie Hounds by Charles Walter Simpson (1885–1971).

principles of the successful breeder of race-horses, as it is invariably found that those animals are most to be depended upon for the perpetuation of their species whose genealogy can be traced in the greatest number of direct lines to great celebrities of olden times.' In other words, study the pedigrees! Whether the Foxhound graces the conformation show scene or parades at Honiton and Peterborough, the breeding behind the hound will come through, backed by informed selection and as always, cheered on by a host of admirers. The Foxhound reigns supreme as the canine athlete.

> Mr Fernie's country lies entirely in Leicestershire. The kennels are at Melbourne, a pretty village on the Welland, but in the extreme corner of the county and of the Hunt. They have about sixty couple of hounds in kennels, a charming pack with the true make, the good loins, the hocks near the ground and the beautiful necks and shoulders which enable them to gallop all day without tiring up and down the hills of their country, and to travel at a pace which is surpassed by no other pack of our time.
>
> Charles Simpson, *The Harboro' Country* (1927)

The Harehounds: Bassets, Harriers and Beagles

Basset Hounds – Hunting for the Real One

Long body, short legs, large back, long leathers, lovely head, lovely voice, the Basset is full of good qualities. It always has a loathing for any beast, but rabbit and hare are particularly favoured quarry; however Bassets are a perfect pure breed for roe deer, wolf and boar. Usually white with black or fawn markings, often their hair is all black and thick with reddish touches under the eyes, over the chest and at the base of legs. Many are griffons and amongst these, many are white with large patches of coffee colour. The other varieties of Basset are primarily distinguished by very pronounced arching of the front legs, their colour is the same as that of the straight legged Bassets; only I know that the griffons are very rare. The Bassets are naturally very much slower than the other hounds.

Basset Hounds in full cry, from a drawing by L. Wain.

Le Comte le Couteulx de Canteleu, *La Venerie Française* (1858)

The above quote is from the most famous French hound breeder of his time and his admiration for the Basset is quite clear. The breed we know best in Britain is outnumbered by those of mainland Europe, such as the Artesien-Normand, the Bleu de Gascogne, the Fauve de Bretagne and the Griffon-Vendeen Petit and Grand. They are still used to hunt hare and rabbit for the gun, excelling in dense cover. But they are also used for flushing game birds, rather like spaniels. There have been theories that the type evolved as a 'sport' from the St Hubert Hound, in its various types, and was then committed to a hunt involving footed rather than mounted hunters. We know that the short leg in the Bloodhound is dominant genetically over the longer leg (Whitney, *How to Breed Dogs*). The short leg is a Basset feature, whether crooked or straight. A sporting writer, Pennell-Elmhurst, who wrote under the pseudonym Brooksby, is quoted in David Hindle's *The Hunting Basset* of 2009, as writing (in 1896):

Straight-legged Hunting Bassets of the 1890s.

A Pack of Basset Hounds of 1894 by Valentine T. Garland.

On Tuesday I had the opportunity of seeing a form of hunting altogether novel to me, viz., the chase of the hare by Basset Hounds, the Messrs Cooper having brought their pack from Delapre Abbey. I confess I was charmed. There was something so sporting in seeing these little hounds (to all appearance first cross between a turnspit and a foxhound) driving along in grass that almost hid them.

He likened their length of leg to the spit-turning dog as no other hound here displayed such a feature at that time. A wealthy London-based sportsman would not have been aware of the Welsh heelers with similar legs or the tendency for some working terriers to carry such a noticeable feature.

Early References
In his most valuable book on hunting, published in the late sixteenth century, Jacques du Fouilloux makes an early reference to Bassets, describing them as badger dogs. He identified two types: those with a crooked front, which he stated were short-coated and

went to ground better, and those with a straight front, which often carried the rough coat and ran game above ground as well as conducting terrier work. Du Fouilloux attributed the first home of these Bassets to the regions of Artois and Flanders. Both these regions have a record over five centuries of producing exceptional hounds.

In his excellent book *The Basset Hound* (1968), George Johnston, who knew his hounds, produced a map of northwestern Europe showing the distribution of the Basset type. This puts the rough-coated variety in northwest France (the Basset Fauve de Bretagne and the Basset Griffon-Vendeen), the smooth-coated variety in the north (the Bassets de Normandie, d'Artois and d'Ardennes) and the south (the Bassets de Saintonge and Bleu de Gascogne), with some smooth-coats on the German-French border in the Vosges and the Black Forest. He also mentions the allied breeds: the Dachshund in Germany, the Niederlaufhund of Switzerland and the Drever of Sweden.

The first French dog show, in Paris in 1863, issued a catalogue which listed Bassets as follows: straight-legged short and long-haired, crooked-legged short and long-haired, Baden Bassets, Burgos, St Domingo, Illyrian and Hungarian Bassets. This shows a Basset diaspora stretching from Brittany to Budapest and from the Black Forest to the Balkans. The Baden Basset would have been the Dachsbracke or badger hound. The Danes had a Dachsbracke too, known there as the Strellufstover, and now embraced by the Drever of northern Scandinavia. These short-legged but usually straight-legged hounds were used to drive game to the waiting guns. It is surprising that, whilst the Swiss have developed several breeds of Niederlaufhunde, the French border areas with Switzerland have none.

The Companion Basset

The Basset Hound had a chequered start as a hunting dog in Britain. As Dr Brian Wilson points out in his *A Bother of Bassets* (2004), throughout Britain, over thirty Basset Hound kennels that had begun to operate between 1872 and 1903 had, by the time the Master of Basset Hounds Association (MBHA) was founded in 1912, come and gone. But the Basset Hound, as a pet or show dog, is now well established in Britain, with more than 1,000 being registered annually. In America in 1977, nearly 15,000 were registered with the AKC, such was their appeal. Other French Basset breeds are now becoming known here, with the Petit Basset Griffon Vendeen proving the most popular. Thirty years ago I found them longer-eared, longer-backed and more heavily coated than desired, but this may have been due to the breeding between the Grands and the Petits allowed up till then. This is hardly surprising for it is a delightful breed, full of character and charm. A first-class book on the breed has recently been published: written by Valerie Link and Linda Skerritt, and published in America by Doral Publishing. Nearly 400 pages long, with a good index, it is a pleasing production in times when so many breed books are disappointingly shallow.

The best show Basset Hound, of all the Basset breeds, that I saw in 2012 was a Petit Basset Griffon Vendeen bitch, Champion Soletrader Peek A Boo,

Petit Basset Griffon Vendeen couple from 1900.

Petit Basset Griffon Vendeen at Crufts, 1991.

bred by Gavin and Sara Robertson and sired by a Dutch import, also from Soletrader kennels' stock. This hound really looked as though she could hunt! (She went on to win Best in Show at Crufts in 2013.)

It is ironic that those with show Bassets who criticize the hunting fraternity for their outcross to the Harrier should choose to overlook pioneer breeder Millais' outcrosses to both the Beagle and the Bloodhound. Of this latter cross, as documented by David Hindle in his *The Hunting Basset* of 2009, Millais stated, at the time (*c*.1892):

> I therefore employed the Bloodhound as the vehicle for importing fresh blood to counteract the commencing degeneration on the part of the Basset, considering that this cross would be of infinitely greater value to us breeders than the importation would be of a number of French Bassets of the same variety, but of inferior type and size.

It's the task of any hound breeder to improve his hounds, not just perpetuate old flaws. Pure-bred Bassets are still represented in the hunting field by the Albany and the Huckworthy. Ten years ago the West Lodge pack was three-quarters Basset, one-quarter Harrier but there were also Griffon-Vendeens in the pack. There are several packs of Petit Griffons-Vendeens hunting in Britain. The Ryford Chase has utilized West Country Harrier, Welsh Foxhound and more recently Beagle blood to make the pack less wilful and more biddable.

The Albany was for some time the Basset Hound Club's pack, with some show dogs hunting with them. The American hunting Bassets are often show dogs too. American hunters find two types of Basset Hound: those with high energy, which are lighter in bone, less chunky and longer in leg; and the lower-energy, more classic hounds which are noticeably more laid-back, in the modern idiom. The former lack the painstaking methodical style of the classic Basset hunt but often 'hunt on' using air scent before picking up ground scent once more. The Americans have trials for hunting in packs and hunting in couples, or brace trials. The American Rabbit Hound Association also has a hunt competition for Bassets. In the future we may well have no Bassets hunting.

The Barony Bassets in Dumfriesshire by Liam Clancy, twentieth century.

The Hunting Packs

In 1908 there were nearly forty hunting packs of Bassets in Britain, against just ten Basset Hounds registered with the Kennel Club in that year. Twelve years ago there were ten packs recognized by the MBHA: six were straight-legged packs, the others crooked-legged. About half were pure-bred Bassets, the remainder mainly the so-called English Basset, the progeny of the Harrier outcross and more recently Beagle, West Country Harrier and Petit Basset Griffon Vendeen blood too. The first pack made up of English Bassets was the Westerby, whose country lies mainly in Leicestershire, and originally pure-bred Walhampton Bassets. The pure-bred hunting basset lacks much of the excessive wrinkle and exaggerated crooked knee of so many show bench hounds. The Fourshire Bassets of ten years ago were good examples of pure-bred working hounds.

Around 1910, the hunting stock declined appreciably, all too many of the hounds displaying gross exaggeration and even malformation. There were stories of Bassets being carried from the hunting field on stretchers made of sheep hurdles. In 1911 the MBHA was formed and only hounds from recognized packs became eligible for registration. KC-registered hounds were refused entry. The majority of MBHA registrations were Artesien-Normandie in origin. A notable exception was the Sandringham kennel of Basset Griffon-Vendeen owned by Queen Alexandra. The First World War, however, almost saw the demise of the Basset Hound in England.

Colonel Morrison's work with the Westerby pack from the 1930s saw a steady improvement in fortune. He started with the Basset Artesien-Normandie for its nose and cry, that is, its scenting skill and musical baying. He made inspired crosses with the Basset Griffon-Vendeen, the Beagle and the Harrier to enhance drive, stamina and pace. Today's show breeders should note that the improved performance was not vaguely 'expected' from a closed gene pool but pursued by a gifted breeder with an open mind. Millais, the pioneer Basset breeder, would have approved.

Lesson Worth Heeding

The desire to see hounds bred for hunting led to the Albany & West Lodge Hounds pack being formed in 1955, as the Working Branch of the Basset Hound Club (BHC). In 1972, the name of the pack was changed to just the Albany and the Working Branch restructured. In 2002, the BHC withdrew support for the Albany when the latter felt the hounds were becoming too heavy and cumbersome. The Albany became a subscription pack and began to outcross to other packs in the pursuit of a working capability in their hounds. Foxhound, Harrier or Beagle blood was never used in these outcrosses. In 2006 the Albany merged with the West Lodge, seeking hounds that could hunt for four hours twice a week. A working hound with its chest at least five inches off the ground was the aim. This parting of the ways can never be good for the breed and is a lesson to be heeded by other hound breed clubs wanting to develop a pedigree breed still able to perform its original function. Could it be that in the Basset Hound of the show rings the long-ago Bloodhound input is proving, even today, too dominant genetically for this breed's best interests, guilty of introducing exaggerations to an unhealthy degree?

Avoiding Excessive Features

A writer in the *Veterinary Record* in 1991, referred to this type, rather unkindly, as 'achondroplasic dwarfs'. Smythe, in his excellent *The Conformation of the Dog* (1957), wrote:

Some breeds exhibit localized deformities; in the Dachshund and Basset Hound the head and body are normal but the limbs show exaggerated achondroplasia. Legs are short, thick and somewhat crooked. Both the head and the limbs are encased in a skin

Krehl's Basset Hounds: Jupiter, End of Paris and Pallas, 1879.

several sizes too large for the dog, with wrinkled folds. The feet are large.

Achondroplasia is a form of dwarfing due to disease affecting the long bones of the limbs before birth; it occurs in cattle and in other breeds of dog. When it is undesired in a breed of dog, the afflicted pups are quickly destroyed.

The inheritance of short legs is complex; Robinson in his Genetics for Dog Breeders of 1989, suggested that shorter legs are dominant over longer legs. He went on to state: 'Although polygenic heredity may be assumed for length for most breed differences, this does not mean that major achondroplasic genes do not exist.' The worry here for me is that shorter-legged breeds can in time become even shorter and not always for the benefit of the breed. Crooked legs can so easily become painfully crooked legs. It is significant that when the Bassets used for hunting in Britain became too exaggerated, it was the leggier Harrier which provided the best outcross, rather than the Beagle, which was also tried. I believe that Basset Hounds, pure-bred and true to type, in France, Britain and America, have occasionally produced a large hound pup, with straight, proportionately long legs, in an otherwise typical Basset litter. Significantly, the Basset Fauve de Bretagne is only allowed a 'slight crook' in its front legs. It is also the shortest-backed Basset breed. Some of the breed here have passed the Schweisshund aptitude test – a tribute to their soundness.

Showing Limitations

If you respect and admire functional dogs then it is with sadness that you might view some Bassets on the show bench. There is all too often a poor lay of shoulder, a short upper arm, a looseness of elbow, flat feet or even splay feet and a lack of a ribcage carried well back. Even more apparent are the over-long ears and the over-bent front legs. A cynic might observe that the Basset Hound is a breed much loved by the nation but not so much by some of its breeders. There is a balance to be found in such a breed between breed type and a degree of gross exaggeration that causes discomfort to the dog. Breed lovers should be dog lovers too. It is worrying to read a show critique by an experienced well-regarded judge at a top championship show in 2012 containing remarks such as: 'I was very surprised at the poor quality...at this show. Too many upright shoulders...flat large heavy ears...eyelids not in contact with the eye...Some were too heavy and close to the ground and were unable to move with any purpose.' An event like this should showcase the breed, not provide ammunition for the anti-showdog brigade.

It was reassuring to read the critique of the Basset Hound judge at Crufts 2013, which included these valuable observations:

> ...my overall impression was that the huge, overdone Basset, dripping in furnishing and confusing weight with substance was on the wane which can only be a good thing. However breeders must not overlook the less overt faults such as flanged and slab-sided ribs, forward shoulders, incorrect bites and most importantly eyes, all of which are both wrong and debilitating, in favour of what appears, from the ringside, to be improvements.

De Burgh hunting Bassets.

Show Basset Hound of 1999.

Such informed and outspoken honesty can only be good for this appealing little breed. So often show critiques seem worded to please the exhibitors and not to benefit the breed itself.

Such an admirable breed should not need protection from its top breeders. The breed elders have much to do if this distinctive breed is to remain healthy and retain both type and public affection. It is refreshing when experienced knowledgeable Basset Hound breeder/owners speak out and voice their disquiet. A decade ago, Vivien Evans, the wife of the late John Evans, who did so much for the Basset Hound Club and was a key figure in the setting-up of the Albany Basset pack, put forward the view that in today's show rings, we see too many heavyweight parodies of the true hound and they often win awards! She considered that many breeders had reinterpreted the words of the breed standard in order to produce excessively heavy creatures quite unsuited to their original purpose, and argued for a weight limit and the making of soundness the prime consideration for ring success. She pleaded for the breed to be saved from the excesses of those who claim to love it. For the sake of this most distinctive of hound breeds, I do hope her wise words are heeded.

> To the Editor of the *Kennel Gazette*,
> Sir, BASSETHOUNDS, Would the exhibitors of the above hounds pardon my ignorance, and kindly inform me whether the bassethounds as exhibited at the late Kennel Club show are intended to be used as 'sporting dogs', in which category I see they are classed, or if they appeared as an advertisement for hounds fatted for show purposes, and as such, no doubt, splendid specimens? Being of a 'sporting' turn of mind I thought I should like to possess a small pack of these dogs, but the appearance of those at the show has quite damped my ardour, as for hunting purposes those dogs could only be of use to one afflicted with the gout, or otherwise incapacitated from the active use of his legs.
>
> *Kennel Gazette*, March, 1888.

The sentiments could have been expressed by a sportsman of today; but the *Kennel Gazette* of today would not print such a letter – any criticism of the pedigree dog is forbidden in this journal. I wrote arti-

Albany Pack of KC-registered Basset Hounds.

cles for it for five years, then dared to express a view, in another magazine, that opposed KC thinking at that time, and was never to write for them again. Sycophancy or blind loyalty can never be in the best interests of dogs.

The Harriers

> What is a harrier? Well, the encyclopaedia tells us that it is 'the English name for the hound used in hunting the hare', and it would be difficult to give a more definite description, for he would be a bold man who would undertake to say that there is now-a-days a distinct *breed* of this nature in the United Kingdom, nor is it worth while to inquire whether there ever was such a breed…many packs consist entirely of dwarf fox-hounds, that being the simplest, most expeditious, and probably the cheapest method of getting and keeping together a 'cry of hare-dogs'.

Those slightly patronizing words from the Duke of Beaufort in his *Hunting* of 1894 quickly illustrate the lack of recognition of the Harrier over the last century or so. That lack of recognition may be rooted in a lack of identity. In his *Hounds in Old Days* (1913), Sir Walter Gilbey wrote:

> It is impossible to dissociate the harrier from the stag- or buck-hound, for the sufficient reason that they were the same breed. For hundreds of years, down to the present time, the same hounds have hunted stag, buck and hare; the Anglesey harriers and the Scarteen black and tan beagles in Ireland, for example, hunt both hare and deer at the present day.

Harehounds of British breeds in France, late nineteenth century.

BELOW LEFT: *Hare-hunting in Britain, late nineteenth century.*

Lack of Recognition

The Foxhound, the Beagle and the Basset Hound are recognized as breeds by the Kennel Club but not at the moment the Harrier. This has not always been the case. Four were registered with the KC in 1913 and twenty in 1925. At the Armagh Dog Show in 1892 the Harrier judge reported in the *Kennel Gazette* in December of that year that: 'Harriers had six couples, all from the same kennel. They were a very even lot…' The KC does, however, recognize harehounds from abroad, as the Hamiltonstovare, the Basset Fauve de Bretagne, the Segugio Italiano and the two Basset Griffon Vendeen breeds demonstrate. The American Kennel Club does recognize our Harrier, to me a sad reflection on our custody of native breeds. But the fortunes of the Harrier have always varied. If you take for example the chronology of hare-hunting in

just Surrey and Sussex from 1738 to 1925, it shows that twenty-four packs of Harriers either disbanded, merged or changed to another breed in that period, a period when hunting was an obsession rather than a pastime. This rate of change has rarely been matched in other breeds of packhounds.

In *The Dogs of the British Islands* of 1878, 'Stonehenge' (alias J.H. Walsh), wrote on this breed that:

> In the present day it is very difficult to meet with a harrier possessed of blood entirely unmixed with that of the foxhound… Breeders still take special care to have a combination of intelligence and high scenting power sufficient to meet the wiles of the hare, which are much more varied than those of the fox…

He also referred to a Rough Welsh Harrier, stating that it 'still exists in a state of comparative purity'; another native breed neglected to the point of extinction.

In *The Illustrated Book of the Dog* of 1879, Vero Shaw writes on the breed: 'It is as a dwarf Southern Hound that the Harrier should be most properly regarded… One peculiarity, however, which distinguishes a Harrier from a Foxhound is the recognition of blue-mottle as a correct colour for the breed'. For hare-hunting, however, the esteemed Beckford, regarded as *the* authority on packhounds in the late eighteenth century and early nineteenth century, favoured a cross 'between the large, slow-hunting

Harrier and the little Fox Beagle'. Rawdon Lee, in his *Modern Dogs, Sporting Division*; Vol I (1897), wrote that: 'Unless some very considerable change takes place, it is extremely likely that the harrier will not survive very many generations, at any rate in this country.' He referred to a smooth-coated Welsh Harrier, black or black and tan in colour, and, separately to a range of shoulder height in the breed from 15½ to 22 inches.

Struggle for Identity

Against that background, it is easy to see why this breed has struggled to maintain its identity over two centuries yet emerged with distinction. In his *Hounds* of 1913, Frank Townend Barton writes on Harriers that 'there are about eighty-five packs in England and Wales, forty packs in Ireland, but only one in Scotland…one of the oldest packs of Harriers is the Pennistone…consisting of thirteen couples of 22 to 24 inch pure Harriers, or hounds of the English type'. He stated that the Holcombe Harriers, 200 years old, was composed of twenty couples of 22in 'Old English Harriers'. I believe there are just over a dozen packs of Harriers still in existence, and, whilst this is a big reduction from the eighty-five of a century ago, the breed has survived rather better than Rawdon Lee's gloomy prediction.

If the breed is to be recognized as such away from the hunting field, what should it look like? Should it resemble the Southern Hound with ears like the Sabueso Español and the Swiss Laufhund breeds? Should it be black and tan like the Welsh Harrier of old and the Schillerstovare, the Slovene Mountain Hound and the Kerry Beagles of the Scarteen pack?

Harriers of mixed type, 1897.

Allix's pack of Harriers, a late nineteenth-century engraving by Scott.

Should it be blue-mottled like the Hailsham Harriers or lemon and mainly white like the Istrian Hound and our own West Country Harrier? The Old English Harrier was cloddier than, say, our Studbook Harrier of today; but is that the right template? Is the Harrier a 16in high hound or one standing at 22in?

Correct Phenotype

Devon and Sussex used to be strongholds of the Southern Hound blood, but there was once a harrier pack in Devon, hunted by a Mr Webber, and predecessors of the Silverton Harriers, which was slate-grey, rather like the Steinbracke of Germany. The wide diversity of view over the correct phenotype for the Harrier led to the Association of Masters of Harriers and Beagles to examine this in 1891 by way of a committee report. This committee found that there were at least a dozen dif-

ferent kinds of harehounds, quite diverse in type, with half their owners claiming theirs to be 'pure Harriers'. The committee recommended that all Harriers should be admitted to the Studbook, and then the book be closed. This led to a division between Studbook and Pure Harriers, which continued to arouse great debate.

The Pure Harriers, like the Holcombe in Lancashire, were said to have better scenting skill; the Studbook Harriers to have too much drive. What is quite clear from this debate, however, is that the aim was to breed a hunting dog to suit the country being hunted by that pack. What is the point of uniformity if a longer-legged hound is required in open country and a slower, better-scenting hound in very close country? In the *Kennel Gazette* of May 1884 there is a description of Harding Cox's Harriers running for seven hours seven minutes over a course of 48 miles. The hounds on this occasion were described as simply racing along and that 'it took some pretty fast galloping to live with them.' There are a number of salient points arising from this account.

Firstly, when breeders of sporting dogs are arguing about the correct shoulder height for their breed, the crucial question should always be asked: what terrain were they designed to work over? Secondly, the physique displayed by sporting breeds is rooted in field prowess and anyone tinkering with a breed standard needs watching. Sporting breeds like the Harrier developed in a hard school in which failure was not tolerated. For breeds that for centuries excelled in the hunting field to appear in the show ring with upright shoulders, under-muscled hindquarters or weak feet is a betrayal of the worst kind. What really is the point of fancying a particular breed if you then set out to sabotage its heritage?

ABOVE LEFT: *An Easton Park Harrier, the Duke of Hamilton's Jesuit.*

Northern Harriers – the Holcombe pack.

The Colne Valley Harriers of 1910.

The Colne Valley Harriers in 1910.

BELOW RIGHT: *Master with the Hailsham Harriers, the last pack of Old Southern Hounds, 1917.*

Pursuit of Field Performance

The wide range of colours that once featured in the Harrier appeals to me. Harrier experts in the nineteenth century considered the blue-mottled or blue-pied hounds the 'true harrier type' but Foxhound blood has introduced the tricolours. The other colours favoured in the last century include hare-pied, badger-pied, lemon-pied, slate-grey or mainly white, especially in the West Country. Old English Red, as it was called, was a famous hound colour in the West, with black and tan favoured in Ireland. The Scarteen pack of Kerry Beagles, perpetuated by the remarkable Ryan family over three centuries, are handsome hounds, with admirers the world over. Few hound breeders breed on colour alone, but favoured a jacket that produced a uniform pack.

Hound breeders are seeking performance, not a mindless observation of the wording of a breed's word picture or standard, so often sadly the case in KC show rings. If an outcross is needed the system permits this, in the packs: a Studbook Harrier dog mated to a Foxhound bitch is listed as 'Appendix' then, when the resultant bitches are bred back to a Studbook Harrier dog, their offspring are then eligible for the Studbook as Harriers; the stallion *must* be a Harrier, not the other way around.

Cross-breeding in the constant search for field performance has given us so many distinguished pedigree breeds. The Harrier has been used successfully – for example when Colonel Morrison used the Studbook Harrier Dunston Gangway to improve

the Basset Hound's conformation, as an outcross. A world in which the closed gene pool is adhered to, no matter how diseased the progeny or short-lived the dogs and no matter how exaggerations exaggerate themselves to the distress of the dog has little appeal for me. Nor am I content to see the ancient Harrier of England lost to us through a change in the law, now that hunting with dogs is legally regulated.

Now is the time to conserve such a distinctive and well-bred hound; it is very much part of our national sporting heritage. We should benefit from the past, not lightly discard it.

For me the Harrier is the perfect hound, handsome and with no exaggeration, representing all

that is best in British hound breeding. The Cambridgeshire Harriers of Betty Gingell a few decades back, especially her Harkaway and her Housemaid, epitomized, for me, near-perfection in hound conformation. We have every reason to be proud of our Harrier. It is immensely cheering to learn of the new young huntsman Joe Tesseyman at the Waveney Harriers, with country in East Suffolk/Norfolk. Aged just twenty-two, schooled at the Cottesmore and before that at the Badsworth and Bramham Moor, he shows great enthusiasm for his twenty-two-couple pack, supported mainly by amateur whippers-in. If a small pack like this can be backed with such commitment and energy then the future of these excellent hounds is in good hands.

West Country Harriers of the late twentieth century.

Studbook Harriers of the twentieth century.

The Beagle

Pour down, like a flood from the hills, brave boys,
On the wings of the wind
The merry beagles fly;
Dull sorrow lags behind:
Ye shrill echoes reply,
Catch each flying sound, and double our joys.

Those words by William Somerville capture the sheer gaiety of the harehound called the Beagle. But for how long in years to come will 'the merry beagles fly' and we go 'hare-ing after them'? In Robert Leighton's *New Book of the Dog*, published in 1912, G.S. Lowe was writing: 'There is nothing to surpass the beauty of the Beagle, either to see him on the flags of his kennel

or in unravelling a difficulty on the line of a dodging hare. In neatness he is really the little model of a Foxhound.' He went on to point out that 'Dorsetshire used to be the great county for Beagles. The downs there were exactly fitted for them, and years ago, when roe-deer were preserved on the large estates, Beagles were used to hunt this small breed of deer.'

ABOVE RIGHT: Mr Gorman's rough-coated Beagles.

A kennelman and three and a half couples of Beagles by Richard Ansdell, 1870.

Rough-Coated Beagles

He recalled the Welsh rough-coated Beagle and its look-alike, the big Essex Beagle, going on to state that, 'A very pretty lot of little rough Beagles were recently shown at Reigate. They were called the Telscome, and exhibited by Mr. A. Gorham.' He suggested Welsh Hound or even Otterhound blood to get this coat and the increased size of the Welsh and Essex varieties. But from his illustration of Gorham's hounds, a distinct Basset Griffon Vendeen (Grand) look can be detected. An interchange of French and English or Welsh hound blood has centuries behind it. Coat texture apart, the Gorham Beagles have the set of ear, ear length and facial expression of the French hounds. Beagle breeders would have known of these 16in-high Griffons and, to avoid introducing much greater size, would have seen much merit in resorting to the blood of the Basset Griffon Vendeen (Grand).

In his *Rural Sports* of 1801, the Rev. W.B. Daniel wrote:

> Beagles, rough or smooth, have their admirers; their tongues are musical, and they go faster than the Southern hounds, but tail much…they require a clever huntsman, for out of eighty couple in the field during a winter's Sport, he observed not four couple that could be depended on. Of the two sorts he prefers the wire-haired, as having good shoulders, and being well filleted. Smooth-haired Beagles are commonly deep hung, thick lipped, with large nostrils, but often so soft and bad quartered, as to be shoulder-shook and crippled the first season they hunt; crooked legs, like the Bath Turnspit, are frequently seen among them…

'Shoulder-shook' is an old hunting field expression for the jarring caused by badly-placed shoulders and is an apt one. There is no hint of a uniform breed of Beagle in this passage.

Daniel also considered that: 'The North Country Beagle is nimble and vigorous, he pursues the Hare with impetuosity, gives her no time to double, and if the Scent lies high, will easily run down two brace before dinner'; he went on to describe a pocket Beagle, writing:

> Of this diminutive and lavish kind the late Colonel Hardy had once a Cry, consisting of ten or eleven couple, which were always carried to and from the field in a large pair of Panniers, slung across a horse; small as they were, they would keep a Hare at all her shifts to escape them…

So we have smooth, rough and wire-coated Beagles, some with crooked legs and some of small terrier size, that is, pannier-size. There was clearly no attempt to seek a standardized breed, just a competent harehound of varying coat texture and shoulder height.

The Brighton and Storrington pack by Lionel Edwards, c.1960.

Lord Percy's Beagles by Lionel Edwards, 1933.

The country being hunted often dictated the size of hound, but performance was everything, never appearance alone.

Shoulders and Size

There seems to be an endless debate about shoulder height in Beagles. Writing in *Hounds* magazine in November 1987, Beagle expert Newton Rycroft gave the view that: 'Height alone does not govern pace in beagles. Shoulders and stride are also most important', going on to describe how one of the smallest bitches in kennels often performed best in the field *because she was the only one with perfect shoulders*. He finished his article by stating: 'Finally, the 16-17 (inch) beagle. Rightly or wrongly those who breed these get little sympathy from this quarter! If they cannot catch hares with 15 inch beagles then I feel they need not bigger hounds, but better ones.' A reader subsequently wrote in to state that after a mating that produced exceptional quality at 14 inches, a repeat mating produced a litter of five, all over 16 inches. Do you cull quality because of shoulder height? In another issue of the same magazine, 'Hareless' was stating:

> Reduce your size down to 14/15 inch? Well, fine in the lowlands, but too small for a rough moorland country. Quality 15 inch beagles can soon lose their followers on the right day, but as long as they turn with their hare and retain a god cry do not be put off by the grumblers. It seems illogical to spend ten to fifteen years breeding your hounds to perfection,

then start taking notice of people who say they are too good.

I do wish the breeders of show Beagles would take more notice of those who breed the hunting hounds.

Show Flaws and Pack Faults

The differing needs of those who hunt Beagles and those who only show them can lead to the production of two different hounds. Breed type is sometimes over-played by the show fraternity; the requirements of the pack, and purely function can produce plain-headed, lightweight hounds with more 'hounds general' than pedigree Beagle in their appearance. This dilemma is hardly new. Writing in the Beagle Club's Yearbook for 1901, Walter Crofton gave the view:

> The fact is, Peterborough, supported by Masters keeping Beagles for hare-hunting and catering only for such, has for some years encouraged the breeding and showing of well-made speedy little hounds and altogether neglected some of the beautiful and typical head points of the Beagle, and with these have gone a few of his working characteristics. On the other hand, the country gentleman and farmer (sometimes for generations) has kept in the family a little 'cry' of Beagles for shooting over, has bred to maintain the style of work he admires, and the typical Beagle expression and head, which he loves, but he has often been careless about body parts…

Springhill Beagles by Henry F. Lucas-Lucas, 1914.

It must be the aim to breed for function without losing the breed. It's quite possible to 'lose the breed' in the packs but more likely in the show ring.

Exhibiting Faults

At the final championship show of 2012, the Ladies Kennel Association's, the Beagle judge was commendably honest in her remarks about the entry. Although the prevalent faults she found are hardly new, it was of value to persist in drawing attention to them. Flat and splayed feet are a handicap to a running hound: the breed standard requires them to be 'tight and firm'. The commonest cause of such a flaw is a lack of hard exercise; hounds of any breed put before a judge should be in the very best condition. Tails curling over the back, spitz-fashion, spoil an otherwise sound exhibit and this judge was right to resent it. This has been a long-standing fault in this breed – I can remember seeing it fifty years ago. Show breeders have habitually blamed the packs for this, but I see few signs of it there.

The New Forest pack by T. Ivester Lloyd, 1936.

The first show Beagle I ever saw, in the 1950s, was an outstanding hound, Ch. Barvae Paigan, and he came from the pack bloodlines. I was also impressed by a very sound show dog, Glenivy Intrepid, a decade or so ago, really looking like a harehound. In recent years, from the ringside, I have been impressed by Ch. Nedlaw Barbarian, a wonderfully symmetrical little hound. But show Beagles have, for me, too heavy a body, their legs are too hefty and their feet too large for my liking; the latter may not be helped by a breed standard that specifies feet that are 'well knuckled-up' and 'not hare-footed'. This may be rooted in the distant past when such standards were first written. The Foxhound breeders have moved on; let's hope we don't have a 'mini-shorthorn' tendency in this fine breed. It was depressing to read the critique of the Beagle judge at the Scottish Beagle Club's show in April 2008: 'Front movement coming on was as bad as I can ever remember, many hounds had large open feet, far too many had short ribcages and long loins…' Did the exhibitors of such hounds truly not know what made a sound Beagle?

Hunting a Pack

Ever since reading Roger Free's *Beagle and Terrier* (1946), as a fourteen-year-old, hunting with a small pack of assorted dogs has appealed to me. He wrote in times when individual freedom had greater respect but a future need for vermin-control could see his style of operating in the field on the way back and to a greater degree. Free kept and hunted a small mixed pack of 14in Beagles and Terriers for hunting rabbits for the gun. 'Dalesman' described Free's pack as one of 'which any huntsman might be proud,

Roger Free with his bobbery pack.

Newcastle and District Beagles of 1947, by T. Carr.

because they have all those attributes which go towards excellence. Some of these are bred in the hounds – courage, stamina, nose and tongue – but the rest must be taught and instilled with patience and knowledge of hounds and their work.' What a challenging self-set task for any ambitious sportsman! Free, not surprisingly, considered that more pleasure was to be derived from hunting your own hounds than from being a follower of a pack hunted by another.

Free argued that whereas gundogs are taught by man, scenthounds frequently learn to hunt without the assistance of man and are therefore more self-reliant. He wasn't decrying the merits of gundogs but stressing the need for a different approach to the training of hounds. He advocated choosing a dog that was not afraid to look you in the eye. He preferred to guide a dog rather than 'break' it. He looked for boldness, perseverance, eagerness and biddability. He

emphasised the latter and was aware of the menace of self-hunting hounds, oblivious to all recall.

Free concentrated on hunting the hounds and did not himself carry a gun. He normally used four or five couples of Beagles with two or three terriers, finding the latter better in really difficult cover. This meant handling a dozen dogs single-handed, a testing task. Some sportsmen find controlling one gundog quite beyond them! Generally speaking, terriers and scenthounds demand far more skill in their training than gundogs, partly because of their different instincts and partly because they are often expected to operate in the field *as a pack*. Gundogs have been bred for centuries to respond to human direction in the field; terriers and scenthounds have striven for several centuries to defy all human instructions.

In the United States, the American Rabbit Hound Association registers rabbit hounds bred to meet its

American rabbit hunt with Beagles.

standards. Founded in 1986, with 140 clubs in over twenty-eight states, the ARHA promotes hunting competitions and offers a programme of organized rabbit hound hunts. There are six types of hunt competitions: gundog brace, gundog pack, big pack, little pack, progressive pack and Basset. The objective of these field events is to identify those hounds with the best ability to search (that is, locate the rabbit), flush and drive the rabbit back to the hunter. At the end of each hunt competition, there is a conformation show to try to identify the best-constructed hounds. A comparable parent body in the UK might concentrate the minds of rabbit-hunters.

Value of Rabbit Control

In Australia they have an even bigger problem with rabbit damage than we do here. Yet, despite developing their own heeler and terrier, they too have never produced a specialist rabbit hound by name. This may be because the breeds taken there from Britain were deemed adequate for the task. In his informative book *Australian Barkers and Biters* of 1914, Robert Kaleski paid tribute to the Beagle, writing:

> Of late years another job has arisen for the Beagle in Australia, and he, like all good Australians, has risen to the job. This job is a very important one. Every grazier knows that after his country has been absolutely swept bare of the grey curse there is invariably one here and one there overlooked in some inaccessible places which pop up and start breeding again. Ordinary dogs do not bother with odd ones like these in bad places; but the Beagle, with whom chasing rabbits is an age-old instinct, goes after these 'last rabbits' with joy and never leaves them alone until run down and secured.

It is this sheer persistence, massive enthusiasm and scenting prowess that make the Beagle such a superlative hunter – and a handful sometimes for a novice Beagle owner not versed in their avid trailing instincts whenever strong scent is encountered! These instincts are being perpetuated by the working section of the Beagle Club and I applaud their efforts in these difficult days for sporting breeds. The best Beagles that I see come from the Dummer pack; they always look capable of providing a great day's sport and appearing far racier and more workmanlike, yet

Beagle from the Dummer pack.

Beagle at a KC show.

still handsome, than those in the KC show rings. The show exhibits for me possess too much bone, walk too stiffly and are often heavy-headed. A recent Crufts critique stated that the most prevalent faults in the entry were wide fronts and what was termed 'flapping feet'; short, steep upper arms were reported at a number of championship shows, a certain cause of restricted movement. The judge at the Welsh Beagle Club's November 2009 show wrote, 'I am saddened by the state of the breed at present particularly in males… I found many exhibits with large splayed feet and, accompanied by a weakness in pastern…' This is not good news for any hound breed.

Long-Distance Runner
In his informative book *Beagling* (1960), Lovell Hewitt makes some instructive points on the construction of the little hound. He considered that Beagles were all too often judged on their fronts and criticized the desire for absolutely straight front legs. He pointed out that Squire Osbaldeston's rightly famous stallion hound Furrier 1820 was only drafted to the Belvoir because he was not quite straight in front. He stressed that the Beagle was a long-distance runner not a sprinter, emphasizing the importance of strong, well-muscled loins and quarters. He wrote that Beagles tend to become weedy with successive generations and a narrow chest was a warning of this. He liked the fuller waist and disliked dippy backs. He found that a hound with a short head also lacked persistence. He was strongly against the exaggerated cat's foot, once the preference in the hunting kennels.

In Sweden, Norway and Finland, the Beagle is a popular dog for hunting; the Swedish Beagle Club being founded in 1953. In these Nordic countries the Beagle is hunted singly, not in a pack, and not just on hare; in addition to hare, in Finland on fox, in Sweden on fox and roe deer and in Norway on fox, roe deer and deer. Each year around 300 entries at field trials are made in both Sweden and Finland. In Sweden a Beagle cannot become a show champion unless it first gains the field trial champion award. In Britain, Beagles from the show world can gain a working certificate; for the packs there used to be beagle trials like the West Country Beagle trials in March each year. Perhaps it's time for another Charlie Morton. He hunted a small pack of Beagles solely for rabbiting with the gun, from about 1877 to 1919; his pack, consisting of three couples of 16in hounds, often produced returns of over seventy rabbits a shoot. He never carried a horn, just used his rich deep voice. He worked his hounds two or three days a week but insisted on a day's break between shoots. He never used a van or a hound trailer, walking his hounds to each meet. Many of his hounds lived to well over ten and he hunted his pack for over forty years. Local farmers greatly valued his work on rabbit-control; rabbit damage in Britain nowadays costs our economy tens of millions of pounds. Bring back the Beagle-shoots!

Since starting these annual shows at Peterborough and the formation of the stud-book, a marvellous change for the better has taken place in both the harrier and the beagle, but in the present instance, of course, my

Working Beagles.

The pack on parade at Ragley Game Fair, 2008.

remarks must be confined to the latter. No beagle can now be entered in the stud-book with a direct harrier cross nearer than two generations back. Under the association, classes are arranged at the annual show for beagles not over sixteen inches which are entered in or are eligible for admission into the stud-book, and during the year 1893 there was a strong entry of these hounds. Leaving the association, I will endeavour to describe the best kind of beagle for hunting the hare, and I may remark that the little beagle of about twelve or thirteen inches, very pretty, and useful for rabbit hunting, is absolutely of no use whatsoever.

The Duke of Beaufort et al., *Hunting* (1894).

There are at the present moment, according to the Rural Almanack, 119 packs of harriers in England, 2 in Scotland, and 28 in Ireland, making a total of 149 for the United Kingdom; and there are 48 packs of beagles… Sir W Harcourt's Act 'For the better protection of occupiers of land against injury to their crops from ground game', or 'The Hares and Rabbits Bill' was passed in 1880; and everybody knows the enormous destruction of hares which took place as soon as that Act came into operation; in many places, indeed, they became practically extinct…

The Earl of Suffolk, The Encyclopaedia of Sport (1897); he goes on to state the sportsman's role subsequently in increasing hare numbers.

To sum up, therefore, which we should look for in our favourite hounds are perfect symmetry of build to insure strength and staying power, an intelligent and alert expression, a shapely neck, well-balanced shoulders, a compact sturdy body with good depth and width of chest, well-rounded and muscular loins and thighs and straight well-boned forelegs with perfect cat-feet. Of faults silently to shudder at, when seen in a neighbouring pack, and to turn a blind eye to, if seen in our own, are tendencies to straight shoulders, flat open splay feet, short throaty bull-necks, weak thighs, slack loins and flat sides, while knock knees with knees turned in and toes out or calf-knees with knees over-extended and actually bent slightly backwards, cannot fail to make us groan aloud in any circumstances in sympathy for the poor hound which possesses them.

Dr D. Jobson-Scott, *Beagling for Beginners* (1933)

Only 70 years ago Wilfred Scawen Blunt quoted his Old Squire as saying:

I love the hunting of the hare
Better than that of the fox
I like to be as my fathers were
In the days ere I was born.

This attitude still lives on amongst the dyed-in-the-wool followers of harrier packs in the West Country and East Anglia, and amongst beaglers almost everywhere. They know that the hare, with its bewildering speed when fresh, its cunning, its shifts and stratagems and fading scent as it tires, is a more elusive if not so enduring a quarry as the fox, and that to hunt and catch a hare represents the art of venery at its highest.

Wilson Stephens, *The Farmer's Book of Field Sports* (1961)

Conserving the Otterhound

It is not too much to say that almost every description of hound that hunts by scent has at some time or other been employed in the chase of the otter: true Otterhounds, foxhounds, staghounds, harriers, bloodhounds, rough-haired Welsh foxhounds and harriers and crosses of these with each other, and especially with the Otterhound proper.

Captain L.C.R. Cameron, in *Deer, Hare & Otter Hunting*, The Lonsdale Library Vol. XXII (1936)

No One Type

In his *Rural Sports* of 1870, Delabere Blaine records, on the subject of otter-hunting:

Dogs of every variety were also employed, and the whole rather resembled a conspiracy than a hunt…it is but seldom that we meet with an organised and in-and-in bred pack…Dwarf foxhounds, crossed either with the water spaniel, or with the rough wire-haired terrier, are used; but the best otter-dog, in our opinion, is that bred between the old southern harrier and the rough crisp-coated water spaniel, with a slight cross of the bull breed to give ferocity and hardihood.

That informative account reveals at once the mixed blood behind today's Otterhound, as well as

Hunting exuberance – The Find by Walter Hunt, 1900.

Head Study of Otterhounds *by Reuben Ward Binks, 1921.*

a disregard for pedigree, the sacred cow of the last century.

Sir John Buchanan-Jardine, in his *Hounds of the World* of 1937, states that there was really no true breed of Otterhound before 1880. There were of course precious few *true* breeds of dog at that time by the judgement of today's five-generation pedigree. I suggest that Otterhounds (identified by their function not as a breed) were dogs bred mainly from scenthound and water-dog blood and then perpetuated as the type we recognize today. If you want a hound that will work well in water, why not combine the nose and perseverance of the scenthound with the coat, feet and instincts of the ancient water-dogs? Look at the old prints of the water-dogs and then deny any similarity with the Otterhound of today! In the middle of the nineteenth century, many believed the best pack to be that of Squire Lomax of Clayton

Hall, hunting the Ribble, the Lune, the Kent and the Hodder in Lancashire. Squire Lomax inherited these hounds and so their pack type was long established. In 1904 there were twenty-four packs hunting the otter in Britain but only four were pure-bred. I believe it is fair to say that from around 1900 to 1930, Otterhounds were not renowned for their hunting qualities, enjoying the scent more than the catch.

Troublesome Past

The great huntsman and naturalist of Edwardian times, Lauchlan Rose, wrote in *Field Sports* magazine in 1910 (when the Masters of Otterhounds' Association was formed):

> In Edward II's reign a royal pack of otterhounds was kept and even in those days they were distinguished from other 'dogges' by their great heads and large ears, well long and hanging down, great legs and strong and great feet, round and great claws. There is little doubt that they were hard in coat and rough

Otterhound at Crufts, 1991.

in hair, much as they are at the present day. I wonder what other breed of dog can show such a long, unbroken strain or type. There is some legend that the French griffon has been used to resuscitate the old breed, some say, even the wild timber wolf, but I have been unable to trace authentically such a cross.

He may have something there. He noted a distinct improvement in the breed in the period 1890–1910, especially in the tightening of the feet. At the end of the nineteenth century, a great supporter of the Otterhound in France was the very knowledgeable Comte de Tinguy who bought and sold whole packs of them, on either side of the channel.

In The Lonsdale Library's *Hounds & Dogs* of 1932, Captain L.C.R. Cameron, writing about the aptly named hound Dreadful, stated that: 'But in kennels he was very troublesome, constantly starting fights in which the rest of the pack joined forces against him, so that he always came off worsted. He would obey no rate but mine…' Griffon blood would bring a defi-

A working Otterhound from the packs.

nite obstinacy with it. The blood of a wolf could have brought quarrelsomeness to a pack animal. Hounds used to hunt mink have to be every bit as determined as those formerly used to hunt otter. Such resolution and spirit once gave Otterhounds quite a reputation in kennels. One authority recorded: '…it happens that the breed has become unusually savage and that they are constantly fighting in kennels. Indeed, instances are common enough of more than half being destroyed in a single night, in the bloody fight which has been commenced by perhaps a single couple.' The KC has recently amended the breed standard to include the words: 'Signs of aggression or nervousness should be heavily penalized'. The Otterhounds that I see nowadays however, whether on the bench or in the field, are sociable, amiable and thoroughly likeable.

Value of the Hound

Otho Paget, in his *Hunting* of 1900, wrote of the breed:

> The pure-bred otter-hound is generally of a tan colour, varying from light to dark, and occasionally showing patches of white, but when this occurs I think it is evidence of a cross at some period. He has a rough wiry coat, and the harder the texture of his hair, the better… Nearly all packs of otter-hounds have a large proportion of foxhound blood mixed up with other breeds.

Those words illustrate the mixed blood flowing in the veins of today's Otterhound. The composition of the minkhound packs shows the differing views of huntsmen: Greg Mousley formed the Dove Valley Minkhounds in 1988 with seventeen couples made up of English Foxhounds, Welsh Hounds and Otterhounds; the Pembrokeshire & Carmarthenshire Minkhounds consisted of thirty-five couples of pure Otterhounds. Whatever the mix, a highly individual breed of dog has resulted, with a characteristic jacket, the obstinacy (or determination, when on scent) of the hound breeds and a much more affection-earning appearance than the other large scenthounds.

Rightly, in these times, the otter is no longer hunted. But it is easy to overlook the enormous damage inflicted on fish stocks by otters in past times, when fish was a far more important source of human food. The ancient fish-ponds represented the freezers of today and were often 'holding' pools for fish caught elsewhere but not needed immediately for the table. Wild creatures raiding these stocks like the cormorant, the heron and the otter were regarded as vermin – a threat to the wellbeing of humans. (Otters have been known to kill domestic poultry too.) The otter was subsequently hunted for sport but the kill ratio, relative to that of other country sports, was low. The Rev. John Russell, of eponymous terrier fame, stated that he had hunted over 2,000 miles before encountering his first otter, even though the ground was being hunted for them throughout this distance. The otter's lifestyle did not make hunting easy. Nowadays the mink, even with a different modus vivendi from the otter, is similarly difficult to catch.

L-r: A. N. Other, A. N. Other, P. O'Callaghan, Dick Longford, Paddy Doyle, Timmy O'Mahony, John Murray M.O.H. with Bruiser, Driver, Donovan and Rapid from the Clonmel Otterhounds.

The Clonmel Otterhounds in the 1930s.

Otterhounds Searching for Scent *by Reuben Ward Binks, 1930.*

Too Much Variety

The Otterhounds in the show ring seem to vary enormously, not just in breed type, but in size, substance, coat, condition, skull shape, set of eye, mouths and movement. I do hope this admirable breed of dog is not about to join the 'coat' breeds, breeds where the coat becomes the main asset of the dog. Some I see have head hair more appropriate for a Briard or a Bearded Collie both in length and texture. I also dislike seeing a gay tail in this breed; for me the breed should move giving the impression of a dog that has a function: a determined stride, head down and tail out behind. The lack of hard muscle in some entries too is disappointing. These hounds were famous for their staying power. There are sadly many contemporary examples of breeds being bred mainly for coat, being judged mainly on coat and their physical condition neglected. It would be most regrettable if this breed, still not long from the packs, went this way too.

Ears and skulls are a worry in the breed and the breed standard's wording compounds the problem. Once a dog's ears are described as a 'unique feature of the breed' alarm bells ring for me. The concept that this breed has to have a fold in its ear to improve waterproofing doesn't seem to apply to any of the water-dog breeds or the Newfoundland. Ears that 'easily reach the nose when pulled forward' and have

to possess a 'curious draped appearance – an essential point not to be lost' encourage the exaggerators. In twenty years time, I suspect the breed will have the most unsightly ears and be judged on them as a breed point. It would be safer, and healthier for the dog undoubtedly, for the shorter ear to be favoured without the characteristic breed feature being lost. (When I wrote similarly in a sporting magazine article, my views were described by one breed show stalwart as 'dangerous'!) The standard of mouths, dentition especially, can deteriorate away from the packs; strong teeth, even teeth, and a scissor bite are all important in a hound.

Penalties of Pure-Breeding

Variation in shoulder height is not a bad fault in scent hounds, where packs are bred to suit country, as long as the hound is balanced, free-moving, vigorous in action and not clumsily cumbersome through being too rangy. At the Otterhound Club's championship show a couple of years ago, the judge reported that 'some hounds were underdeveloped behind, with floppy hocks, which brushed, or even plaited, as they moved away'. This is a bad fault in a hunting breed. A fault to be penalized in any scenthound is when depth of rib does not reach back the whole length of the ribcage; lung room is vital. Dumfriesshire Cy-

Otterhound used on mink.

pher at Trevereux would be my favourite example of a balanced well-proportioned Otterhound. I recall his being a grandson of US Ch. Andel Little Big Man, brought in by the Dumfriesshire pack; any resort to really good blood from outside must be a bonus to the breed. Cypher's grand-dam was another fine hound of the pack, Jezebel.

The Otterhound Dumfriesshire Cypher.

It is pleasing that the breed standard permits all recognized hound colours, which must mean scenthound colours; liver and white is not permissible in the breed but is found in Whippets and Greyhounds away from the show stock. The wording of the breed standard on gait/movement is, for me, bizarre: 'Very loose and shambling at walk, springing immediately into a loose, very long-striding, sound, active trot. Gallop smooth and exceptionally long striding.' Words like these could give excuse to loose or upright shoulders (good, well-placed shoulders are underrated in far too many sporting breeds), a lack of coordination and even pacing. The Deerhound is expected to have a long stride, the Greyhound a free stride, the Basenji a swift, long, tireless, swinging stride, the Grand Bleu de Gascogne to be long striding, the Hamiltonstovare to be free-striding and long reaching and the Ibizan Hound to have a long, far-reaching stride. The word 'exceptionally' used to describe the long stride of the Otterhound is, relative to these other breeds, absurd. It literally suggests a longer stride than that possessed by the sighthounds.

Writing in *Hounds* magazine in 1991, Greg Mousley, a Master of Otterhounds, gave the view that:

The problems suffered in the hindquarters with poor hocks and stifles are I'm sure, due to the fact that otterhounds are usually over angulated in this area. Any breed of dog that tends to be over angulated in the hindquarters is susceptible to these problems unless an outcross is sought. The present day breeders of Kennel Club registered otterhounds are unable to strengthen their lines by doing this as the offspring are unregisterable, regardless of the fact that they are vastly superior due to their new found hybrid vigour… Years ago otterhounds were reinforced by a dash of Welsh or other blood on a regular basis to ensure they remained sound in conformation.

The show ring, and the mindset of its devotees, is capable of producing outstanding hounds; it is also, sadly, more than capable of just exemplifying *pure-breeding* whatever the cost to the health, vigour and soundness of the entry. This has to be rethought; the health of the hounds must *always* come first.

Show-Ring Destiny

Lively and lovable, with the intense curiosity of a Basset Hound, the single-mindedness of a Bloodhound, yet without the obstinacy of either, the Otterhound is conserved today in the show ring, although only thirty-eight new registrations were recorded by the Kennel Club in 2011 and thirty-seven in 2012. Having lost their role, the future of the *breed*, despite their use in minkhound packs, needs care. I have worries about their becoming in, say, twenty years time, over-coated, featuring giant ears, of a standard colour and no longer prized as a sporting scenthound breed in the field. From their long and mixed ancestry, it would be a tragedy if their appearance became increasingly exaggerated, as so often happens with longer-coated and longer-eared breeds. The coat of the French Griffon breeds – rough, harsh, stiff but never long or overstated – could be the model for this breed too.

The Otterhound is still here today only because of the vision, dedication and enterprise of a relatively small number of devotees. It is their work that has saved a distinctive British sporting breed from extinction. It is not the job of the Masters of Minkhounds to conserve the purebred Otterhound; it is their job to control the menace of mink, legally, wherever that considerable threat to wildlife exists. If they happen to use some pure-bred Otterhounds for this purpose so much the better. The fate of the breed of Otterhound now rests with show-ring breeders. It is a challenge and a considerable responsibility.

Otters no longer pose a threat to our larders and are rightly conserved. So too must be the hounds

Otterhounds from the pack.

which once hunted them, they are an important part of our sporting heritage. If we do not respect their sporting past and only breed them for their coats, the 'uniqueness' of their ears, a 'very loose and shambling' gait and 'exceptional' stride then we will be betraying the work of Squire Lomax and his ancestors, and Captain Bell-Irving with his Dumfriesshire pack, and his. May Otterhounds, whether in minkhound packs or in the show ring, go from strength to strength – a very individual hound well worth saving.

Although originally employed in the chase of many sorts of quarry the Otterhound in Britain, in the absence of wolves and wild boar, seems always to have been kept to the pursuit of the otter: the only really savage beast of the chase left in these islands. That this is undoubtedly its proper quarry is proved by the facts that: (i) it enters readily to the scent of an otter without any trouble; (ii) it does not often riot on any other species of quarry unless misled by the presence of hounds of other breeds in the same pack; (iii) it can own the scent of an otter when no other hound can recognise it, and (iv) it is a natural 'marking hound',

Teme Valley minkhound.

Group of Otterhounds by John Emms, 1880.

BELOW: Otterhounds by Joseph H. Sharp, 1900.

The Devon and Somerset Staghounds, 1931.

BELOW RIGHT: Luxury – a Royal Staghound, *engraving by F. Babbage from a painting by R.B. Davis.*

and when it speaks at a holt the Huntsman may be sure his quarry is at home. These qualities alone give it precedence over all other hounds used for Otter Hunting…

> Captain L.C.R. Cameron writing in *Deer, Hare & Otter Hunting*, Lonsdale Library Vol. XXII (1936)

As to otterhounds versus foxhounds, I am convinced that finance, or rather the lack of it, is the only reason why draft foxhounds are preferred to otterhounds – breeding hounds on a big scale adds enormously to expenses – if an MOH breeds otterhounds on the same lines that foxhounds are bred, breeds by selection, breeds each year enough puppies to get a big enough young entry the following year – big enough not only to be able to put down any physical crock that may come in, but big enough to allow for drafting a certain number – during and at the end of their first season, you can have, in my humble opinion, a pack of purebred otterhounds, not only not inferior to, but superior to any pack of draft foxhounds.

> William Thompson of Giggleswick, in the introduction to *The Book of the Otter* by Richard Clapham (1928)

Celebrating The Staghound

No pack of hounds in England could show a cleaner or more direct pedigree than could the staghounds of

Staghounds of today.

Staghounds on the flags, 2001.

course, the Hunting Act of 2004 has undermined the core function of Staghound packs, but these have long been much-admired hounds, with a clear identity and distinct value for the hound devotee. In his *Modern Dogs* of 1897, Rawdon Lee wrote of them:

> …this hound is neither more nor less than a foxhound under another name, but trained for a different purpose… He has been used, or at any rate, a somewhat similar animal to him has long been used, for staghunting, and we are told by historians that, in the times of the Normans, villages were depopulated, and places for divine worship overthrown, in order that the nobles might have their parks in which to keep their deer.

North Devonshire up to the year 1825… The history of the Devonshire hounds can be traced in a single line back to the year 1598, when Hugh Pollard, Elizabeth's Ranger, kept a pack at Simonsbath.
The Duke of Beaufort, *Hunting* (1894)

Lee remarked that the change of quarry 'does not appear to have made any difference in the character and disposition of the animal. The staghound is just as fast, and is said to possess as good a nose; in coat, colour, and formation they are identical—and hard, thick feet, good legs, with strong loins…'

You don't hear much about the Staghound these days, and by Staghound I mean the scenthound of the packs, not the loose name for a big, rough-haired lurcher both here and in Australia and the United States. Of

Hunting Prowess

In Lee's day there were eighteen packs of Staghounds in England and seven in Ireland; he mentions Her Majesty's Staghounds or Buckhounds, kept by the

Old English Staghounds by Henry Rankin Poore.

Staghounds of the 1890s.

State and kennelled at Ascot; the Devon and Somerset and Sir John Heathcote Amery's at Tiverton; Lord de Rothschild's thirty couples in Bedfordshire; the Enfield Chase with twenty-three; and the Surrey and the New Forest with twenty-five, although the latter were called the New Forest Deerhounds, hunting both the wild fallow and red deer. The stamina of the hounds in these packs was awesome, with more than one 70-mile run being recorded. Delabere Blaine, in his *Encyclopaedia of Rural Sports* of 1870, referred to a 'breed of yellow pie', considered as the genuine buckhound, of the old Southern hound stamp. Thomas Johnson, in *The Sportsman's Cyclopedia* of 1831 claimed that, 'The staghound may be regarded as the first remove from the bloodhound – we mean the staghound of ancient days.' Depictions of staghounds of his day did display a distinct Bloodhound impression; this heavier build being attributed by some to Talbot blood, with the Talbot tan still cropping up in packs to this day.

In his *Hounds of Britain* (1973), Jack Ivester Lloyd wrote: 'As a distinct breed, the Staghound disappeared from Britain when the old North Devon pack was sold in 1825. It is thought they went to Germany, except for a few retained by Parson Froude and…influenced the breeding of the Welsh Hound as well as, probably, the West Country Harrier.' The old North Devon Staghounds, predecessors of the Devon and Somerset, were considered too slow and too heavy to hunt that country, so a Foxhound cross was instigated. The result earned this tribute:

> A nobler pack of hounds no man ever saw. In height twenty-six to twenty-eight inches, colour hare-pied, yellow, yellow and white and badger-pied. Long ears, deep muzzles and deep chests. In tongue they were perfect and even when running at speed they gave plenty of tongue and their great size enabled them to cross the long heather and rough sedgy pasturage of the forest without effort or difficulty.

Their cry was important since it was considered that less tongue was thrown on the scent of the red deer than on fox or roe deer. The great Nimrod described these North Devon Staghounds as having 'deep and sonorous' tongues, but thought them short in the neck and slack in the loins.

Old Breed

Sir Walter Gilbey, in his *Hounds in Old Days* (1913), gave his own view of our old breed of Staghound, writing: 'The superior size of the old staghound, its longer head, its exceptional scenting power, and, not least, its colour – yellow, lemon and badger pied – all suggest a cross at some period with the principal breed of French hound.' Today, in France there are over thirty packs of staghounds, made up of breeds like the Poitevin, the quaintly named Billy, the tri-colores and, interestingly, the Blancs et Orange. I believe that the Chaudenay hunt, in the same family since 1830, uses pacey, tricoloured Poitevins that have an infusion of Foxhound blood. The red stag is their quarry. A stockier staghound once there was the Chambray type, more like our old type in build and coat colour. Is it too much to hope that the Frenchman's constitutional right to hunt might one day have some influence on EU law-makers, rippling outwards into the newer Eastern European countries, where greater affluence could see old styles of national hunting reintroduced. We might then rethink our national posture – supported by EU law!

For those who look back on the old days with a sense of loss, they can find enrichment in books like Fred Goss's *Memories of a Stag Harbourer* (1931), which he dedicated to 'The seven masters of the Devon and Somerset under whom I had the honour to serve'. Are we ever likely to see such a dedication again? The knowledge, expertise and, notably, the affection for the quarry in this man's words are quite remarkable. Deer control in his time was conducted by countrymen with extraordinary compassion and backed not by a recent degree in animal studies but by tapping into centuries of acquired knowledge, a commitment to responsible hunting and immense respect for the country used by the hunt. Michael Brander got this right when he wrote, in his inspired book The Hunting Instinct, of 1964, 'Every living thing is in danger and it is the hunter's natural if contradictory impulse to preserve what he hunts. A truce to all pettiness, let's look to the future.'

So much, then, for the two main varieties of the authentic staghound as known to more or less contemporary history. That is to say, first, the lemon pye, magpye, and badger pye, like George III's hounds which Colonel Thornton took to France, and like the Epping Forest hounds which went to North Devon; and, secondly, the black and tan St. Huberts or Talbots of Mr Nevill and Lord Wolverton. It is as well, both for their own sakes and for that of their admirers, that they have either gone abroad or disappeared. They would have been sadly ridden over in these

Staghounds at rest, 1904.

Royal Staghounds, 1856.

days, when riding is the avowed principle of so much hunting, and especially of stag-hunting.

Lord Ribblesdale, *The Queen's Hounds and Stag-hunting Recollections* (1897). Ribblesdale also writes, in a footnote, that 'Mr Darby described the old Epping Forest staghounds as 'pointer fleshed, with a stalliony look about them.'

When Lord Graves gave up the North Devon Staghounds in 1812, he wrote to his successor, the 1st Lord Fortescue, with suggestions as to the way hounds for the country should be bred. This letter was privately printed along with Lord Fortescue's diary for the years 1812 to 1818. This is what was written on the subject: 'It is to be observed that there is only one sort of hound adapted to Stag Hunting on Exmoor. The heavy Staghound is totally inadequate to get over the strong fences of the country and the foxhound from his nature is altogether unqualified to try the water, the constant resort of the red deer when pressed by hounds. Yet resort must be had to both

the heavy Staghound and the foxhound. First cross: Put a heavy Staghound dog to some large foxhound bitches, the result being half stag and half foxhound. Second cross: Put the bitches to a Staghound dog, and to some heavy Staghound bitches put those dogs of the first cross that are most promising. The product of this last cross is the sort required.'

Colonel W.W. Wiggin, Master of the Devon and Somerset Staghounds, 'Stag Hunting on Exmoor' in Deer, Hare & Otter Hunting, Lonsdale Library Vol. XXII (1936)

Buckhounds

'A buck is a diverse beast, he hath not his hair as a hart, for he is more white, and also he hath not such a head.' Those words from *The Master of Game* show the mild distinction made between the types of deer in times when stag-hunting was very widely practised. In the fifteenth century, however, the method of hunting the stag and the smaller buck differed;

Staghounds at rest, 1904.

BELOW LEFT: New Forest Buckhounds of 1936.

in the former, the stag was tracked using a limier, or leashed hound, rather like the tufters of the West country staghound packs; in the latter, the pursuit was conducted as a par force hunt, or 'sight and scent steeplechase'. Buck-hunting had a special importance attached to it during the reign of Edward III when the royal pack for this was acknowledged and its Mastership allocated to the Brocas family. Buckhounds were lighter and faster than their staghound equivalents, the different style of the chase demanding pace ahead of nose. Artistic licence apart, depictions of them show a Harrier-like hound rather than the heavier-boned, noticeably bigger staghound. Eventually, the buckhound became subsumed into the staghound fraternity and any differences between them nullified.

The Dalmatian

The Dalmatian has become known as the coach-dog, the spotted dog used to escort the horse-drawn coach, sometimes to keep the village curs from frightening the horses. The breed's name has led, fancifully in my view, to the conclusion that the name itself means that this breed hails from Dalmatia, with patriotic dog-lovers there convincing a number of kennel clubs of their claim to this as their native breed. I can't find any historical evidence for this claim. Yet just about every book covering or referring to breeds of dog links the

Dalmatian-like Hound depicted in E. Junco's Tableau *(Diplomate Espagnol).*

origin of the Dalmatian with Dalmatia. My own theory, which I am happy to have challenged, is that this breed name comes not from the country but the medieval Old French expression for a deer-hunting dog: *dama-chien, dama* being an Old French word for deer. (In her *Dalmatians Today*, 1997, breed expert Patches Silverstone quotes the detailed case I make for this.) There are a number of old paintings that depict such a spotted dog performing in the deer hunt. Certainly, in conformation, the breed is remarkably hound-like. It has significance; if they were hounds of the chase then they belong in the Hound Group, to be judged using the criteria applied to hounds. In 2012 I saw a top-quality specimen of this breed, Champion Offordale Chevalier, bred and owned by Jenny Alexander, that looked the epitome of a well-constructed hound of the chase, a genuine 'deer-dog'.

Meissen porcelain depicting spotted hound in the deer hunt, 1790.

Hunting of a fallow deer, whether it be a male or female, in common parlance is called buck hunting, as we say stag hunting, whether it is a stag or a hind we pursue… Fallow deer are hunted by staghounds, by foxhounds or by harriers. There are, however, regular buckhounds; such as we have seen resembled dwarf staghounds, and were bony, without too much weight, and deep toned. Regular packs of buckhounds are supplied with deer from a park… Buckhounds are met with but rarely now in England. They are, however, more common in Scotland.

Delabere Blaine, *An Encyclopaedia of Rural Sports* (1870)

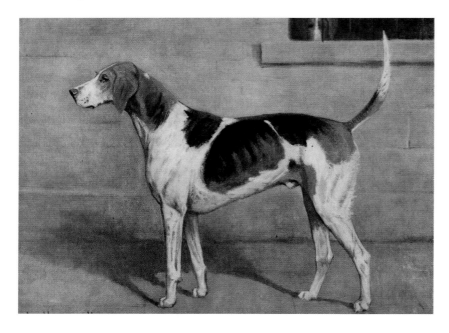

Bellman the famous Staghound, a 1935 print by G. Paice.

The Trail Hounds – the Racing Scenthounds

Outstanding Hounds

Forty years ago when walking in the Lake District, I saw in the valley below me what appeared to be a

Fit, lean, athletic trail hounds. (Photo: John Coughlan)

pack of Foxhounds in full flow. From a distance they looked like repeated splashes of milk as they poured in unison over stone walls and wire fences. But a closer examination, through strong field-glasses, revealed that these hounds were not following either a visible quarry or ground scent; and they were not hunting as a pack. They were following air scent, with noses high, great pace and huge stamina, giant enthusiasm and considerable scenting skill. They were trail hounds racing along a laid scent-line at a speed one could only marvel at. This was a re-enaction of a medieval par force hunt but without a quarry.

As an increasingly urban society regards quarry hounds with a critical eye, hound-trailing, or hound racing as some prefer to call it, may provide an alternative outlet for redundant packhounds across Britain. The skills are not the same but it is one way of saving superb canine athletes from extinction. Walking in the Lake District is testing enough; racing over demanding country for mile after mile at high speed calls for remarkable staying power, superb muscular condition, astounding determination, highly effective hearts and lungs, keen noses and more than efficient feet. These hounds are superlative middle-distance runners being used as steeplechasers over long distance courses; quite outstanding sporting dogs.

Superbly fit and skilfully bred, these hounds are much-loved pets too. Now justifying recognition as a distinct breed, they have been honed by performance rather than breeder whim, emerging as sound, unexaggerated, functional animals yet still most attractive, as well as being genetically healthy and temperamentally sound. Those used to seeing soft-muscled, overweight exhibits in our KC-licensed show rings would regard these sleek, superbly conditioned, hard-muscled hounds as being either skinny or underfed, such is the contemporary ignorance of dog and dog care. Hounds in exemplary condition for sports such as hunting, racing or coursing display the hard condition, the athletic leanness, the extreme tuck-up and show of rib, the extra-svelte physique and rippling muscle tone that might lead the uninitiated to report their owners to the RSPCA – and nowadays this body would probably find cause to investigate!

Joe and Sheila Smith with Senior Champion Max.

Match Races

It has long been the tendency of man to test his hounds against those of others to trial their speed, stamina and scenting skill. This has led to the rag-dog races of the north-east, the racing Greyhound stadiums of the Western world and the 'match-race' competitions in the Foxhound fraternity of old. The latter produced the quite remarkable feat of Bluecap (1759). Mr Smith-Barry's Bluecap and his daughter Wanton (1760) were run against Mr Meynell's couple from the Quorn pack. In 1762, a drag was laid over a four-mile course on Newmarket racecourse. Bluecap won in a little more than eight minutes; sixty horses started with the four hounds; only twelve finished. This feat led to Bluecap being portrayed by the noted sporting artist John Sartorius, whose painting depicted a hound very much like a Fell Hound.

Bluecap 1759, owned by John Smith-Barry, from a painting by John Sartorius.

Merkin, depicted by Sawrey Gilpin.

In his *Rural Sports*, Rev. Daniel records the feat of Merkin, a Foxhound bitch bred by Colonel Thornton, who 'was challenged to run any hound of her year five miles over Newmarket, giving 220 yards, for 10,000 guineas, or to give Madcap 100 yards, and run the same distance for 5,000. Merkin had run a Trial of Four Miles, and the time she performed it in was seven Minutes and half a second.' This would have been over level grassland; she may have had Greyhound blood. Thornton favoured all manner of outcrosses.

Hound-racing or trailing came from match-races conducted by MFHs of packs based in the Lake District, out of the same competitive ambitions as those of Smith-Barry and Meynell. Packs like the Blencathra, the Coniston, the Eskdale and Ennerdale, the Melbrake and the Ullswater by their very names

give an idea of the country hunted over. The College Valley pack in Northumberland, once alleged to be the fastest pack in Britain, was of Fell type too, as demanded by their hill country. *The Reminiscences of Joe Bowman and the Ullswater Foxhounds* of 1921 made this observation:

The development of the sport of hound trailing has spread the interest in the sport over a much wider area, and the rivalry between the northern and southern sections of the country is now very great. The north are claiming to produce a faster hound, a claim which was put to a practical test over an end-away trail from Wythburn to Ambleside. It justified the old opinion, 'each hound to his own country' – the fell hounds to the scree, rock and bracken, and those trained in open country to the easier going ground.

Trail Hounds slipped.

The legendary Joe Bowman stated that Lord Lonsdale set the seal of popularity with his annual Lowther Castle trail, with an attractive meeting also at the Grisedale Hall trail near Hawkshead, where 'there is about a mile of straight. Here a splendid finish can be seen, when the scent is where it ought to be – breast high.' This illustrates the main difference between ground scent hounds like Bloodhounds, with their extreme persistence, nose-to-the-ground style and placing of accurate precise tracking before pace; and the air scent hounds, the par force hounds, with their high heads, high pace and great drive. The steeplechase of the par force hunt using air scent hounds was long preferred in continental Europe. In Britain, 'hunting cunning', or the painstaking unravelling of ground scent, eventually prevailed. This decided the development, or extinction, of our packs of hounds.

Fell Packs

Out of the Fell packs and on to the trails came the fastest air scenters, with hounds from the Patterdale 'foxers' once coming first, second and third at the Grasmere Sports. In his *Foxes, Foxhounds and Fox-hunting* of 1928, Richard Clapham, a noted authority on hounds in northern England wrote: 'Our fell hounds trace their origin back to the old Talbot tans, while later they acquired a certain infusion of pointer blood. The latter was introduced in order to make hounds carry their heads higher.' He pointed out that white predominated in the Fell Hound's coat so that the hounds could be better seen by their foot followers. The infusion of Pointer blood to ensure a high head carriage may have had the added value of ensuring sound feet; sportsmen in South Africa and South America valued such an infusion because of this latter benefit.

Clapham described the Fell Hound in these words: 'The general impression afforded by a fell hound is a complete antithesis of that provided by a hound of Peterborough type [that is, standard hound show type]. Instead of size, weight and power, we have lightness, activity, and pace, coupled with wonderful stamina…' In his *Hounds of the World*, Buchanan-Jardine described the Fell Hound as around 23in in height, with long, sloping shoulders, an elegant neck and a long lean head, usually with a slightly pointed muzzle. This reminds me of the French hound breed the Poitevin, which displays a similar head. Buchanan-Jardine interestingly observes in his book that 'the foxhounds

The Trail Hound Mountain, 1921, owned by Joseph Kitchin.

of the Cumberland Fells, no doubt owe the most to the old "Chien blanc"', that is, the famous royal white hounds of France, which originated in a white hound given to Louis XI by the squire of Poitou, where the breed of Poitevin comes from.

Harrier Blood

In a letter to *Hounds* magazine in 1992, John Mawson wrote from Cumbria to state:

The Hound Trailing Association hounds are descended from the harrier mainly the Brampton Harrier, that were disbanded at the start of the First World War. This line comes from a harrier, a bitch called White Rally and approximately half of today's trail hounds go back to this bitch. Another line, further back, comes from the Holme Harriers, a dog (hound) called Macduff. His grand dam was by a

ABOVE: Fell Foxhounds by T. Ivester Lloyd, 1934.
BELOW: The start of a hound trail.

bloodhound… There has been one or two outcrosses in the last forty years to fell hounds… Today, hounds do not have the opportunity to show their speed, stamina and strength because there are so few trails over thirty-five or forty minutes and therefore nothing to show their true prowess.

He also expressed concern about inbreeding in to-day's trail hound, arising in part from that sport's fanciers not knowing enough about contemporary Harrier packs. But since the early twentieth century, a number of outcrossings have occurred.

The trail hound may have been founded on Fell Hound and local Harrier blood but since then has developed separately into its own distinctive type. In 1919 the blood of the Windemere Harrier Cracker

Hound trail start, Grasmere Sports, August, 1899.

Assembling for a trail race, 1897.

was introduced; in 1922 Harrier blood from Lanca-shire packs was used and again, to greater effect, six years later when a Harrier sire, Beware, was utilized to produce a litter which subsequently proved domi-nant in the trail hound dynasty. (Trail hunts were held in the country covered by the Holcombe Hunt and the then Rochdale Harriers.) In the mid-1920s a Pointer-Harrier cross, the bitch Gravity, was intro-duced and helped to found today's bloodlines. In the 1950s a Greyhound-Irish Setter cross was tried; then a West Country Harrier (from the Dart Vale) and in 1962 a couple of Kerry Beagles also tried but none of these outsiders proved impressive in breeding terms.

It would be interesting to try a Saluki lurcher, bred for enhanced stamina, a Rampur Hound from India, the lighter-built American Foxhound, the Segugio from Italy or the podencos of the Mediterranean lit-toral, for example from Portugal and Ibiza, as trail hounds. They possess the type of anatomy and the hunting instincts to succeed, the latter forming the basis of the trailing desire. One outstanding trail hound called Singwell joined the local Foxhound packs in the winter and proved itself as a dual-pur-pose hound. Joe Bowman once wrote that:

Denise Bland with Senior Champion Huntsman's Choice III.

Donna and Tracey Hill with their puppy Maiden.

The 1999 Champion Puppy Cristy, with owner Carole Jackson.

Hunting of the aniseed and oil drag has been reduced nearly to a science by the fleet-footed hounds, but little doubt is entertained that the average hounds from the five Lakeland foxhound packs are little if any behind the drivers of the bloodless trail in point of speed, whilst in courage and stamina they will probably excel.

It is interesting that in these trailhounds an occasional silky coat can crop up in litters, possibly from the surreptitious use of outside blood long ago.

Speed with Stamina

The sport of hound racing has long been highly competitive and a mainly working-class pursuit. An early star, and first hound to win a hundred prizes, was Rattler, trained by an Ambleside cobbler but sadly poisoned, allegedly by a rival trainer. Rattler had a son, Ruler, which was clever enough to run with the other hounds without trailing its own line, then sprint in to triumph as an accomplished finisher. In contrast, one of the fastest early hounds, a bitch called Ruby, was a poor finisher, often overtaken when in sight of the finishing line. Speed alone is not enough in these races. Trail hounds race an 8- to 10-mile course over the most testing country in England and complete it in 25–45 minutes, the time range indicating the different terrain between each course set. Twenty years ago, a superb hound called 'Hartsop Magic' was the star of the trailing circuit. In 1985 she had thirty-two wins, a year later twenty-six and another thirty-three in 1987. Clapham claimed that hounds have been timed to do 15½mph over a course rising to 1,250 feet in the first mile and a half. The sport's governing body, the Hound Trailing Association, formed as long ago as 1906, can withhold prize money if a particular course is completed too quickly or too slowly. This may well be a shrewd method of reducing the chances of fixing a race.

This is a 200-year-old country sport, which I very much hope will survive, with the sustained support of local farmers and landowners, another 200. Held between March and October each year, run over a circular course, with a separate outward scent from the home run, with each hound marked with a dye to ensure those that finish actually started, this could be the hound sport for the future. The morally vain can find little to criticize in this quite admirable canine activity. The hounds taking part, however, are still hounds; one once finished the course with a rabbit in its mouth and the ambitious outcross to a so-called Russian Retriever produced a hound that preferred mutton to the thrill of the race! It is a well-regulated sport too and, with land being taken out of agricultural use and hunting with dogs under threat, one to be considered more widely than just in the Lakes.

Unrecognized Native Hound Breed

I have nothing but the greatest admiration for the country people of Cumberland and Westmorland who have kept these hounds going over many years in such magnificent shape. As a lover of functional dogs, I congratulate them on their superb hounds and salute their achievements and efforts. I have thirty books on hounds that make no mention of trail hounds. But in the present political climate it is more likely that these hounds will survive than many others. The trail hounds registered with the Hound Trailing Association now represent an important English native breed that deserves recognition as such. They are distinctive; they breed true to type; they have a long distinguished *and* recorded pedigree, and they are a huge credit to English breeders.

As a nation we are far too casual, even neglectful, about conserving our native breeds of dog and far too eager to import inferior foreign breeds. From the KC's lists have gone the English White Terrier and the Harrier. Sportsmen never bothered to protect the Llanidloes Setter, develop the Norfolk Retriever or preserve the English Water Spaniel. Sheep farmers failed to perpetuate the old sheepdog breeds: the Welsh Hillman, the Old Welsh Grey, the Blue Shag, the Smithfield Sheepdog and the Black and Tan. Of course some contemporary breeds carry their genes or perpetuate their type, but that has never been part of a planned conservation scheme.

The sporting dog is under unprecedented threat; there is a greater need now to safeguard our precious remaining breeds than ever before. The quarry hounds could disappear unless a function for them is found. Packs overseas may snap them up – as the renowned Dumfriesshire pack has been – for their prowess is acknowledged throughout the sporting world. But these are native British hounds, so very much part of our sporting heritage. We would be extremely foolish to leave their future development to foreign fanciers – or, even worse, politicians! Hound-racing may not suit those looking to admire the work of a *pack* or please mounted followers. But which do we prefer? Hound trailing…or nothing?

> …the trailers use a mixture of aniseed, paraffin and turpentine to lay the trail that the hounds follow. And that is the essence of hound-trailing – a group of super-fit hounds following a scent round a course that could be anything up to 10 miles long, over field and fell, from the slip (start) to the finish, in a time that should be around 30 minutes – trails run in less than 25 minutes or more than 40 minutes are declared void. Unlike the various forms of hunting, the humans involved in hound trailing do not physically follow the hounds. Instead they watch from vantage points, experience and superlative eyesight picking out and identifying the lead hound, while to the non-hound trailer the dogs could be so many ants scurrying across a distant surface…
>
> John Coughlan, Hound Trailing (1998)

The Bloodhound

> The sleuthhound derives its name from its readiness in tracing the sleuth, slot, or track of the deer. Gratius, who wrote before the Christian era, and Strabo, who flourished somewhat later, notices the importation of dogs of this kind from Britain into Gaul as common, in consequence of their excellence…their exquisite powers of scent were put into requisition to trace human marauders and blood-stained culprits, from which they gained the name of bloodhound in England, while they retained their appellation of sleuthhound in Scotland.
>
> Delabere Blaine, *An Encyclopaedia of Rural Sports* (1870)

Sleuth Hound

In some ways, it might have been better for the breed to become our Sleuth Hound or Slough Hound, as the Scots would have it. The word 'blood' in its title conjures up images, for some, of a bloodthirsty attack dog rather than an amiable scenthound more interested in scent than taste! And the Bloodhound is *the* scenthound. The breed title matches that of the 'blood' horse in its origin. In his treatise *Of Englishe Dogges* of 1576, Dr Caius wrote:

St Hubert Hounds depicted by Eubussy, c.1870.

Bloodhounds being secured – Coupling Hounds by John F. Tayler (1806–89).

For whether the beast, being wounded...and escapeth the hands of the huntsman; or whether the said beast being slain is conveyed cleanly out of the park (so that there be some signification of bloodshed) these dogs, with no less facility and easiness than avidity and greediness, can disclose and betray the same by smelling: applying to their pursuit, agility and nimbleness, without tediousness. For which consideration, of a singular speciality they deserve to be called Sanguinarii, Bloodhounds.

Breed Title

In its *Illustrated Breed Standards* the KC records: 'The home country of the breed is Belgium and ancestry can be traced back to the monastery of St Hubert. In Belgium the Bloodhound is known by his other name of St Hubert Hound. It is most probable that this hound was one of those brought to England by the Normans in 1066.' Apart from the fact that Belgium did not become a country until 1830 and the hounds of the monastery were all black, the great French hound expert of the nineteenth century, Count le Couteulx de Canteleu, held that *all* French hounds were descended from the St Hubert strain, a claim disputed by other hound experts. The monastery is in the Ardennes, a region long famous for its *schweisshunds*, but for black ones. The naming of the Bloodhound as the Chien de St Hubert, and the recognition of Belgium as its origin source, was done unilaterally by the FCI, the international kennel club based there. I think it is far more likely that the modern *breed* of Bloodhound was developed in Britain. The noun 'bloodhound' has been used loosely to describe hounds developed as far apart as Cuba and South Africa. The naming of breeds of dog has rarely been impressively accurate.

English Ingredients

In *The Sportsman's Cabinet* of 1804, there is an interesting statement about the provenance of the Bloodhound:

> ...it is fair to infer (particularly as no proof whatever has been adduced to the contrary), that the original stock of the blood-hounds in this country partook, in nearly an equal degree, of the large, strong, bony, fleet stag-hound, and of the old English southern-hound, still maintained in the low and swampy parts of the

kingdom. Those destined to one particular kind of pursuit, and used merely as blood-hounds, were never brought into the chase with any distinct pack for the promotion of sport with any species of game; but they were preserved and supported (as a constable or Bow-street runner of the present day,) for the purposes of pursuit and detection...

I later describe how breeders in the late nineteenth century made use of Southern Hound blood and other ingredients, including several breeds of French hounds in the pursuit of an improved Bloodhound. Both kennel clubs and breed historians are quick to attribute origin of favoured breeds to overseas breeds of the same coat colour in an attempt to romanticize their breed.

St Hubert Past

One French-Canadian enthusiast, Christiane Bernard, claims a separate strain as the genuine St Huberts, with her hounds of that name reaching as

Christiane Bernard's recreated St Hubert Hound.

Handsome red Bloodhound.

much as 34in at the shoulder and weighing around 145lb. One of her male dogs was said to measure 36in and weigh 160lb, but she admits he was exceptional. A breed of comparable size and coat colour is the Greater Swiss Mountain Dog, which can weigh 135lb, with the smaller Polish Scenthound (Gonczy Polski), the Austrian Brandlbracke and the bigger variety of the Hungarian Erdelyi Kopo featuring the same physique but lacking the hugely elongated ears and throatiness. Similar breeds were known in the Baltic States, with the impressive Finnish Hound standing out at World Dog Shows for sheer soundness, matched by handsomeness.

Big, strapping, black and tan or tricolour scent-hounds can be found all over Europe, from the Jura type in Switzerland to the Bavarian Mountain Hound, as well as in the United States, with their coonhound breeds, and in South America, where the Fila Brasileiro embraces a strain of distinct Bloodhound type. Perhaps the French hound expert, Count le Couteulx de Canteleu, had a point in considering the St Hubert Hound as the founder of all European hound breeds rather than one distinct one from the Ardennes, in what became Belgium. It's far more likely, though, that the St Hubert strain is behind just the Bleu de Gascogne, Gascon-Saintongeois, Ariegeois and Artois-Normand packs.

Individual Breed

Any spirited sportsman seeking a highly individual breed and one to challenge the world he lives in would be well suited to the breed of Bloodhound! Writing on 'The Bloodhound As A Sporting Dog' in *The Badminton Magazine of Sports and Pastimes* of 1902, Russell Richardson gave the view, 'That the bloodhound fails to occupy the high position amongst sporting dogs to which, by reason of its high qualities, it would seem to be entitled…must

Jura Hound from Switzerland.

Fila Brasileiro at the World Dog Show 2003, revealing its Bloodhound ancestry.

be a matter of surprise and regret to all who have any personal knowledge of their capabilities…' In a world where conforming is all and copying others appears the name of the game, the sheer facial appeal alone of this breed should attract the individuals left among us. Richardson went on to express the pleasure to be obtained from hunting the 'clean boot' with such a dog, a pursuit that can surely antagonize no one. No doubt followers of the remaining Bloodhound packs still enjoying this pastime will echo his views.

Sporting Hound

Writing in *With Hound and Terrier* (1904), West Country sportswoman and knowledgeable dog breeder Alys Serrell gave an interesting view of the Bloodhound around that time:

> Mr Holford's hounds were well known, and his Matchless and Diligent were among the best specimens of their day. Another famous breeder was Mr Brough, whose kennel has had a long series of show successes. Unfortunately the bloodhound has not been exempt from the dangers of a show career… In process of time, some of the show bench hounds became a sort of canine tadpole – all head. Legs and feet, back and loins, and all that propelling power without which a hound is not worthy of the name, were neglected as matters of small importance compared to an exaggerated wrinkle, a narrow high-peaked head, a deeply sunken eye, and a disproportionate length of ear. The bloodhound indeed was apparently doomed, because the extreme views of the fanciers would leave him neither the power to hunt nor the brains to be a companion. Then came the happy idea of making him again an instrument of sport, in the direction to which his hereditary qualities seemed to point. The leading bloodhound-owners trained their hounds to hunt the clean boot…and when the first trials were arranged, very general interest was excited.

Her summary tells you a great deal about show ring excesses penalizing a sporting breed – an activity not confined to this breed.

Colour in the Gene Pool

In the late nineteenth century it was not unknown for Bloodhounds to feature white markings: a white star on the chest, a white tip to the tail and even the spotted 'snowstorm' coat with flecks of white along the saddle, rather like the early Labradors known as 'hailstone-coated'. The writer and author of a century ago, Frank Townend Barton, once bred a pure white whelp in a pure-bred Bloodhound litter and, to his subsequent regret, consigned it to the bucket as an 'undesirable' anomaly. Genes act in a random, not a mathematical manner; the range of a breed's gene pool will always reveal its past in time. A deep red with tan markings was once much more common, with some fanciers preferring a tawny hue, mixed with black, on the saddle. Today's KC-ordained breed standard stipulates: black and tan, liver and tan (red and tan) and red, but allows darker colours sometimes interspersed with lighter or badger-coloured hair and sometimes flecked with white. A small amount of white is permissible on the chest, the feet and on the tip of the tail. I have yet to come across a show breeder who welcomes white markings in his stock. Truly, there is no threat to any breed from the colour of its coat; the only threat to a hound breed comes from an inability to hunt.

Historically, Bloodhounds were very much part of the chase, featuring in Landseer's paintings of the deer hunt, with their unique tracking skills leading to their use all over the world. The 'father' of the breed here was Edwin Brough, whose hounds were as much admired in the show ring (where his kennel won over 700 prizes, including 386 'firsts'), as employed as scenters by a variety of users. His hounds were sound physically, lacking the super-elongated ears, excess of loose skin, distressing display of haw and over-abundance of dewlap/throatiness – condemned by Alys Serrell a century ago but still seen in the show rings today.

Mixed Blood

The pack Bloodhounds are much more like Brough's hounds; show breeders recently expressed dismay when the KC accepted new blood into the breed from the Readyfield pack, when more informed breeders favoured an outcross to a different pack – of *their* choice. It is encouraging, however, to see the acceptance of blood from outside the show lines. The obsession with pure-breeding, even when to the detriment of a breed, is very twentieth century and needs to be relegated to the history books. A wider gene pool is being encouraged too, in this breed, with blood coming in from Czech, American and Norwegian lines. The blood of the Bloodhound was valued by our sporting ancestors when seeking to enhance the scenting performance of other breeds.

In the valuable *The Kennel Encyclopaedia* of 1907, the well-informed editor J. Sidney Turner gave Bloodhound expert Edwin Brough nearly ninety pages to cover his breed and his words are enlightening, if paraphrased, here:

> During the last century each keeper in the New Forest was required to maintain a couple of hounds, which they called Talbots but were probably more likely to be degenerate Bloodhounds, to hunt wounded deer. Mr Thomas Neville, a great sportsman, bred his pack from one or two couples purchased from a keeper in the New Forest and in 1876 Mr Edwin Nichols procured from Mr Neville a bitch called Countess, eventually breeding-on a bitch called Restless to a dog hound called Luath XI, from which mating came the best of their time. To one of these, Bravo, Mr Brough put a purebred Southern Hound, Clara, which in the third generation produced Ch. Victor, born 1890. Mr Mark Beaufoy imported a bitch, Babylone, from France, who was a mixture of Bloodhound, Vendee and St Hubert from the Ardennes. She was behind Chs Bettina and Pitmilly Ulf but her name does not appear in any of the champions pedigrees.

The Bloodhound Luath XI depicted by R.H. Moore.

Against that background, it does seem somewhat strange for today's breed fanciers to be opposing proposals to use pack blood to reinvigorate the modern pedigree breed. Mixed blood made the modern Bloodhound; mixed blood could improve the hounds of today.

Brough also made known his views on uninformed, unimaginative pedigree dog breeding of that time with these words:

> A little later came the blind worship of pedigree, which, for the average breeder, consisted of a string of meaningless names representing animals quite unknown to him. His only idea was to bow down to the fetish 'thoroughbred', not realising that a pedigree composed entirely of thoroughbred wasters might be vastly inferior to one consisting chiefly of animals representing the best of their breed, which had continuously reproduced the required qualities for many generations, although containing a slight admixture of different blood.

Those words from a great hound breeder should be posted up alongside Adrian Jones's statue of Forager, the Pytchley Foxhound, standing outside the Kennel Club in Piccadilly!

Valued Blood

The famous Foxhound Harlequin was one quarter Bloodhound and considered by the great hound expert of the twentieth century, Sir John Buchanan-Jardine, as the best hound in the field he ever saw.

Edwin Brough's Burgundy.

The Southern Hound Clara of 1884.

Another great hound expert, Sir Newton Rycroft, wrote in *Hounds, Hunting and Country* (2001):

What is the potential value of such crosses both for fox- and deerhunting? Here I believe a very sharp

distinction has to be made between pure bloodhound and working bloodhound with an outcross. When first considering the pure bloodhound, the best and, I believe, only the very best have retained the nose… As regards cry, stamina and constitution, I believe the pure bloodhound of today is far too weak to be a practical proposition for crossing.

Hound expert Jack Ivester Lloyd, writing to *Hounds* magazine in September 1989, gave the view that the Bloodhound both before and after the Second World War was 'all in' after hunting a 4-mile line, blaming inbreeding due to the small numbers of the breed in those times.

It is worth noting that when the East Anglian Bloodhound pack was set up, they went for a three-quarter Bloodhound, together with blood from the Dumfriesshire Foxhounds and also the French Gascogne, and produced a more pack-orientated hound. Breeding for performance has to be the way with hounds.

The French Hound Babylone.

Tracking Prowess

A famous tracking pack was the Ledburn – usually about five or six couples hunting at least once a week in the winter in the Vale of Aylesbury until the outbreak of the Second World War. They were famous for their voice too. Ledburn Boswell and Ledburn Baal each, separately, hunted his man twenty-four hours cold over Corrie Common in Dumfriesshire before the Second World War and, after the war Mrs Oldfield's hound won the Brough Cup for hunting a six-hour cold line for 3 miles in 20 minutes. In his *Dog Breaking* of 1909, General Hutchinson remarks on the value of this breed in tracking poachers: '… for the fear poachers naturally entertain of being tracked to their homes at dawn of day would more deter them from entering a cover than any dread of being assailed at night by the boldest armed party.' I give many marks to those stalwarts who still carry out tracking trials, drag-hunting or hunting the 'clean boot', for their hounds and retain the famous ability in these majestic animals. Scope for gamekeepers here!

Hunting the 'Clean Boot'

In *The Badminton Magazine of Sports and Pastimes* Vol. XV (1902), Russell Richardson wrote:

> From what has been briefly written it will be seen that hunting the clean boot may easily be added to the pleasures of country life; however limited one's own property may be there should be little difficulty in obtaining the necessary permission to cross sufficient

Bloodhounds on a trail – Sir William Q. Orchardson's Escape of 1874.

Brough's famous tracking Bloodhounds Barnaby and Burgho, used in the hunt for Jack the Ripper.

land to make up any number of good runs, and this form of hunting has the advantage that a course can always be chosen in the direction one desires to take, and no damage whatever need be done. Most interesting and instructive experiments might be easily tried by means of the bloodhound, and many points on which hunting men differ might be put to a series of useful tests – such, for instance, as whether scent is destroyed by a sudden frost, and, if so, whether totally or only temporarily, and in the latter case whether the line could be taken up again immediately on a thaw setting in…

He makes a simple case for the sport to become much more widespread than the present tracking programme, with huge benefit both to hounds and their owners. It was good to read of the Association of Bloodhound Breeders restarting the Marlwood Chal-

lenge Beaker contest on the Pennines at Todmorden in which qualified hounds must successfully hunt a line 20 hours cold and no less than 3 miles long; in 1981 it was won by a really good Bloodhound WT Ch. Rushton Rochester, a valuable competition won by a fine hound.

New Look at Exaggerations

The American vet and sportsman Leon Whitney, who probably bred more cross-bred dogs than anyone before or since, in his informative *How to Breed Dogs* (1947) lamented the 'rage for 'bone' in the breed by show breeders, the strange desire for 'heavy ankles' and 'heavy wrinkle', contrasting the usefulness of such dogs with the much more workmanlike hounds produced by those breeding 'trailers'. His remarks come to mind when you have seen say the Peak pack

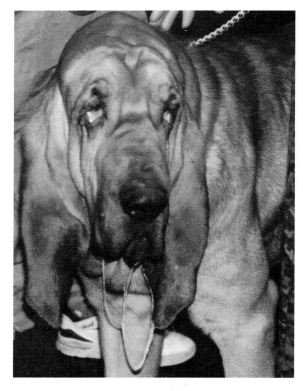

TOP: *Drooling, sore-eyed Bloodhound that qualified for Crufts in 1994.*

BOTTOM: *Top-class show Bloodhound Ch. Quiet Creeks Double Or Nothing for Heather.*

or the Coakham hounds and compared them to show Bloodhounds. At the Richmond championship dog show of November 2011, one of the best show judges in Britain gave the view that this was the worst entry of the breed that she had ever judged, with some prizes being withheld. With tiny entry figures, some rosettes are hollow victories and I dread to think of some of the show dogs being bred from. Sadly, I have seen some show-ring hounds with quite a variety of mouth and jaw faults, with both over- and undershot specimens and excessive narrowness at the muzzle. Bloodhounds 'taste' scent and deserve sound mouths. When working in Europe, I saw the hounds of Robert de Messemaeker in Belgium at shows and admired their heads – no excess facial skin or over-wrinkled brows there, but good sound dogs.

The KC is viewing needless exaggeration in breeds of dog with greater scrutiny nowadays. Commendably, they have removed expressions like: 'especially noticeable loose skin about the head and neck and where it hangs in deep folds', and, again on head skin, deleted 'appears abundant, but more particularly so when head is carried low, skin falling into loose pendulous ridges and folds, especially over forehead and sides of face.' The KC has also introduced new wording: 'Signs of any obvious eye irritation must be heavily penalized.' Over the last thirty years I have seen Bloodhounds in the show ring with red-raw eyes and such a superfluity of head skin that their eyesight has been impaired. And some of them won prizes! One Bloodhound exhibitor informed me, and he believed it, that it was important that the head skin hung right over the dog's eyes 'so that it was forced to seek scent on the ground'. When I gently reminded him that all the famous man-trailers had tight head skin and no impaired vision, he merely shrugged and strolled away. Before the devotees of pack Bloodhounds feel superior, the past seeking of heavy ankles and massive bone in Foxhounds was just as misguided. As always it is the dogs that bear the brunt of human foolishness.

In the American show rings, the exhibits appear less exaggerated; a colleague recently back from there, with experience of hunting the breed, told me that the best hound he had seen for years was the American Champion Quiet Creeks Double or Nothing for Heather, sound yet full of breed type, tighter-skinned than our entry. St Hubert would have admired such a hound!

Bloodhounds of the Pack by T. Ivester Lloyd, 1937.

Pack Activity

It was pleasing to see hounds from the Four Shires Bloodhounds (a pack hunting the Derbyshire, Staffordshire, Nottinghamshire and South Yorkshire country) succeeding at a recent Peterborough Festival of Hunting – the result of a clear, enlightened breeding programme. The Bloodhounds 'of the packs' contain valuable breeding material, especially for the widening of the gene pool in the show kennels. Their unforgettable 'voice' has long been treasured, with some sportsmen in France long favouring this breed in the hunting field. I have a distant memory, when working in Germany over half a century ago, of a British cavalry regiment to the south having a Bloodhound pack, called, I think, the Weser Vale Bloodhounds. I have a memory too, from working in Northern Ireland, of a pack in County Antrim, the Holestone Farmers Bloodhounds, working over very heavy going quite successfully. It was sad to learn of the break-up of the East Anglian Bloodhound pack in 2013; run by farrier Roger Clark on the Essex-Suffolk boundary, it was formed in 1992. It was good, however, to learn recently of a new Bloodhound pack being formed, the Highmoor in North Yorkshire, with drafts from the Southdown and Eridge, the Readyfield and the Coakham hunts. These are very special hounds, so much a keystone of all hound work and so worth conserving.

The bloodhound, in every literary transmission to be found upon record, is unanimously admitted to have been about seven, or eight and twenty inches high, of substantial, firm, strong, compact, and muscular form; the face wide upon the forehead, gradually narrowing to the nose; the countenance attractively serene, and solicitous of attention; nostrils wide and expansive; ears large, soft, and pendulous, broad at the base, and narrowing to the tip; tail long, with an erective curve, particularly when in pursuit, with a voice awfully loud, deep, and sonorous.

The Sportsman's Cabinet (1804)

No breed can vigorously thrive on the strength of past greatness, nor can it always rely on finding financially able and generous backers as it has in the past. The breed cannot thrive solely by its presence at dog shows and occasional Field Trials. Those who love these hounds must breed for good temperament, for active brains, and for the ability to fit into the home life of to-day. In order to do so some exaggerations of type may have to be swept away, but this price would prove well worth while.

Douglas H. Appleton, *The Bloodhound Handbook* (1960)

Bloodhounds of the pack at Ragley Game Fair.

Bloodhounds in Full Cry by T. Ivester Lloyd, 1934.

Having sampled the delights of hunting the clean boot across wild and beautiful countryside myself, I have no hesitation in advising others to do the same. But I will lay odds that, if they are persuaded to act as runners and lay the trail, the sound of hounds on their line will send shivers down their spines!

Phil Drabble, writing the Foreword to Brian Lowe's *Hunting the Clean Boot* (1981)

The Boarhounds

Undaunted in courage, the true boarhound would rush on his game without hesitation and almost as certainly he ran on his destruction. These valuable dogs, therefore, were not so frequently allowed to attack the boar 'at force', as formerly, at the first onset, but were purposely restrained until the boar had become somewhat exhausted.

Delabere Blaine, *An Encyclopaedia of Rural Sports* (1870)

Dangerous Prey

Next to the rhinoceros, the wild boar is generally acknowledged to be the most dangerous prey in the world for the hunter. Extraordinarily strong, amazingly fast, apparently fearless, with a keen sense of smell, very sharp hearing and a low centre of gravity propelled by 300lb, any dog facing one has to be a little bit special. With a power-packed muzzle, tailor-made for rooting in the hardest ground and formidable tusks designed to slash and tear, the wild boar makes a terrifying adversary. The Greeks considered the boar hunt to be the supreme test in the chase for the hunter and his hounds. Many of the hounds were killed on each hunt. Xenophon recommended Laconian hounds for the pursuit and Indian hounds at the kill; the boar being despatched with a spear not by the dogs, although at times they would be holding on to the boar when the kill was made. The Laconian or Spartan hound was harrier-size and a superb tracker; the 'Indian hound' was bigger, heavier – well described as a hunting mastiff. These 'Indian hounds' were not from India but from Hyrcania on the Caspian Sea.

Special Hounds

It is important to appreciate that boar hunting was not just another form of hunting. In his valuable book *Hounds and Hunting in Ancient Greece*, published in 1964, Denison Bingham Hull stated: 'It was the very danger of the boar hunt that made it fascinating to the Greeks; victory was essential, for there was no safety except through conquest. It was that urge to display courage that made the boar hunt the highest manifestation of the chase'; the hounds of course were always in greater danger than the human hunters. Hull quotes from Xenophon's *Cynegeticus* as recording that boarhounds 'must by no means be picked by chance, for they must be prepared to fight the beast'. These were clearly highly respected and rather special hounds.

In *Sport in Classic Times*, published in 1931, A.J. Butler noted interestingly that Oppian mentions big-game hounds that are blue-black and considers 'a tawny colour' denotes swiftness and strength. He also refers to boarhounds that have light-coloured bodies with patches of black, dark red or blue. All the above are coat colours occurring in the German Boarhound, the Great Dane. In *Hunting in the Ancient World* (1985), J.K. Anderson quoted Arrian as reporting: 'The best bred hounds have a proud air and seem haughty, and tread lightly, quickly, and delicately, and turn their sides and stretch their necks upward like horses when they are showing off.' (That sounds very Great Dane-like to me! *See* later coverage.)

ABOVE RIGHT: *Slate-blue Great Dane.*

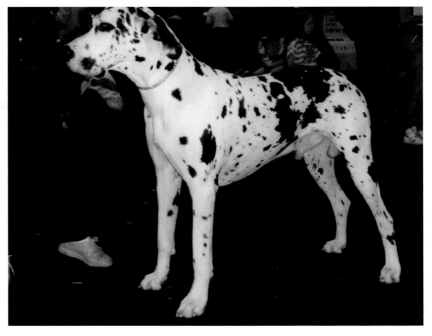

Harlequin Great Dane.

Loose Nomenclature

The ancient Greeks; Gaston Phoebus, Count of Foix (1331–91), in the fourteenth century; the Bavarians in the seventeenth century; and the Czars in the nineteenth century used hunting dogs of different types in unison according to function. Greyhounds, scenthounds and hunting mastiffs were used together and not hunted separately, unlike our more specialist packs. Boarhounds could therefore be the loose term to describe all hounds on a boar hunt, whatever their function in the chase and kill. Casual researchers can therefore look at a painting of a boar hunt or read accounts of one and jump to all sorts of false conclusions about what boarhounds could look like in past times. The illustrations in Comte de Foix's well-known *Livre de Chasse* depict scenthounds, sighthounds and hunting mastiffs being used complementarily in the hunting field. In Turbervile's *Booke of Hunting* of 1576, he describes bloudhoundes, greyhoundes, mastiffes and a variety of scenthounds being used in support of each other. But as firearms developed, both in range and power, the role of the killing dog became obsolete; hounds of the chase and the hunter with the gun could get by without 'holding and killing' dogs.

Dangerous Amusement

In England, in the reign of Henry II, the wild boar was hunted with hounds and spears in many wooded areas, from the Forest of Dean to Warwickshire and beyond. King James hunted the boar at Windsor, this being described as 'a more dangerous amusement than it was likely he could find any pleasure in'. Turbervile, writing in the late sixteenth century, recorded that hounds accustomed to running the boar were spoiled for game of scent less strong. They were alleged to be less inclined to stoop to the scent of deer or hare and disinclined to pursue a swifter quarry that didn't turn to bay when out of breath. The sheer ferocity and remarkable bravery of the boar at bay was legendary amongst those who hunted with hounds, across several centuries. There was an old German saying to the effect that if you wanted boars' heads, you first had to sacrifice those of many dogs.

No hunter wants to lose his best scenthounds to the tusks of a wild boar, and because of the high risk of canine death, two practices were introduced. One was to protect the hounds with protective clothing like chain-mail. The other was to introduce less valuable, more expendable, huge, cross-bred dogs for the killing stage. Later on, when firearms were invented, the hounds were used to bay the boar, which was then despatched by a special knife-like sword or by shooting, rather like modern staghunting. Phoebus considered the killing of a charging boar with a sword on horseback as being the finest feat any hunter could achieve.

Bear Baiting *by Hondius, 1650 – the 'seizing and holding' hounds.*

The Italian boar hunt of 1880 – the hunting mastiffs at work.

The great forests of central Europe provided endless opportunities for hunting. In the nineteenth century the pursuit of wild animals with hounds was conducted on a vast scale. In France there were over 350 packs of hounds. In 1890 the Czar of Russia organized a grand fourteen-day hunt in which his party killed forty-two European bison, thirty-six elk and 138 wild boar.

Protective Coats

Artists like Snyders, Tempesta and Desportes have recorded great hunting scenes for us and portrayed the dogs involved with their customary accuracy. But these portrayals have sometimes led to needless confusion. The boar, for example, was pursued by boarhounds but seized by catch-dogs or boar-lurchers, the boarhounds being too valuable to be risked 'at

Desportes' La Chasse au Sanglier, *depicting a protected 'seizing hound'.*

German 'seizer' or boar hunt catch-dog, heavily protected.

the kill'. It is likely that more dogs were killed on big game hunts than the quarry. Favourite hounds in the pack were protected with padded jackets of brown fustian (a thick, hard-wearing twill cloth) or bombazine (a twilled fabric of worsted and silk or cotton), with whalebone on the chest and belly to reduce the ripping action of the boar's tusks. To reduce canine casualties, the hounds had to support each other.

The wealthier hunters furnished their hounds with coats made of chain mail, on a quilted canvas and leather base. The Duke of Coburg's old sporting armouries near Gotha produced such coats. We should remember the sheer dash and reckless courage of the dogs that wore them. 'Extreme persistence' is now sadly one of the 'points' looked for by ignorant policemen when assessing powerful dogs under our shameful anti-dog laws. What a reward for centuries of selfless service doing man's bidding! We might strengthen the case for the defence in such sad prosecutions if the powerful, determined dogs being persecuted were recognized, at long last, as *hounds*. The role of hounds varied but they worked in a team.

French Packs

There are still over 100 packs of hounds in France with the status of *'la grande venerie'*, that is, hunting stag, roebuck and boar. The hounds for this are such breeds as the Poitevin, the Gascon-Saintongeois and the crossbred Anglo-Français. These breeds have great voice, pace and nose, if lacking the drive and stamina of our

Foxhounds. There are still fourteen packs concentrating on the boar hunt. Two of these packs are composed of the quaintly named Billy breed, fast hounds, full of cry and strongly made, though lacking the power of the Poitevin. The Griffon-Nivernais, a long-backed, rangy, wire-haired breed and the Grand Griffon-Vendeen are also used as boarhounds. In France, the boar is still hunted using the Vautrait, originally a pack of running mastiffs, now mostly Anglo-Français tricolores, supported by the odd Foxhound. The Tiens-Bon Picard, the only pack in northeastern France still pursuing the ancient skill, uses twenty-five couples, plus *limiers* (our tufters) made up of a Foxhound, a Griffon Nivernais and an Anglo-Français, operating under a harbourer (*valet de limier*) to locate the quarry. These hounds only bay the boar; holding or seizing dogs are not used in such a hunt.

French hounds hunting boar, as well as other quarry, are covered in more detail in Chapter 3, as are hounds from the Americas and Asia. In 1850, an English sportsman spent two seasons hunting wolves and boar in France with the bigger Brittany hound, describing these hounds as 24in high and 'big powerful animals, wire-haired, deep-tongued, with grand heads, and supported by plenty of bone... I don't think I ever saw a harder driving lot in chase in my life'. It is from such Brittany hounds that the modern Vendeen gets his rough coat. The rough-coated Welsh Hound has also been linked with such French hounds. The Greeks and Romans admired the rough-coated hunting dogs of the Celts.

A wild boar is a fearsome adversary, its speed in the charge is like lightning, its tusks can rip through the flanks of a dog and its underbelly with devastating effect. In *A Month in the Forests of France* of 1857, Grantley Berkeley related how one old boar at bay killed or rendered hors de combat fourteen of the eighteen hounds attacking it. He considered this a higher canine casualty rate than usual but expressed no surprise at the fact that dogs were routinely killed in such a hunt. The attitude towards the recklessly brave dogs which closed with the wild boar at bay is aptly summed up in *The Master of Game* of 1406:

> They are almost shaped as a greyhound of full shape, they have a great head, great lips and great ears, and with such, men help themselves well at the baiting of the bull and at hunting of the wild boar, for it is natural to them to hold fast [that is, seize and hold] but they are so heavy and ugly, that if they be slain by the wild boar it is no great loss.

Forest Hunts

A similar lack of sympathy towards dogs existed in the hunting field, especially in the boar hunt. Historians list the appalling totals of quarry killed but never the number of dogs that lost their lives in such hunts. Elector John George I of Saxony (1611–56) held hunts in which nearly 32,000 wild boar were killed; his son only managed 22,000 in his lifetime! But it is likely that several dogs died for every boar. The scale of hunting in the seventeenth and eighteenth centuries was quite staggering: on 12 January 1656 on Dresden Heath, 44 stags and 250 wild boar were killed; in Moritzburg in 1730 the haul was 221 antlered stags, 116 does, 82 fallow bucks, 46 fallow does and 614 wild boar. It may well be the case that on Dresden Heath on 12 January 1656, several hundred dogs died in the hunting conducted that day.

In AD802 Charlemagne hunted wild boar in the Ardennes, aurochs in the Hercynian Forest and later had his trousers and boots torn to pieces by a bison; all three quarry were formidable adversaries and were hunted by the same huge hounds. Between 1611 and 1680, game books reveal that around 40,000 wild boar, sows and young boars were killed in Saxony. In 1737, King Augustus II himself killed more that 400 wild boar in the course of a single hunt in Saxony. John George II killed more than 22,000 wild boar in twenty-four years.

In Poland's Bialowieza Forest in 1890, in a fortnight's hunting, 42 bison, 36 elk and 138 wild boar were killed.

This is the frame in which to picture the Great Dane type as a bison hound, aurochs hound, staghound *and* boarhound. In central Europe there were once huge dogs used in the boar hunts of the great forests of what is now Germany, western Poland and the Czech Republic. They were known as *'hatzruden'* (literally big hunting dogs), huge rough-haired, cross-bred dogs, supplied to the various courts by peasants. They were the 'expendable' dogs of the boar hunt, used at the kill. The nobility, however, bred the smooth-coated *'sauruden'* (boar hounds), also referred to as *'saufänger'* (boar catcher) and *'saupacker'* (literally, member of a pack used for hunting wild boar). The *'sauruden'* were the equivalent, in the late 18th century, of the hunting alauntes of the fifteenth century, with the Bullmastiff being the modern equivalent of the 'alaunts of the butcheries'. The specialist *'leibhund'*, literally 'body-dog', was the catch-dog used to close with the boar and seize it.

Alaunt Link

It is worth noting that the Italian name for the Great Dane is Alano, while the Spanish still have a hunting mastiff called an Alano. The alauntes (resembling

Silver, gold, glass and enamel brooch. French, c. 1890.

Head study of Alaunt-type seizing hound, French, 1890.

Brindle Boarhounds with pups, print by H.B. Chalon, early eighteenth century.

a mastiff-sighthound cross and represented today by powerful bull-lurchers) were the fierce dogs of the Alans or Alani, who invaded Gaul in the fourth century AD, with settlements on the Rhine and the Elbe. Place names of Alanic origin are Kotzen near Brandenburg, Kotschen near Merseburg, Kothen near Bernberg and Choten-Koppeldorf near Sonnenberg. One variety of the alauntes depicted and described in the Comte de Foix's great work, *The Book of Hunting,* in the late fourteenth century is very much of Great Dane type. So too are the hounds portrayed by Antonius Tempesta of Florence in the late sixteenth and early seventeenth centuries.

It must be kept in mind that alauntes varied in size and shape, as did the *'beissers'* used on different quarry. The Count describes three principal types: one resembling a strong-headed Greyhound, another a powerful hunting mastiff of Great Dane construction and a third a short-faced butcher's dog or catch-dog, the ancestor of the baiting dogs. Alauntes were a type of dog for a particular function, not a breed or even a breed type. I believe it is perfectly reasonable to regard the modern breed called the Great Dane (in English-speaking countries) or Deutsche Dogge (German mastiff) as the inheritor of the *saurude* or boar hound mantle.

The Great Dane – German Boarhound

On the continent of Europe, the Great Dane is known as the Deutsche Dogge (or German Mastiff, liter-

ally), but the boarhound/running mastiff ancestry is strangely denied by a number of kennel clubs, including the club of Great Britain, which classifies this breed, not as a hound, but in the Working Group, for show purposes. The mis-classification of a breed has far-reaching consequences; the show-ring judges don't judge them as *hounds,* breeders do not expect them to perform in the field and do not seek a hound conformation. Great Danes are mis-classified. Theo Marples FZS, editor of *Our Dogs* in the 1920s, comments on this odd classification in his book *Show Dogs,* stating: 'The two breeds [the Great Dane as a boarhound and the Borzoi as a wolfhound] are exactly on all fours with each other in their sporting use and English relationship, which makes it difficult to understand by what line of logic the Kennel Club has thus differentiated between them on its register' (the Borzoi being in the Hound Group, unlike the Great Dane). Three-quarters of a century later this 'registration rationale' is even harder to understand or support. Now accepted by the FCI as a German breed, its emergence as a pedigree breed was in no small way due to English Victorian fanciers of the breed, who formed The Great Dane Club several years before a comparable breed club had been formed in Germany.

What do the more authoritative writers say on this subject? The esteemed 'Stonehenge' in *The Dog* of 1867 wrote, on the subject of the Boarhound: 'This is the Great Dane, and is used for boar-hunting in Germany and for hunting the elk in Denmark and Norway.' Drury, in *The Twentieth Century Dog* (1904), refers to 'the great Dane, or boarhound, as it is also called.' Dalziel, in his *British Dogs* of 1881, stated that: '...the Saxons brought with them their Great Danes, and hunted boar with them in English forests and fens.' Wynn, in *The History of the Mastiff* of 1886, wrote: '...readers and translators should be very guarded how they render molossus as a mastiff, for the true molossian was an erect-eared (altas aure) slate coloured (glauci) or fawn (fulvus) swift footed... dog, identical or almost so, with the modern Suliot boarhound.' This is a significant statement coming from such a mastiff devotee, perhaps stressing the role of the *running mastiff*. Hamilton-Smith, writing at the end of the nineteenth century, stated that Great Danes were most likely the true Molossian hound of antiquity. Interestingly, he also states that Caelius and others refer to a race of blue or slate-coloured Molossi (Glauci Molossi). The strangely underrated Scottish writer James Watson, in his masterly *The Dog Book* (1906), wrote on the Great Dane: 'As to the origin of the dog there is not the slightest doubt whatever that it is the true descendant of the Molossian dog.'

'Dogge' means Mastiff

In what is now Germany, names such as Ulmer dog, Deutsche Dogge, boarhound or Great Dane eventually became standardized into one breed name: Deutsche Dogge or German Mastiff. It has been argued that this decision was born out of the need of a reunified Germany to have a national dog after the war of 1870, rather than any pursuit of historical accuracy. Heavy 'par force' hunting mastiffs imported into Central Europe from England were similarly known as Englische Dogge. It is important to note, however, that artists such as Tempesta, Snyders, Hondius, Hackert and Ridinger produced paintings, etchings or drawings of boar hunts featuring not just prized highly bred hounds of the chase but also the 'catch-dogs': huge, savage, expendable, broadermouthed, rough-haired cross-breeds. These dogs, which the French called *'matins'*, went in at the kill so that the valued hounds of the chase were spared injury from deadly tusks. After all, who wants their favoured, carefully bred hound of the chase portrayed and then confused with more casually bred 'killing dogs'? Sadly, too, once that kennel clubs around Europe later on wrongly accepted the Molossian dog as a broad-mouthed or mastiff-type dog, the genuine possessors of the Molossian dog phenotype – modern breeds like the Great Dane, the Dogo Argentino and the Broholmer – were lost to hound groups.

The word 'Dogge' in medieval Europe meant a hunting mastiff not a catch or capture dog like the broad-mouthed breeds. Hartig, in his *Lexicon for Hunters and Friends of the Hunt*, published in Berlin in 1836,

German boarhound with friends, late nineteenth century.

wrote that 'The stature of the English Dogge is beautiful, long and gracefully muscular. The stature of the Bullenbeisser is less pleasing.' In referring to the 'English Dogge' Hartig meant the hunting mastiff from England. The Bärenbeisser (literally bear-biter), like the Bullenbeisser, was a catch-dog, the ancestor of the Boxer.

German 'Running' Mastiff

In his celebrated work, *The Illustrated Book of the Dog* (1879), Vero Shaw refers to the Great Dane as the German Mastiff. He mentions a letter from a Herr Gustav Lang of Stuttgart, an authority on the breed at that time, which stated: 'The name 'Boarhound' is not known in Germany. In boar hunting every possible large ferocious 'mongrel' was used.' If you extend this logic, you should no longer call a Harrier by that name because lurchers also hunt hares. Do you stop calling an Elkhound an Elkhound because other breeds also hunt them? I think not. Herr Lang was, however, making two points that I do not dispute: firstly that there was no *breed* of boarhound in Germany, the bigger quarry being hunted separately using the same hounds; and secondly, the boar hunt utilized large, fierce 'killing dogs' of mixed breeds, as well as hounds of the chase.

No nation in the world has a breed with boarhound in its title. This is because large hounds did not specialize as a rule. The same hounds hunted stag, boar and sometimes bear and wolf too. In this way, the French used breeds like the Poitevin, the Billy, the Grand Griffon-Vendeen and the Grand Bleu de Gascogne for *'la grande venerie'* generally. Our own huge scenthounds ended up being called Staghounds, but it was a description of function rather than a breed title; before the loss of wild boar to Britain such hounds would have been used in the boar hunt too. Herr Lang never disputed that the breed called both the Great Dane/Deutsche Dogge had once been used as a boarhound; he was disputing the title, not the function. The breed title of Deutsche Dogge was bitterly opposed by British breed club officials in 1883, despite Germany being regarded as the breed's host country.

Rawdon Lee included the Great Dane in his *Modern Dogs, Sporting Division: Vol 1* of 1897, stating : '...that he was used for these purposes [to hunt the wild boar and chase the deer] long before he came to be a house dog there is no manner of doubt... This is the reason I place him in the Group of Sporting Dogs.' The first official record of a Great Dane at the

Head studies of the various 'Doggen' or mastiff type, by Johann Ridinger (1698–1767).

Kennel Club was in the KC studbook of 1878, Marko no.7893, described as an Ulmer Dog. A second Marko, registered in 1879, was actually described as a 'Royal German hunting hound'! No doubts about a hound ancestry there. Hounds that hunted boar were often killed in the hunt and boar hunting in Central Europe down the ages was massively conducted. Perhaps because of the wholly arbitrary division of hounds today into scent or sighthounds, multi-purpose hounds that hunted 'at force', using scent and sight to best effect, have been neglected. This has been covered in earlier sections, but its significance reaches across many headings.

Wrongly Named

I can find no reason for the Great Dane to be so named. The French naturalist Buffon (1707–88), responsible for so many canine misnomers, called it *'le grand Danois'* but, knowing his fallibility, he could have been mishearing the words *'Daim'* (buck) or *'Daine'* (doe), French for fallow deer, *'daino'* in Italian, when packhounds used to hunt deer were referred to by sportsmen. Other references to a Danish dog could have been directed at the Danischer Dogge or Broholmer, the mastiff of Broholm Castle, a Great Dane-like if smaller breed, now being resurrected by worthy Danish enthusiasts. In his authoritative *Encyclopaedia of Rural Sports*, published in 1870, Delabere Blaine recorded: 'The boarhound in its original state is rarely met with, except in some of the northern parts of Europe, particularly in Germany…these boarhounds were propagated with much regard to the purity of their descent…'

The Great Dane, as a breed type, is believed by some to have been originally brought here by the Saxons, quoting the words 'He who alone there was deemed best of all, The war dog of the Danefolk, well worthy of men', in Hel-Ride of Brynhild. The breed was certainly known here in the late eighteenth century as the well-known paintings at Tatton Hall in Cheshire indicate. Two of the breed were presented to HRH The Duchess of York in 1807, being described as Wild-Boar Hounds or Tiger-Dogs from Hesse-Cassel. It is important to note that in the early days of dog shows, for example the Birmingham Show of 1884, the breed was actually listed as the boarhound. Wynn, in his *History of the Mastiff* of 1886, always refers to boarhounds rather than Great

Great Dane in full stride – looking every inch a hound.

Danes. In 1780 the German artist Riedel portrayed the breed and described it as a Grosse Dänischer Jagd Hund, or great Danish *hunting dog*.

Could this be anything other *than a hound?*

Mistaken Identity

So what should today's breed of Great Dane, a distinguished running mastiff, be called, and, more importantly, how should it be most appropriately grouped? It can be argued that if you get the breed title right you are more likely to get the grouping right. Dealing with the breed title, there is no credible direct association between Denmark and this breed. It was just as wrong to call this breed *'le grand Danois'* as it was to call the harlequin Pinscher *'le petit Danois'*. Buffon at least acknowledged the latter error but went along with what became common usage. He appears to have made the 'grey matin' into the Great Danish Dog, perhaps confusing the hybrid catch-dogs with the hounds of the chase. Professor Gmelin, updating Linnaeus in 1792, referred to these catch-dogs as 'boar-lurchers' (*canis laniarius fuillus*), drawing attention to their strongly made heads.

The title Deutsche Dogge is fine if people realize that 'dogge' means a running mastiff and not a broad-mouthed breed like the Neapolitan Mastiff, the Bordeaux Mastiff or the Bullmastiff. There is compelling evidence that the Great Dane is the nearest descendant of the ancient Molossian dog, the hound variety of that name. It was a pity that the Germans didn't name their national breed 'The German Hunting Mastiff' and thereby made it immediately identifiable as a sporting breed.

The Germans already have scenthounds and mountain hounds by name, the Hanoverian Schweisshund or scenthound and the Bavarian Mountain Hound. A similarly precise title for the Deutsche Dogge would have made good sense. Even the German artist Riedel, two hundred years ago, realized it was a hunting dog. It might be advantageous to rename the breed here: The Great Dane (German Hunting Mastiff), which would embrace the Deutsche Dogge title even more accurately and not offend those who are only comfortable with the status quo. The amendment of the title 'Alsatian' to German Shepherd Dog shows what can be done. Originally registered here as the Alsatian Wolf Dog, the 'wolf dog' was dropped in due course and the breed became the Alsatian (German Shepherd Dog) and then finally The German Shepherd Dog. A similar path could be followed by the Great Dane, in a comparable pursuit of greater accuracy.

Par Force Role

In *Great Danes – Past and Present* (1928), Dr Morell MacKenzie was concerned that 'if the Great Dane is considered a hound he is the only representative (although he responds to 'pack law') which does not carry his tail erect or like a flag when on the track.' This reveals the ignorance of the writer; such hounds were not purely scenthounds, they were 'par force' hounds that hunted by scent *and* sight. Why should such a versatile hound carry its stern like a scenthound when it is a more complete hound than that? The Great Dane, as a boarhound, had to have speed and the construction which produces it. The breed needs the pelvic angulation that permits a good forward reach of the hindlegs, more like the sighthounds than the scenthounds. Such a desired pelvic angulation decides set of and carriage of tail in the breed. I was concerned by a 2012 show report on the breed that set out worrying faults being encountered in the show entry: poor rear ends with very straight stifles, prominent breastbones, hindlegs not parallel and exhibits stacked with their hind feet too far apart to allow a natural posture from the dog. Showing off a dog in the ring should mean displaying a handsome exhibit standing and moving *quite naturally* – exaggeration has to be denied by judges and exhibitors.

Importance of Groups to Judges

Once the hound origin evidence is accepted, the pressure for this breed to be transferred to the Hound Group will be irrefutable. Just as the Airedale is King of the Terriers, so too will the Great Dane (German Hunting Mastiff) be King of the Hounds. It will no longer be exhibited on the same day as the sled dogs, herding dogs, flock guardians, heelers, water dogs and broad-mouthed gripping or holding dogs and be judged by those who know such breeds best – and possibly favour them. It might even lead to a concentration on anatomical soundness and functional athleticism in the breed rather than the mere production of statuesque canine ornaments unable to move with power and purpose.

The very expression 'Working Breed' undermines and demeans the noble associations and rich sporting heritage of these outstanding dogs. It is time to heed the views of Marples, 'Stonehenge', Drury, Dalziel, Hamilton-Smith, Rawdon Lee, Leighton, Wynn and Watson – can all these distinguished writers really be wrong? Surely Great Dane fanciers should listen to their combined wisdom and then strive, in their own lifetime, to improve the stature of their beloved breed. Breed titles do matter; breeds no longer bred for an historic function soon deteriorate. In his *Dogs and All About Them*, published in 1914, the well-respected writer Robert Leighton stated: 'The Kennel Club has classed the Great Dane amongst the Non-Sporting dogs, probably because with us he cannot find a quarry worthy of his mettle; but for all that, he has the instincts and qualifications of a sporting dog...' Allocation to an FCI or KC grouping *does* matter; being judged by judges used to hounds must suit a breed with this construction, let alone its 'instincts and qualifications' as Robert Leighton put it. Come on, Great Dane breed clubs, what was your breed *for*? How can you breed successfully without a functional design? Against which criteria do you judge a breed that has no accepted purpose? Is your magnificent breed not worth *your* determined efforts to get it properly classified after all its selfless service to man?

Giant Amongst Dogs
In the quaintly titled *Dogs: their Whims, Instincts and Peculiarities* of 1883, edited by Henry Webb, these words are used to describe the German Boarhound:

This giant amongst dogs is placed by strength, activity and courage, in the front rank of his race; as guardian or protector he has no superior, and but few equals. If you look at him when he stands, with all his qualities fully aroused, involuntarily the thought strikes you, I should wish that dog by my side in the moment of danger, well sure I should find in him a staunch friend and mighty champion.

Over a hundred years later we continue to deny such a breed its rightful sporting place in dogdom and are surely lesser people in so doing. The best Great Danes I've seen were in Holland in the 1980s; they really did look like giant *hounds*. In 2012, when studying a stunning black Great Dane, Champion Internos Challenger, and noticing its superb hound conformation: well-placed elbows, deep brisket, good spring of rib, solid topline and powerful hind movement, I mourned the absence of such an outstanding hound from its rightful place in the Hound Group classes. We owe this distinguished breed its rightful recog-

nition without any further delay. As I have striven to establish, the Group into which breeds of dog are placed by kennel clubs has considerable significance for both breeders and judges, and in consequence for the breeds concerned.

...his great size, strength and courage make him one of the best of all possible guards, which is the only use he is put to in this country, though, considering that he is bred on the same lines as his hunting forefathers, and inherits all the instincts of a sporting dog, it seems something of an anomaly that he should be relegated by Kennel Club definition to a place amongst the 'Non-sporting' division of breeds. With his strength and speed he could be made very useful for hunting big game, and his scent is remarkable...
E. MacKay Scott, writing on the Great Dane in *The Kennel Encyclopaedia* (1907)

The Boarhound of Denmark
The Broholmer, or Mastiff of Broholm Castle in Denmark, is not likely to appear in Britain for some time, for its fanciers in its native land are determined to retain stock until such time as their own gene pool is satisfactory. The Broholmer Society now has more than 300 members, with some 200 dogs registered. The rule over selling abroad will only be reconsidered when there are 300 dogs registered from eight different lines. The selection programme began in 1974 and within fifteen years 100 dogs suitable for registration had emerged. It was in 1974 that enthusiast Jytte Weiss wrote an article, 'In Search of the Broholmer', after the last specimen of the breed was believed to have died in 1956. A responding telephone call to her brought to light an eleven-year-old dog, 31in at the withers and weighing almost 176lb. This dog, when examined, met the demands of the 1886 breed standard. Other dogs of this type were then discovered.

At one time, it was believed that fawn was the classic colour for the breed, but researches revealed that there had been a black variety in the Grib Skov region of North Sjelland. The Danish kings apparently favoured the fawns in the hunting field, but farmers, butchers and foresters in that region preferred the black variety, the colour favoured too in the night-dogs at the Tivoli Gardens in Copenhagen. This colour was accepted by the FCI in 1982, when the standard was accepted by them.

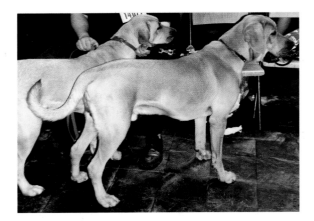

Broholmers – Danish mastiffs.

From an engraving by Richard Blome in his " Gentleman's Recreation" (1686).

King of Denmark out hunting, 1686, from Blome's Gentleman's Recreation.

As the breeding programme developed, blacks were mated with fawns but this produced tricolours, rather like the Swiss Cattle Dog breeds. Black to black matings were eventually dropped because the progeny lacked essential breed type. Fawns, from fawn parents, were bigger and stronger. The extant standard permits just three colours: clear fawn with a black mask/muzzle, deep fawn and black, usually with small white markings on the chest and toes. The ideal size is considered to be between 30 and 32in at the withers. Great size is thankfully not desired and, commendably, balance, virility and health are considered a higher priority. Leading fancier Jytte Weiss has stated that 'we have paid particular attention to the very good character and mentality of the Broholmer'. Although the guarding qualities of the breed are valued, a stable, good-natured temperament, the famed magnanimity of the mastiff breeds and, especially, tolerance of children are wisely valued more. The more powerful the dog, the more caution has to be exercised in today's society. A disciplined, biddable dog is also required by hunters. A bad-tempered hound is a menace in kennels; spirit and tenacity must never be confused with undesired aggression.

Royal Boarhound

This breed is very likely to have been the boarhound of the Danish kings. The Great Dane or German boarhound may well have developed from this breed, the added stature coming from an infusion of Suliot Dog blood, the latter being favoured as the parade dog of German regiments. The Suliot Dogs came from the Suli Mountains in Epirus, base of the renowned Molossian dogs. An underrated figure in the survival of this once famous breed is Danish archaeologist Count Niels Frederik Sehested from Broholm. In the middle of the nineteenth century he had his interest aroused from old prints depicting the breed. His work led, in time, to 120 pups being placed with notable Danes who promised to promote the resurrected breed. Two of these were King Frederik VII and the Countess Danner, who referred to his pups as 'Jaegerspris' dogs, after the name of his favourite estate. One of these, Tyrk, can be seen, preserved, in the Museum of Zoology in Copenhagen. Large fawn dogs were subsequently bred on the estates of the Count of Broholm. Dogs of this appearance were also utilized by cattle dealers and, rather like the

Rottweiler in Southern Germany, became known as 'slagterhund' or butchers' dogs.

As most were in the Broholm area, the breed was renamed. The first breed standard was cast when the first Danish dog show was held in the gardens of Rosenberg Castle in 1886. In his monumental work *Dogs of all Nations* of 1904, van Bylandt described the breed as The Danish Dog or Broholmer, 29in at the shoulder, weighing about 125lb and fawn or 'dirty yellow' in colour. He illustrated the breed with two dogs, Logstor and Skjerme, owned by J. Christiansen and A. Schested (sic) of Nykjobing. These dogs displayed bigger ears than the contemporary breed. The extant breed standard sets out, as faults, long ears and a long-haired coat, faults which English Mastiff breeders must now face. No mastiff breed will retain type unless faults are acknowledged and then remedied. English Mastiffs have relatively big ears, despite the standard's words on ears, as well as a lengthening of the coat, which is not being penalized. If essential breed type is to be conserved, all breeds must be bred to their standard. It is pleasing to know that the Broholmer is in safe hands.

> In Sweden, the Danish dog was formerly used in couples to support a smaller breed of hounds, called elk-finders, in the chace of that powerful animal, to retard it until the horsemen came up.
> Hamilton-Smith, writing in Volume X of *The Naturalist's Library*, edited by Sir William Jardine (1840)

> The Danish dog, which is generally large and smooth hair'd…while he is near you, nobody dare touch you or any thing belonging to you.
> *The Gentleman Farrier* of 1732

The Boarhound Legacy

The East India Company introduced hunting dogs from England into India in 1615; on one occasion a mastiff from England shaming 'the Persian dogs' at a boar kill. In India, a breed called the Poligar, 26in at the shoulder, stiff-coated and light brown in colour, was used to hunt the pig, accompanied by hunters on foot with spears. But of more interest is the Rajapalayam, 30in high and 120lb; black, silver-grey, red and harlequin but more often ivory-white and, with the slightly smaller Alangu, famed in the wild boar hunt. A huge brindle breed, the Shenkottah,

was once used in the big game-hunting grounds of the Trivandrum District. The better known Rampur hounds were used to hunt the boar, as a sighthound. Robert Leighton describes the breed in his *New Book of the Dog* of 1912. The Sindh hound, rather like a Great Dane in appearance, had a long history as a boarhound. Sindh is in the Indus delta and Rampur further north towards the Himalayas, where the headwaters of the great rivers Indus and Ganges originate.

The true boarhound, a hound of the chase or *chien courant*, as opposed to a huge cross-bred dog once used at the killing of the boar, deserves our respect. Such a hound was required to pursue and run down one of the most dangerous quarries in the hunting field. It needed to be a canine athlete, have a good nose, great determination and yet not be too hot-blooded. Both the Fila Brasileiro and the Dogo Argentino have been used in the boar hunt in South America. American Bulldogs are still used as catch-dogs on feral pig in the USA. In our modern, so-called more tolerant society, such powerful, determined hunting dogs are stigmatized and even banned in some allegedly liberal countries. These are not happy times for hunting dogs bred by man to be determined, strong and extraordinarily capable. Sadly, they are also irreplaceable. The boarhound legacy, in the shape of a specific breed's use, is not likely to survive.

> …out of a pack of fifty hounds that start on a boar chase often scarce a dozen return to the kennel whole and sound.
> Jacques du Fouilloux, sixteenth century.

The Heavy Hounds

> A mastiff is a manner of hound.
> Edward, Duke of York, *The Master of Game* (1406)

> The mastiff is a huge, stubborn, ugly and impetuous hound.
> William Harrison, *Description of England* (1586)

In the 6th [Forest Law] of Edward the First [king of England, 1272–1307] it was ordained, if any mastiff be found on any deer, the same mastiff being expe-

Mastiff and her puppies in an outhouse by C. Huet, 1734. Note the wider range of coat colours than in today's pedigree version.

BELOW LEFT: Resting Hound by Johann Ridinger, Augsburg, 1750; note the Great Dane type.

ditated [made lame], then the owner shall be quit of that deed…the mastiff in those ages was a very different animal from the massive creature of later times.

George Jesse, *Researches into the History of the British Dog* (1866)

In the very specialised circumstances of the Tudor animal fight, the mastiff was really very much at a disadvantage. It had never been bred, originally, as an animal-fighting dog at all. It was a hunting dog.

Carson Ritchie, *The British Dog* (1981)

Hunting Mastiffs

The Hound Group, as recognized by the KC, embraces a distinguished and extremely varied collection of breeds of dog. The scenthounds are well represented, from the lugubrious Bloodhound to the lively Beagle, with more foreign breeds like the Basset Fauve de Bretagne, the Petit Basset Griffon Vendeen and the Hamiltonstovare, entering the list with each decade. The sighthounds also feature strongly, from the aristocratic Afghan Hound to the once humble Whippet. The group even includes a breed which works to the gun, the Finnish Spitz, and a breed better classified as a terrier, the Dachshund. But there is a serious omission in this group, that of the heavy hounds, sometimes called the hunting mastiffs.

The type of giant hound used in seventeenth-century hunts.

Boar seized by a boarhound by G.A. Cassana, c.1702.

The omission of the Great Dane (as mentioned above), once a renowned boarhound, from the Hound Group has long been not just a significant loss from the group but also a threat to the credibility of the group system itself. That omission is, however, much more understandable when related to the omission of the hunting mastiffs altogether. Why should wolfhounds feature in this Group but not boarhounds and the heavy hounds once used to hunt other big game, such as wild bulls, buffalo, bears and even wild asses? I suspect that one reason is the influence that Victorian writers on dogs had on the emerging KC. The former offer us fascinating reading material and provide quaint quotes but their scholarship, particularly any objective corroborated research, is sadly lacking. Regrettably, such sources are always the first resort of the eager breed historian or the overnight dog expert. A fair general summary might be that the Victorian writers on dogs were all too often gundog enthusiasts only too willing to portray other breeds in their contemporary rather than their historic setting.

From such a background, the mastiff type became embraced by the Working Group and a breed like the Bulldog, so much a sporting dog in previous centuries, became a Utility Group breed, a description that even sounds disparaging. Small wonder that this splendid breed developed more and more into an unathletic exaggeration of its former sporting self. We may thankfully not actually want our Bulldogs to bait bulls nowadays, but, to be true to their origins they should be physically capable of doing so. Our Otterhounds don't hunt the otter anymore but they retain the physical ability to do so – *and* expect to be judged as hounds born to hunt. The Bulldog seems to be judged mainly on its head.

Kennel Clubs Confusion

Unfortunately the FCI too has got itself into a considerable muddle over the heavy hound breeds it recognizes and Britain does not. The Fila Brasileiro and the Dogo Argentino, both still used as heavy hounds in their native countries, are not classified as hounds by them, but collected together with a real hotch-potch of breeds, including what they dub Molossers and Dogues, mainly the broad-mouthed breeds. Even overlooking the fact that the Molossian dog took two forms, a big flock guardian and,

separately, a huge hound, and did not include the broad-mouthed breeds, such a grouping wrongly transplants the descendants of the heavy hounds into the guarding breeds.

This betrays their rich heritage and seriously misleads breeders and judges of such admirable dogs. Group 2 under the FCI system includes Pinschers, Schnauzers, 'Molossian Type' and Swiss Cattle Dogs. In other words, terriers from Germany, hunting dogs from South America, a boarhound from Germany, flock guardians from the Pyrenees and the Caucasus, the mastiff breeds of Europe, the Bulldog and a water dog from Canada, the Newfoundland, are considered to have some sort of collective bond or rational congregation. Scenthounds are in Group 6.

This means that scenthounds like the Grand Bleu de Gascogne, the Grand Gascon-Saintongeois, the Anglo-Français Blanc et Noir and the Français Tricolore, all around 26in high, are candidates for Group 6 but hounds from South America of that size are not. The Fila Brasileiro was developed from a number of breeds, including the Bloodhound and the Great Dane, but is assessed by the FCI to be not a hound but purely a guarding breed. Our KC puts the Bloodhound in the Hound Group, the Great Dane in the Working Group and the Bulldog in the Utility

The Mendelan – the now-extinct Russian bearhound.

Group. There is some very muddled thinking going on here and it can't produce judges with the desired experience or knowledge in the right rings. Hounds by their very birthright have to be judged as such.

Of course the loss of function once the hunting of big game with hounds lapsed led to the disappearance of many types of heavy hound: the Bullenbeisser in Germany, the Mendelan, a huge bearhound, in Russia and the Suliot Dog in Macedonia/Greece, for example. The huge Staghounds of Devon and Somerset, disbanded early in the last century, were 27in high and described as follows by Dr Charles Palk Collyns in *The Chase of the Wild Red Deer*:

> A nobler pack of hounds no man ever saw. They had been in the country for years, and had been bred with the utmost care for the express purpose of stag-hunting...their great size enabled them to cross the long heather and rough sedgy pasturage of the forest without effort or difficulty.

Lost Hounds

Sir Walter Scott, in *Woodstock*, produces an interesting description with his words on Bevis: 'It was a large wolf-dog, in strength a Mastiff, in form and almost in fleetness a Greyhound. Bevis was the noblest of the

A 150lb Fila Brasileiro from the Doerrhund Kennels in Canada.

Bullenbeisser from Germany in the eighteenth century.

Bullenbeissers at work , supporting the Saupackers after their chase.

Hunting Mastiffs used in the Scottish deer hunt.

kind which ever pulled down a stag, tawny-coloured like a lion, with a black muzzle and feet.' That, at the start of the nineteenth century in Britain, is a good description of the alauntes, or hunting mastiffs, of Gaston de Foix 400 years earlier. Topsell, writing in 1607, stated that: 'There be in France, dogs brought out of Great Britain to kill bears, wolves, and wild boars', describing such dogs as 'singularly swift and strong.' We have clearly lost a distinctive type of heavy hound.

Denmark has also lost hound breeds, the Augustenborg Hunter and the Strelluf Hound, for example, but has saved the Broholmer, an ancient type of hunting mastiff. The word 'mastiff', now utilized precisely to describe a specific British breed of pedigree dog, has long been used, and misused, by scholars to describe huge, fierce dogs of all types. This has allowed researchers in the breed of Mastiff to indulge in all kinds of whimsical thinking, as Adcock, Taunton,

Kingdon and MacDona demonstrated a century ago. In his valuable book *Hunting and Hunting Reserves in Medieval Scotland* (1979), John Gilbert writes of references to mastiffs in the Scottish Forest Laws; capable of attacking and pulling down deer, they wore spiked collars and were used to attack wolves and hunt boar, when they hunted to the horn.

Respecting Function

Gilbert was referring to a heavy hound, not what is now the modern breed of Mastiff, whose appearance and especially its movement is scarcely hound-like. This makes a point for me. Directly you stop breeding a dog to a known function, even one long lapsed, then the breed that dog belongs to loses its way. We saw this in the Bulldog and now see it increasingly in the broad-mouthed dogs, worryingly too short in the muzzle and progressively less athletic. Their fanciers forget the sporting origins of their breed, foolishly to my mind, and pursue obsessions with heads, bone and bulk. This is not only historically incorrect but never to the benefit of the dog.

The heavy hounds were highly rated in the ancient world, from China to Assyria and throughout Europe. Their function may have been overtaken by the invention of firearms and the march of time, but those which survive should not be insulted by being bred as unathletic yard-dogs, described as 'Utility' breeds and removed from the sporting division, to be lumped with the herding breeds or sled-dogs. The Hound Group both in the FCI and the KC interpretation urgently needs a truly radical rethink.

As discussed separately, the answer lies in a move away from the rather arbitrary division of hound breeds into scent- or sighthounds. All hounds hunt by sight at times, and versatile hounds like the Ibizan use sight, scent *and hearing* to equal effect. A better separation would be between those that hunt using stamina, like most of the scenthounds, those that hunt mainly using their sheer speed, like the sighthounds, those that hunted using scent and sight as par force hounds and those that were employed 'at the kill', as holding and seizing hounds. This would bring the hunting mastiffs into the Hound Group, but more importantly bring them under judges who are used to assessing animals that were designed to hunt their prey. Movement, construction, athleticism generally, and probably feet and 'bite', would soon improve.

The German Bullenbeisser, their heavy hound.

Heavy Hound Heritage

The mastiff breeds, whether huge like the Mastiff of England, as small as the Bulldog of Britain, cropped-eared like the Cane Corso of Italy and the Perro de Presa of the Canaries, loose-skinned like the Mastini of Italy or dock-tailed like the Boxer of Germany, are not only fine examples of powerful but good-tempered dogs but form part of their respective nation's canine heritage. It is vital that they do not fall victim to show-ring faddists or misguided cliques of rosette-chasing, over-competitive zealots. A giant Mastiff that can hardly walk, a muzzle-less Bulldog that can hardly breathe and a Bullmastiff dying young from an avoidable inherited disease are all sad reflections on the moral sterility of twentieth and twenty-first-century breeders.

May twenty-first-century breeders wake up to such unacceptable excesses, honour the proud heritage of these distinguished breeds and respect them for what they are: the light heavyweights of the canine world, quick on their feet and devastating at close quarter protection when threatened. They are not mountain dogs or draught dogs needing massive bone but strongly built hounds with their own distinct type, which must be conserved. Such magnificent canine athletes deserve the very best custodianship, with every fancier respecting their hound ancestry, remembering their bravery at man's behest and revering their renowned stoicism. Long live the heavy hounds of the world!

…in a pack there may be some individuals which have the special capacity to herd and round up animals for the kill, and others of more massive build who in the main do the attacking. We see the projection of these two types exemplified in our domestic dogs, especially in those of collie type which are pre-eminent as sheep and shepherd dogs, and in those of mastiff type – the massive dogs – which attack the larger animals in the hunt.

Richard and Alice Fiennes, *The Natural History of the Dog* (1968)

Guillot le Mastinier, called Sonot, for his expenses in the Forest of Dyrmon in seeking 24 mastiffs borrowed for the King's sport in his boar-hunting in the Forest of Halatte, and for his lodging for this purpose and for bringing these mastiffs to the Forest with the boar-hounds for ten days…

The French Royal Hunting Accounts of Philippe de Courguilleroy, Master Huntsman to the King, 1398.

Mastiffs were still kept as guard-dogs, but their value in hunting disappeared with the wild boar.

Roger Longrigg, *The English Squire and his Sport* (1977)

Tempesta's boar-hunting engraving of 1602.

Ridinger's Boar Hunt *of 1710, showing the famed Englische Doggen.*

CHAPTER 3

HOUNDS ABROAD

Hounds in France

It was asserted by King Charles IX of France, in his book, *La Chasse Royale*, that all breeds of French hounds descended from one or other of what he described as the Royal Races, four in number. They were 'Chien blanc du Roi', 'Chien de St Hubert', 'Chien gris de St Louis', and 'Chien fauve de Bretagne'. From the 'Chien blanc de Roi' and the 'Chien de St Hubert' descended the Normandy hound that exercised such an enormous influence on the evolution of the modern English hound.

C.R. Acton, *The Foxhound of the Future* (1953)

Unique Heritage

In his introduction to Johnston and Ericson's *Hounds of France* (1979), Dr Emile Guillet, Master of the Hounds of the Rallye Kereol, wrote: 'With six or seven hundred thousand hounds, divided into 40 breeds or varieties used by 400,000 hunters, France possesses a national heritage unique in the world.' How sad for British sportsmen, especially those who risked their lives to free France just over half a century ago, to note that we have lost much of our sporting heritage, whilst they have retained all of theirs. It's worth noting that with over 8 per cent of the vote, against our 2 per cent of the vote here, the French countryman still has a political voice. It is worth noting too that hunting is enshrined in the laws of the French constitution; we hunt within the law, they hunt by it.

Just as sad is that two of our national assemblies, those of Scotland and Wales, seem almost keener than Westminster to destroy our rural ways. There is a stark difference between, say, Brittany and Wales in attitudes to hunting with dogs. Yet the historic connections between Brittany and Wales are many;

The Hunt Meeting *by Charles Olivier de Penne, 1872;* grande venerie *in style.*

The end of the Hunt *(circle of Constant Troyon, French, 1810–65).*

the rough-coated Welsh Hound has a distinct 'griffon' look to it. The chestnut Basset of Brittany, or Fauve de Bretagne, now established here, has that griffon look too, with a harsh, dense, flat coat. I am impressed by the hounds from the Mochras kennel, with their Harmonie de L'Echo de L'Aube imported from the hunting pack of Rene Gourves of Finisterre in Brittany, famed for its type and quality. It was good to see Ch. Mochras Melchior come Reserve Best of Breed at Crufts 2013. In France there are over 1,000 registrations a year of this breed, most of them in the packs. Betty Judge has now brought in the Grand Griffon Vendeen and the smaller Briquet Griffon

A Grand Griffon Vendeen.

Vendeen (recreated using Harrier blood after the Second World War), to reinforce the Vendeen Bassets already here. Our favouring of smooth-coated scenthounds has left us with just the Otterhound of our packhounds with a griffon flavour, although I suspect that the French would have named our Airedale not a terrier but a griffon.

Ancient Attitude

Hunting in France continues the ancient and aristocratic attitude to 'venery', the exercise of the art and science of hunting. It is divided into two types, depending on the quarry: *la grande* and *la petite venerie*. The former, with quarry of stag, roebuck and boar, is steeped in tradition, with a pageantry and formality passed down from a bygone aristocratic era; it is supported by over 100 packs. The wolf was hunted until its extinction in the 1930s. Most packs of *la petite venerie* hunt the hare, but 20 per cent hunt the fox. The French breeds of hound have great voices, pace and nose but have been accused of lacking drive and stamina. This has led to infusions of Foxhound blood from here. Some packs are Anglo-Français, but most have retained the old breeds, preserving the great ringing cry of the classic French scenthound.

Just as the blood of our Foxhound has been used to the benefit of French hounds, so too has the blood of theirs been used here. In 2013, a litter of puppies bred by the South Devon Hunt are due to begin a hunting future with the Rallye Amor Hunt in Brittany. The South Devon is twinned with the French hunt, which hunts red deer with their Anglo-Français

Basset Fauve de Bretagne – a trio from the Mochras kennel.

Tricolore. The Foxhound blood was sought to inject greater drive in the French pack, with these pups sired by a South Devon stallion put to a French bitch. This is merely a repeat of what has been happening over two centuries.

European Stock

It has been argued, with strong dissent from Celts, that, without the Norman Conquest, we would be without our scenthounds. It has been argued too that all the scenthounds in the world come from either British or French stock, or a blend of the two, as in the United States. Hound expert Sir John Buchanan-Jardine has argued a role for the Norman Hound, now extinct as such, having acquired the name here of Talbot Hound, citing the words of Gervase Markham, Delabere Blaine and T.B. Johnson (*Hunting Directory*, 1826) as evidence. Markham wrote that 'The shag-haired Talbot, preferably grizzled, were… chosen to hunt the fox, badger and other hot scents.' The Bresse breed from eastern France was brought here to form the basis of Welsh hounds; they were shaggy and grizzled. The Griffon-Nivernais would be today's equivalent.

The St Hubert hounds have also been dubbed Talbots, a name which some believe is an English misuse of Taillebois, the Abbot of St Hubert's Monastery in the seventh century. Because of their scenting prowess, the St Huberts were distributed to the French aristocracy in all parts of France; they were bred with local stock but played a major role in the development of scenthounds on both sides of the channel. In early days each local breed of French hound was found in three versions: *chiens d'ordre* or full-sized; *chiens briquets* or medium-sized; and *chiens bassets*. The latter were subdivided into three sub-types, according to the structure of the foreleg: straight-

Chien de Saintonge, 1904.

Poitevin displaying a hunting wound.

Grand Bleu de Gascogne.

legged, half-crooked and full crooked. Nowadays we tend to think wrongly of all true Bassets being only the full crooked foreleg version. The contemporary straight-legged English Basset, achieved with the help of Harrier blood, is a quite legitimate Basset, not a modern innovation.

Breeding Base

Of the old pure French strains of hounds, there are two in particular that stand out as the ones to which the modern French hound owes most: the Saintongeois and the Poitevin. A tricolour hound is often referred to as having the latter's blood, a black and white one the blood of the former. But both markings can occur in the same litter. The less pure-bred, smaller type are dubbed Briquets, featuring both smooth- and rough-coated hounds, with the latter embracing the Griffon Vendeens, usually lemon and white, with the Griffon Nivernais, larger and darker-coated, sometimes black and tan.

Coupled Billy – fine old breed.

A Blue Gascony Griffon – a Beagle type from the southwest.

The Gascon and the Norman may have owed most to the St Hubert, long famed for its 'extreme delicacy of scent' and 'wonderfully powerful deep voices'. French sportsmen have always rated voice in their hounds higher than we have here. To this day, I still hear the hounds featuring the blue marbled coat referred to as 'the Frenchies', after the Bleu de Gascogne variety. Since 1980, when the Petit Griffon Bleu de Gascogne, one of the four Gascony blue breeds, was considered to be the rarest hound breed in France, the situation has changed for the better. In 1998, well over 700 Griffon Bleus were registered with the Société Centrale Canine; only Basset Hounds, Beagles and Bassets Fauve de Bretagne registered more. I can see why Dr Castets, in his book *Les Chiens Courants* of 1916, stated rather quaintly, that: 'There is not, among our breeds of hounds, a more noble beast than the **Bleu de Gascogne**, with its majestic allure, height, shimmering coat, powerful voice, archaic aspect and aristocratic melancholy.' It should, however, be acknowledged that Gascony was under English rule from 1150 to 1450, with noblemen moving between the two countries with their hunting dogs.

Wide Range of Breeds

French scenthounds like the quaintly named Billy, the Français Tricolore and the Poitevin resemble our Foxhound, which has often supplied new blood to the French packs. There have long been exchanges of sporting dogs between Britain and France. Ear length sometimes distinguishes French scenthounds from ours, as the Porcelaine demonstrates. But their native bassets, such as the Artesien-Normand, have much shorter ears than our show type of Basset Hound. There are nearly thirty breeds of French scenthound and nearly all of them are little known here. The Vendeen Griffons and the Grand Bleu de Gascogne are now making progress here but most of the others are restricted to France and the Franco-Swiss border country, like the Bruno de Jura, a handsome black and tan breed. I was recently told of a hound breed I've never seen listed: the Rouge du Comminges.

There are over 300 packs of hounds in France: 35 staghound, 73 foxhound, 61 roebuck, 114 harehound and 14 packs of boarhound. Much of their hunting is conducted in woods, not over pasture as here. In their single-minded pursuit of hunting excellence, the French have long sought performance ahead of purity of canine race, even producing the Beagle Harrier, created by blending two of our hound breeds, to suit the country over which they were expected to hunt the hare.

A Griffon Vendeen – Barbaro after the hunt.

BELOW: The Griffon Vendeen of 1910.

The Griffon Vendeen Family

One of the four rough-coated Vendeen hounds coming out of southwest France, the Grand Basset Griffon Vendeen owes its origin to the largest of them all, the Grand Griffon Vendeen, with French hunting tastes leading to the breeding down to a smaller variety in time. This Griffon Vendeen family was bred to cope with the rugged terrain of the Vendée and dense thorny vegetation, with testing weather variations. A hunting hound had to possess high scenting ability, great stamina and a coat resistant to bramble and thorn. The powerful, harsh-coated Grand Griffon was gradually bred down to the shorter-legged Basset Griffon Vendeen and eventually subdivided into the Petit Basset and the Grand Basset. Both sizes were used on a wide variety of game, from rabbit or hare, up to fox, deer and even wild boar. In the late 1880s the Dezamy family patronized both breeds, with the '42 Dezamy' tag still representing the 42cm (16½in) ideal maximum height. The Dezamy type displayed slightly longer legs, stronger bone and the more classic well-sculpted head. The Club du Griffon Vendeen catered for all four sizes of this type of French hound, with hunting trials established. This family of hounds can sometimes produce coat colour anomalies: one sable and white Petit dam producing black and tan and pale cream whelps, and a Grand producing fauve or chestnut offspring. French sportsmen have been known to use the blood of the Teckel and the Bleu de Gascogne in the pursuit of a hound more suitable for their country.

Hound Competitions

It is good to know of hound competitions being conducted in France, an activity once held here, especially in the early to mid-nineteenth century; a revival would be valuable here nowadays. A *brevet de chasse*, with over 100 held each season, is organized by a hound breed club and is held for breeders; a *concours* is held for hunting people. Each pack is scored out of 200 points, based on such basic aspects as voice (prized by the French) and ability to hunt as a pack. At a *brevet*, each hound is examined and judged individually as well. At one *concours*, for example, the hunt would be on foot, the quarry roe deer, with around twenty 'packs' of between two and four couples each, made up of a wide selection of breeds: Bleu de Gascogne, Porcelaine, Anglo-Français, Griffon Nivernais, Aregeois (solid white), Griffon Vendeen (the type resembling our Otterhound), Griffon Bleu, Beagle (used on deer in the southwest) and Beagle Harrier. This one could be followed by another one on hare that might attract some thirty 'packs'; The event is social, too, with scores being allotted to the various huntsmen as well! The camaraderie engendered at such events is immense.

ABOVE: *The 'ideal' Basset-Griffon de Bretagne.*

LEFT: *Head study of a Gascon-Saintongeois Hound, distinctively blue-mottled.*

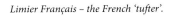

Limier Français – the French 'tufter'.

The Porcelaine of 1910.

Chien de Virelade of 1904.

Chien de Franche-Comté of 1904.

Gascon-Saintongeois Hounds of the Levesque type.

Lost Breeds – Safe Hands

Strangely, the French, with their great passion for hunting, have never developed their own sighthound, although to be fair neither has any mainland northern European country, with coursing long banned. Lost too are the scenthound breeds of Saintongeois (pure-bred), Limiers Français (their 'tufters'), Levesque, Bresse, Artois, du Haut Poitou, Normandie, Virelade, de Franche-Comte and Gris de St Louis, (mostly subsumed into other packs, as some pack titles denote). Their best and most carefully bred packs hunt roe deer, one of the hardest animals to run down with hounds, thereby presenting the bigger challenge to the genuine hound man. The sincere affection in France for rural France, together with its distinct way of life, is in stark contrast to urban attitudes here, where ignorance, indifference and even hostility to country traditions prevails. The hounds of France are in safe hands; ours, despite their global respect amongst real hunting people, are threatened – from within. One French pack, very appropriately, enjoys the freedom of hunting near a British cavalry war cemetery; fighting for ancient freedoms is of no great account in Britain these days. RIP British cavalrymen.

The French judges do not like our catlike feet – a Saintonge hound has a hare's foot – and the lameness which besets English hounds after four or five season's work in France is attributed to the shape of our foxhounds' feet.

Lord Ribblesdale, *The Queen's Hounds and Stag-hunting Recollections* (1897)

Several types of hound are used for hare-hunting in the South of France; they present many variations, according to their origins, but can be placed in the following three categories:

1. The pure-blooded grand chien or chien d'ordre, whether of Gascony, Saintonge or Bordeaux.

2. The Briquet (a harrier-sized hound, of much the same breeding as the various breeds of French hounds but often cross-bred and sometimes not even entirely of hound blood).

3. The cross-bred hound or the improved briquet.

The chien d'ordre or pure hound, which only a few enthusiasts have, with great trouble, preserved in all its original purity, has some fine qualities…

Comte Elie de Vezins, *Hounds for a Pack* (1882)

Here is another bit of news about necks and shoulders; the experience of an expert. It appears that the English insist upon a hound with a long neck, so that he can stoop to a scent; this is a proof, according to the oracle, that most of our foxhounds have not very good noses. The Saintonge hound – an ancient and eminent French breed – hunted with his head up (*le nez au vent*), without deigning to stoop. This is still a characteristic of a well-bred hound – both in pointers and hounds – but M. de Chabot goes on to say that he has often remarked slow-looking hounds keep right up at the lead, and throw their tongues admirably owing to the way they carried their heads and the way their heads were put on. In our love of drive and pace the French think we have sacrificed nose…

Lord Ribblesdale, *The Queen's Hounds and Stag-hunting Recollections* (1897)

From Hound To Hound-Dawg

Few people realize that there are, perhaps, several hundred thousand hounds hunting foxes and wolves in all parts of the United States. There are thousands of other hounds used for mountain lion, bear, and deer; beagles and 'rabbit dogs' run into tens of thousands; and as for coon dogs, – frequently a cross between a hound and something else, with some of them running mute and some giving cry, – their number is legion. Perhaps this estimate is conservative, in view of the fact that the Dog World recently estimated the total number of hounds of all sorts in this country as 1,500,000.

Joseph B. Thomas MFH, *Hounds and Hunting through the Ages* (1937)

In North America, there are still large and aggressive predators to be hunted. They include mountain lion (also called cougar or puma), bobcat, Canadian lynx, brown bear, black bear, gray or timber wolf, red

Joseph B. Thomas's pack of American Foxhounds.

wolf and coyote. Some of this game had existed in Europe but has not been hunted for centuries. For this aggressive quarry the hound requires special agility, tenacity, and aggressiveness, called grit… Other game such as the raccoon and the opossum did not exist in Europe. Its pursuit requires a special hound not only with grit but that bays at the tree onto which the game has fled.

Andreas F. von Recum, *Hunting with Hounds in North America* (2002)

It is hard to overstate the value of hunting dogs to settlers in America in past centuries: from conquistadors to colonists, they needed food, and hounds aided their survival substantially. The hounds developed in the United States are largely unknown to hound fanciers in Britain. This is partly because they are mostly working types, not recognized by the American Kennel Club (AKC), but also because the distinctive hound breeds there have usually been underrated by the working hound fraternity here. It is true too that American styles of hunting, allied with different quarry, saw the development of hounds with a quite different purpose from ours. The Americans too use some of our breeds in the hunting field when we have long since failed to do so. Airedales, sometimes weighing up to 90lb, have a hunting role there that perpetuates the sporting instincts of this admirable breed. In America also a much wider variation in hunting techniques was called for – with hounds to match. In his book *Hunting Hounds* of 1972, David Michael Duffey wrote:

> Hounds that work raccoon are definitely tree hounds; those running lion, lynx, bobcat, and possibly bear would also normally be called tree hounds since the chase most frequently ends there. But dogs used on the other species – boar, deer, coyote, wolf and fox – would be trail hounds…From there we go into specifics. That gives us coonhounds, foxhounds, deerhounds, cathounds, bearhounds, boarhounds, and wolfhounds – if the hounds are 'straight' on these game species…

We could never match such variety of quarry in Britain.

Yet our Beagle has proved consistently popular in the United States. In *The American Hunting Dog* (1919), Warren Hastings Miller wrote:

Head study of an American Foxhound.

The popular and ubiquitous beagle, rich man's and poor man's dog alike, is very plentiful in our country. We have three kinds, the standard 15 inch, the pocket variety about nine inches at the shoulder, and the large beagle which takes after the harrier and stands over twenty inches, making a good dog for fast snowshoe hare, and good also on plain Molly Cottontail. Our first standard beagles were General Rowett's pack, imported from England…

Since then the Beagle has excelled both in the hunting field and on the bench. The Beagle reigned as America's most popular registered breed from 1954 to 1959;

Redbone Hound.

Bluetick Coonhound.

it is the only breed there to have featured in the top ten list since 1915. In 1976, for example, over 44,000 were registered there, while here in the 1970s and 80s we struggled to exceed 1,000 Beagle registrations a year. In America, field trials for Beagles are highly popular and reach very high standards for hunting hounds.

The American packhounds are easily outnumbered by the ad hoc or 'bobbery' packs kept by families or individuals there, with the hounds bearing colourful names: Big 'n Blue (American Blue Gascon Hound), Black Mouth Cur, Bluetick Coonhound, Treeing Tennessee Brindle, Redbone Coonhound, Redtick Coonhound and the Plott Hound from the Great Smoky Mountains of Tennessee and North Carolina. The Black and Tan Coonhound and the American Foxhound are recognized breeds, with the latter having three strains in the South: the Walkers, the Triggs and the Julys or July-Birdsongs. All of these breed true to type, excel in the hunting field and perpetuate the blood of many European scenthound breeds, mainly French and English. From the Louisiana Bayou, the Ozark Mountains and other remote areas came French 'Staghounds' or Blue Gascons, with the Bluetick Coonhound claiming the blood of the French hound breed of Porcelaine. There are now six coonhound breeds recognized by the United Kennel Club (UKC) but only one, the Black and Tan Coon-

hound, by the AKC, the US equivalent of our KC. There are also the Majestic Tree Hounds, a St Hubert type of Coonhound-Bloodhound mix, standing at around 28in and weighing over 100lb, with their own association, formed in 1980.

The more orthodox formed packs in the United States are not short of catchy names either. There is the Why Worry Hunt in South Carolina, with many lemon and white hounds, the Plum Run hounds in Pennsylvania, with their tricolours, the Hidden Meadow Beagles also in Pennsylvania and the Sandanoma Harehounds in New York State, with their sturdy Basset Hounds. The Aitken hounds in South Carolina feature some strapping hounds, a number of them mainly white. With anti-hunting legislation now enacted here, there could be a whole new emphasis on sporting tourism over there. There are close links between the hunting communities of Britain and America.

Today there are studbooks for the American Foxhound and the English Foxhound and the Pen Mary Del – a distinct hound breed there. Traditionally found in the states of Pennsylvania, Maryland and Delaware, hence the breed tag, and once known as the Eastern Shore Hounds, these are leggier, longer-eared, multicoloured hounds – some blue mottled, some black and tan, a few white with tan heads and black-patched bodies – and with 'mouths like bells'. Of 140 registered Foxhound packs in the USA, only sixteen are registered as Pen Mary Dels or PMDs.

Repeated Importations

The import of hounds into America has gone on for well over 500 years. One historian described an embarkation for America in 1539 of De Soto 'with his Portuguese in shining armour, his horses, hounds, and hogs'. These hounds were, however, hunting mastiffs for use on native Indians. From England, the Cavalier Robert Brooke sailed for America in 1650, taking forty of his family – and his pack of hounds. These hounds are behind the Trigg and Walker hounds and their descendants were followed by the Brooke family well into the twentieth century. Dr Thomas Walker imported hounds from England into Virginia in 1742, using them to hunt buffalo, elk, bear, deer and even turkey!

In 1785, George Washington received seven hounds from France, which were described as being

Porcelaine or Franche-Comté hounds.

'of great size'. French hounds were imported into Louisiana in the late seventeenth century, of the Normandy breed – Franche-Comté, known locally as Porcelaines. An importation from Ireland in 1830 had a major influence on the Henry, Birdsong (of Georgia) and Trigg (of Kentucky) strains. These are believed to be Kerry Beagles, 24in, black and tan, red or black in colour. The Walker hounds were re-vitalized with English blood in the late nineteenth century. American hounds were bred solely for performance rather than on some model of physical perfection. In Graham's *The Sporting Dog* (1904), Charles Mather wrote:

> I never saw a hound in America which I thought could possibly improve a good English hound by crossing. The crossing has all been done – by those who know anything about it – by breeding their best-made American bitches to a pure-blooded English hound. All the 'American' hound men breed to first-rate pure blood whenever they get the chance. Yet, if you call the result an English hound, they feel offended.

National pride is usually admirable, but the blood of English Foxhounds has long been prized all over the world. The English Foxhound has yet to make its mark in the KC show rings, but in America, the American Foxhound is widely favoured. In 2013, at the Crufts-equivalent Westminster Kennel Club dog show, an American Foxhound, Ch. Kiarry's Pandora's Box, won the Hound Group – quite a feat.

American Exports

The British hound expert Sir John Buchanan-Jardine imported two couples of the best American Fox-hounds and hunted with them for two seasons. He found that in our conditions they lacked stamina. They were more like our Fell Hounds than the stand-

The Black and Tan Coonhound – Best of Breed at the AKC Centennial Show.

An American Foxhound of J.B. Thomas' strain by T. Ivester Lloyd.

ard Foxhound. He reported that their shoulders were inclined to be rather upright and that they 'gave tongue too freely'. To the great credit of the American hound breeders however, they never subscribed to the astonishing and ill-informed desire for massive bone in their dogs, as our Edwardian Foxhound breeders most unwisely did. This era, described by one famous hound expert as the 'shorthorn period',

influenced some Mastiff, St Bernard and Bloodhound breeders here too – and sadly, still does. The American Foxhound was developed for the hunting style used by the hunter; it was used primarily for running in bobbery packs with each hound acting as an individual. This style also developed a hound with a distinctive topline, featuring a slightly arched loin and a higher set of tail. When I see this in our packs, I immediately think of American Foxhound blood.

The English Foxhound, the American Foxhound and the Black and Tan Coonhound (developed from the Old Glory strain) all feature in American show rings. The latter is a big, handsome breed, the first 'cooner' to achieve AKC recognition and allegedly developed from Virginia Foxhounds but used on bear, cougar and wild hog. It is interesting that its breed standard starts off with these words: 'The Black and Tan Coonhound is first and fundamentally a working dog, a trail and tree hound, capable of withstanding the rigors of winter, the heat of summer and the difficult terrain over which he is called upon to work.' If only the comparable standards of our pedigree scenthound breeds could feature such a clear, unambiguous and firm indication of their breed's purpose, value and priorities. The AKC breed standard for this coonhound has over 100 words covering its gait/movement. The KC breed standard of our nearest equivalent breed, the Bloodhound, contains only three words on gait/movement but over 230 words on

The American Foxhound.

the head/skull. It does not mention that the hound is expected to be able to work! The AKC shows do seem to encourage very large Black and Tan Coonhounds, however, whereas the hunters know that the lighter ones are the better hunting dogs.

The English Coonhound

The background to the breed known as the English Coonhound is set out in Whitney and Underwood's *The Coon Hunter's Handbook* of 1952:

> What one of us learned years ago about the true origin of the English Coonhound as repeated by a very old settler is at complete variance with the story that has been told and retold about the type. Our story, in which we have confidence, is that back in the early days of the settlement of Johnson County, Arkansas, the Cazort family brought with them a long, trim, bluetick hound and a true English tricolor. One was a dog and one was a bitch. Both had glorious voices. These two dogs were the ancestors of many of the settlers' coon dogs. They were inbred and occasionally outcrossed, but the two distinct types kept occurring. The bluetick color was no respecter of types and sometimes appeared on the English type and sometimes on the lithe type. In the mountains one still finds both types, with variations between.

This account shows how hound breeds developed in early America, in time, becoming set breeds with their own titles. Most of them not surprisingly, were brought in from Europe with migrating European settlers.

Genetic Tendencies

In their book on coon hunting, Whitney and Underwood set out the aptitudes passed on in such hounds, writing:

> A few general principles in breed crossing to produce coon dogs are interesting and valuable to know. Since, as we have seen, the open-trailing aptitude is dominant over the still trailing, the quality of the yapping voice is dominant over the beautiful hound quality, and the poorer scenting ability of a nonhound is dominant over a hound's keenness of scent, then the product of crossing a fine hound with a nonhound is an open trailer with a yappy voice and

A treeing hound.

without a very keen nose – usually not much better than the nonhound.

We have given less attention to voice in our hounds than the French or the American hound breeders, and for the latter, using hounds for night hunting, it is easy to see the value of distinctively voiced hounds and to know how to perpetuate it in their stock. As Hartley puts it, in his book *Hunting Dogs* of 1909: 'The hound is the master orator, with a command of language that varies from uncertainty, joy, anxiety, conviction, eagerness with great clearness and truth. His shades of meaning are accurately intonated and perfectly comprehendible to the well-versed hunter.' This form of communication is vital during protracted bouts of night hunting.

Wide-Ranging Quarry

Not prized for its voice, but now recognized by the AKC, is the highly respected Plott Hound. Preferred in brindle, weighing around 50lb and standing over 2ft at the withers, this hound breed is described in

The Plott Hound.

its breed standard as: noted for stamina, endurance, agility, determination and aggressiveness when hunting. In his *Hunting Hounds* (1974), American hound expert David Michael Duffey wrote: 'Plotts do breed true to type. They have some characteristics not common to other hounds, including their more hard-bitten, willing-to-mix-it attitude, punishing fighters' jaws, and a stance and appearance that is sometimes "bulldoggy". No wonder their blood is prized by hunters of the fiercer quarry. The standard commendably states that too much bone is a fault, something I can find in no British breed standard, more's the pity. This breed has long been favoured for its courage, which has led to their use in jaguar hunts in the Mato Grosso to the bear hunts of North America. The latter often feature Airedale-hound crosses, Norwegian Elkhounds and local blends, backed by cold-nosed hounds such as Walker, Trigg, July, Redbones and Blueticks.

As in so many breeds, American hound breeds were developed by determined sportsmen, each seeking excellence in his field of hunting. Jonathan Plott left his native Germany in 1750 and went to America with a few of his favourite boarhounds. He settled in the mountains of western North Carolina and initially used his hounds exclusively for bear hunting. He did not outcross for thirty years and bred what can be truly claimed to be a 'family breed', with an awesome reputation on bear and boar. Plott Hounds have since been used on wolf, mountain lion, coyote, wildcat and deer. There has been speculation that his original hounds were of the Hanover Scenthound type and rumours of outcrosses more recently to Airedales and Black and Tan Coonhounds. We may not approve of such hunting but it takes courage for any dog to approach a bear and that degree of courage is worth perpetuating.

Native Hunting Dogs
The Tahltan Indians up in northwestern British Columbia had their own specialist bear dog. They were black or black and white spitz dogs, around 15in high with a brush-like tail, held erect. The Tahl-Tan Bear Dog had a fox-like yap and a coyote yodel; like wild dogs they came into season only once a year. The Indians used them to hunt black and grizzly bears and lynx. They hunted in the Scandinavian spitz dog style, barking furiously to bay their quarry and alert the approaching hunters to the prey. Once registered with the Canadian KC, the last recorded one being in 1948, this distinctive breed may well now be extinct, another loss to the gene pool of the domestic dog.

Almost lost, too, was the American Indian Dog, the native hunting dog of the North American plains, a type reminiscent of the laikas across the Baring Strait, with the Sioux Dog being remarkably wolf-like. Sadly they all looked like coyotes and the early settlers didn't hesitate to shoot them. It is said that in some Indian tribes, an extended family could own as many as twenty, with thousands of them existing across the plains. Man needs hunting dogs!

Developed by Sportsmen
Some, no doubt the owners of red-tick or blue-tick hounds, will link the coat colour with certain traits of value in the field. In Britain, for example, the sportsman Sir Peter Farquhar found that the blue

Catahoula Leopard Dog.
(Photo: Don Abney)

descendants of a hound named Carmarthen Nimrod '24 had better noses than the non-blue. In the greatly respected Dumfriesshire Foxhound kennel the black hounds generally have appreciably more quality than those with more tan in their coats. It is interesting that the setter and scenthound coat colours have developed on parallel lines, whether it is red or blue tick, solid red, black and tan, lemon and white, red and white or black and white. This may be due to more than just sportsmen's preferences.

Colonel Haiden C. Trigg, who also gave his name to a famous pack of hounds, developed his 'long-eared, deep-toned, rat-tailed, black and tan Virginia hounds' in the mid-nineteenth century. He obtained his stock from noted sportsmen such as George Birdsong, Dr T.Y. Henry and the packs created by Walker and Maupin. The foundation of the Walker line was laid by two English importations and a hound literally stolen from a pack whilst actually on the chase in the mountains of Tennessee. One of Maupin's friends noted the outstanding performance of a local hunting pack – and immediately stole one of the hounds taking part! In due course the Trigg Hounds became the most widely used in American fox hunting.

George Birdsong's hounds were probably the foundation stock of the Redbone strain, solid-red treeing and trailing hounds. The Redbone Coonhound tends to be the most uniform in type of the coonhound breeds – for me, having a distinct Hanover Scenthound look

Black Mouth Cur.

to it. Claims have been made for a Scottish and an Irish origin for these hounds, with their name being linked with Peter Redbone, a Tennessee promoter of this strain. Both the Redtick and the Bluetick Coonhounds have been called 'English' at times in their development and it is clear that the British Isles has played a major role in the creation of all these American hounds, with the exception of the Plott hound. Wherever their origin and however widely spread their ancestors, these are valuable, proficient hounds, created a long way away by gifted breeders; they deserve conservation, and our interest.

Two other distinctive breeds, hunting by scent and sight – as described in Chapter 1, and very much still with us – are the strikingly named Catahoula Leopard Dog of Louisiana and the handsome Black Mouth Cur of the southern states.

The Running Mastiff of Louisiana

Very much developed in the United States, in northeast Louisiana, is the rather dramatically named Catahoula Leopard or Hog Dog, Catahoula meaning beautiful clear water. A muscular, Dalmatian-sized hound, but used extensively as a herding dog, they are usually black merle, with their black patches earning them their breed title. They can also be solid-coloured: black, blue, red and yellow-tan, the coat colours long associated with the mastiff breeds. The distinctive black merle is also found in Great Danes and the Norwegian Dunker Hound. Possessing the classic phenotype of the running mastiffs, they are versatile hunting and herding dogs, able to hot track lost stock, bring it to bay when found and then 'hold it'. This is a difficult task with defiant semi-wild cattle and wilful half-wild hogs. These dogs are often used in teams, with specialist roles: leading, herding or rounding up and driving in the destined direction. They combine this testing task with that of hunting dogs, where they can exercise their 'par force' hunting skills, using sight and scent, their great stamina and immense determination.

Skip and Vicki Loudenslager of the Cottonwood Kennels, Lake Odessa, Michigan, have had Catahoulas for two decades and bred outstanding litters in that time. They had the first two UKC champions, the first three grand champions and the first UKC agility champion on record. Quite soon, they produced thirteen UKC champions. Their red dog Trace came second out of twenty-five dogs at the National Association of Louisiana Catahoula's (NALC) show. Skip hunts them on raccoon and is anxious to keep the working instincts of the breed alive. He tells me that his dogs hunt more as sighthounds, do not run cold tracks, bay like a scenthound or have the latter's temperament. He stresses that his dogs will cease tracking once they see their quarry, the classic once-favoured technique of hounds hunting 'at force'.

Don Abney of Abita Springs, Louisiana, the author of a standard book on the breed, is an NALC certified breeder (and trainer of all breeds), using his Catahoulas across a range of skills. This is an extremely versatile breed, able to hunt, track, herd and compete in agility trials. Registered as the Louisiana Catahoula Leopard Dog with the NALC, the UKC (United Kennel Club), the ARBA (American Rare Breed Association) and the SKC (States Kennel Club), but known informally as the Catahoula Cur, the breed is listed in the Herding Group for show ring purposes. That may recognise their pastoral skills but is scant reward for their sheer versatility, including a natural hunting capability.

Some researchers have linked this breed with dogs brought to the Americas by Spanish colonists, to be subsequently acquired by Indians and later by settlers. There are theories too of the introduction of the blood of herding dogs brought out by French immigrants, with the harlequin coat (what the French call *gris avec taches noires* [danoises]') of the Beauceron, perhaps in mind. But there is a genetic difference between harlequin and merle. Smoother-coated, drop-eared dogs like the Norwegian Dunker Hound would be a more likely foreign source. Interestingly, my namesake, the highly successful English lurcher breeder produces collie/greyhound lurchers with this type of physique and striking coat colour and they are superbly efficient hunting dogs. As Sullivan wrote a century ago: 'Form follows Function'.

Known affectionately as 'cats', used successfully as coonhounds, these Leopard Dogs have been described as 'walking sledgehammers' because of their forcefulness and sheer physical power; they are today's equivalents of medieval par force hounds. They are renowned for their remarkable eyesight when night hunting; those using them in the hunt say that they have never known such keen eyes in any other hound breed. With their unique 'double-glass' eyes, with one sometimes having a different colour from the other, their use on deer, bobcat and wild hog means they have to be adaptable as well as alert and agile. This is a highly individual breed.

The American big game hunter Shelley used hounds from his country in his 'bobbery pack' of lion-hunting dogs in Africa in the 1920s. In his *Jaguar Hunting in the Mato Grosso* (1976), de Almeida wrote:

> …good dogs are essential to a successful hunt. And good jaguar-dogs are the hardest thing to come by in Mato-Grosso… We arranged for Bert to send down to us six hounds of the Plott breed, which were trained to hunt bear in the forests of Washington State, near Seattle. This race of hound is famed for its courage, having been bred over the years strictly for hunting big game… The Plott breed is an overall brindle colour, but varying from orange in some dogs to almost black in others.

Once again, a famous big game hunter is singing the praises of brindle hunting dogs, brindle running mastiffs.

The Running Mastiff of the Southern States

Known affectionately as 'Ole Yeller' because of its coat colour, the Black Mouth Cur or Southern Cur has all the uses and appearance of a running mastiff. Weighing up to 95lb, with a height at the shoulder of up to 25in, these versatile hunting dogs have been used on quarry ranging from squirrel and raccoon to bear and boar. Famous for their long loping stride, great stamina and even more impressive gameness, they hunt and catch their prey, never flinching from closing with fearsome adversary like boar. They can work stock too, as can so many of the mastiff-like breeds.

Short-haired, with a coat varying from light red, through golden yellow to fawn or sandy yellow/tan, they usually feature a black mask and muzzle and sometimes have white toes or a small white spot on their chest. They resemble the Rhodesian Ridgeback, without the ridge. They are silent on the trail, but give a characteristic 'yodel' as they close in on their prey. With a strongly developed desire to please their masters and great hunting skills, they have proved their worth over the years on many remote farms. Such dogs deserve more recognition, especially when you consider that given to purely ornamental breeds that have never worked to help man survive in testing times.

If breeds like these two American breeds, the Broholmer, the Rhodesian Ridgeback, the Dogo Argentino and the Great Dane are to thrive they must be bred in the mould of their hunting field ancestors. The powerful, strong-headed running mastiffs may no longer have a role in Europe as big game hunters, but they are a distinctive element in canine heritage as well as fine breeds in their own right. They *must* be bred, as the Danes insist with their native breed, with superlative temperament and sound character. There is no place in today's society for big, powerful, *savage* dogs. There is still a need, however, for well-disciplined, faithful dogs with a natural guarding instinct and the persistence that allows them to excel in the chase – and that is the challenge for breeders in the twenty-first century.

> …there are few counties in the South or Southwest which do not have their quota of fox-hunting enthusiasts. While not exactly one of the devotees, I can vouch from personal observation for the statement that between the Delaware Bay and the Texas Panhandle nearly every neighborhood has its esteemed foxhounds – toward the Panhandle using them for wolves as much as for the 'beast of stinking flight'… Indeed, if I were writing a volume on American hounds, the most exciting chapters would be descriptions of wolf hunts and the battles with which they conclude. Hounds have to be hounds in this sport; for the hunts are hunts and the battles are battles.
>
> Joseph A. Graham, *The Sporting Dog* (1904)

The Scenthound Diaspora

European Breeds

Less Insularity

Britain's influence in the sporting field across the globe in the nineteenth and early twentieth centuries led to the blood of our hound breeds being extensively exported, Foxhounds especially. Their impressive physical stature, allied with great staying power and backed by nose and voice, made them desired all over the world to improve local hunting dogs, from Swe-

A Foxhound pack en route to India on morning exercise (The Graphic, *1888*).

BELOW LEFT: *The Hobart Hounds of 1900.*

den and Finland in the north, across the channel to France, and even further afield to America, Australia, South Africa and India. Packs of them have been deployed from Gibraltar (the Calpe Hunt) to Tasmania (the Hobart Hunt). It would be wrong, however, not to mention early in this section, one distinctive Irish hound breed, the Kerry Beagle, used in the Scarteen pack; greatly admired in the UK over many years and providing good hunting for many sportsmen from Great Britain. Black and tan Harriers, with other colours allowed – the first show champion, in 1993, was

The Royal Calpe Hunt with the Marquis of Marzales as Master, by Lionel Edwards, 1919.

ABOVE: *Kerry Beagles of the Scarteen pack.*

a blue-mottled dog, Cloudy Fellow – not Beagles in our sense, and like, say, the Tara pack in size, they are claimed to have a continental origin rather than a British Isles background. On the move, they remind me very much of the Dumfriesshire Foxhounds, albeit in a smaller form. May they long continue.

In her book *In Nimrod's Footsteps* (1974), Daphne Moore mentions another black and tan pack in Ireland, the Naas Harriers. She also refers to the Kilkenny Hounds, famous for their strong muscular backs, with a hereditary trait – a spine of 'cloven' muscle running along the topline; I have heard old hound experts stress the capability of being able to roll a billiard ball along a standing hound's back, from withers to rump, without the ball falling off to one side. Strength in the back gives a hound far greater running power.

The rich heritage behind our native scenthounds, together with the ease of introducing superlative reinforcements from just across the channel, has perhaps led us to overlook talented hound breeds from further afield. With more foreign scenthound breeds now becoming known in Britain: the Basset Fauve de Bretagne, the Hamiltonstovare, the Grand Bleu de Gascogne, the Bavarian Mountain Hound, the Norwegian Lundehund and the Grand and Petit Bassets Griffon Vendeen all introduced fairly recently, we are becoming less insular in our outlook.

The Tara Harriers of 1899.

A Tyrolean Hound.

The Styrian Hound from Austria.

A Basset Fauve de Bretagne (Photo: Dalton).

The Brandlbracke (right) by Wouterus Verschuur, 1851.

Lithuanian Hounds from Starting for the Boar Hunt *by A. von Wierusz-Kowalski.*

When working and living three times in Germany, I came across the German, Austrian and Swiss hounds and found much to admire in the Alpine Dachsbracke, the Austrian Hound, the Hanoverian Hound and half a dozen Swiss hound breeds, large and small. At the World Dog Shows in Vienna and Dortmund I learnt of the Styrian Mountain Hound – still sometimes called the Peintinger after its creator, the Tyrolean Hound and the imposing Brandlbracke or Austrian Black and Tan Hound. It's alarming that in Austria, three times as many Golden Retrievers are registered annually as their charming native breed, the Alpine Dachsbracke. We must all conserve our native breeds, they are part of our heritage.

Baltic and Balkan Breeds

The Scandinavian and Baltic hound breeds were very much in evidence when the World Dog Show was held in Helsinki in 1998, with the Finnish Hound attracting a huge entry of impressive hounds. The Baltic hound breeds are, not surprisingly, much alike, with the Estonian, Lithuanian and Latvian (Courland) native scenthounds resembling tricolour Foxhounds in conformation. The black and tan Lithuanian Hound is gradually becoming better known, with distinct similarities to the scenthounds further south. Until quite recently, the Lithuanian hunters using this breed never showed interest in dog shows or even registered their stock with the national kennel club.

The Finnish Hound being used as a tracker.

Posavac Hound – one of the Balkan breeds.

Slovene Mountain Hound.

Montenegran Mountain Hound.

The Balkan breeds – the Istrian (in two coats), the Posavac or Posavski Gonic from northern Bosnia, the Slovene and the Montenegran Mountain Hounds – have distinct similarities too, with the Greek Hound having a comparable appearance. The break-up of the former Yugoslavia has led to each emergent nation renewing its interest in the native hound breeds long established there, with the Yugoslavian Mountain Hound providing yet another variety. It was an Istrian Hound from Slovenia that came first in the solo trial at the 1998 Coupe d'Europe des Chiens Courants hunting trial, staged by the FCI's Hunting Commission, south of Vienna; five of the top ten hounds came from Slovenia and Croatia, no mean feat.

Istrian Hound (smooth-haired variety).

Eastern European Breeds

In Budapest for the World Dog Show, I came across the Polish and Hungarian breeds undergoing a revival in their native countries. With the breakaway of the Iron Curtain countries, scenthound breeds like the Ogar Polski (mainly tan) and the Gonczy Polski (black and tan) in Poland and the Erdelyi Kopo or Transylvanian Hound (in two sizes, 22–26in for wolf, bear, stag, lynx and boar and 18–22in for hare and fox) of Hungary, two similar breeds in type, have been promoted. The Slav influence across borders can be seen in the scenthounds ranging from Slovenia due south of Austria, into Austria itself and on into Serbia and further south. Not surprisingly, the anatomy suits the role of the hound, wherever it's employed. As these countries become increasingly urbanized and westernized, care needs to be taken that such valuable hunting dogs are not briefly celebrated as national emblems then discarded as interest wanes. Here, our KC recognizes the Foxhound but not the Fell Hound, the Welsh Hound, the Harrier or the English Basset. If some of these are not to be hunted in the future, it may well be a question of deciding whether a show-ring future is better than none at all. The Otterhound now features in the show ring as well as in the minkhound packs. Is it not better to conserve genes and await more enlightened times?

Wide Diaspora

In his informative and comprehensive *Hounds of the World* (2000), supported by superb photography from Bruce Tanner, David Alderton covers nearly all the recognized hounds in existence, from the Basenji of the Congo to the Rastreador of Brazil. He mentions both ridgeback breeds, those of Rhodesia and Thailand. He refers to the Dunker, Haldenstovare and Hygenhund of Norway, the Strellufstover of Denmark and the Swedish Beagle. But even such a comprehensive survey as this couldn't find room for the Cretan Hound, the Halleforshund of Sweden, the Alano of Spain, the tribal hunting dogs of South Africa or the Karelian Hound of Finland. In the west, we tend to concentrate on the scenthounds of the packs, overlooking the hounds that work to the gun. But as more nations become aware of their canine

ABOVE RIGHT: *Polish Scenthound (Gonczy Polski).*

Transylvanian Hound (Erdelyi Kopo) – a champion bitch.

Italian Segugios.

Luzerner Niederlaufhund, or hunting Basset.

heritage, more and more identifiable breeds of hound are made known to us.

Scenthounds from overseas have not met with wild success in Britain; our KC recognizes nearly thirty hound breeds, some twenty of these originating from outside Britain, ten of those recognized being sighthound breeds. The four French Basset hound breeds favoured here, and their Grand Bleu de Gascogne, lead the way, with the more recently imported Italian breed, the Segugio, finding fanciers and the Norwegian Lundehund now introduced. It was sad, however, to see a hardy, tough hunting breed like the Segugio wearing coats at Crufts. When

in Italy, I was told of another rare breed, the Little Apennine Hare Hound, being restored by mountain hunters there. In Britain, if you treat the Dachshund varieties as one breed, we only recognized fifteen hound breeds in 1908 and five of those came from abroad. From that list we have lost the Harrier from the show bench but since then registered quite a number of foreign breeds.

The Swiss Breeds

The sporting dogs of Switzerland are little known away from their native country. Not one is recognized by our Kennel Club or utilized by our sportsmen. Yet

The Lucernois (Luzerner) – showing Gascony influence.

Chien Courant Suisse – the national harehound.

they are prized by Swiss sportsmen, with their wide range of harehounds offering unrelated blood in the improvement of the genetic diversity of some of our hound breeds. The Swiss hounds have developed under the influence of those countries adjacent to the various Swiss regions and are sensibly bred to suit the terrain of a region rather than the country as a whole. In this way, we can see the influence of the French hounds in the Jura hounds, of Bavarian hounds in the Lucernese hounds, of German hunting dogs in the Bernese hounds and a more general European look to the Swiss national variety. In each of these four groups: Jura, Lucernese, Bernese and Swiss, there is a Harrier-sized hound or Laufhund and a Beagle-sized hound or Niederlaufhund. The four types of Laufhund are in the 17–22in height bracket, whilst the four types of Niederlaufhund are in the 12–15in height bracket.

The Lucernois or Luzerner Laufhund is similar to the Bavarian Mountain Hound and related to the Hanover Scenthound, and was developed for tracking chamois for the gun, not as a quarry hound. The Swiss Hound, Schweizer Laufhund or *le courant Suisse commun* has proved popular in Norway, with the smaller variety 'improved' by using Dachsbracke blood. The Bernese Hound or Berner Laufhund is usually bigger than the other native hound breeds, with far longer leathers. It resembles the Steinbracke of Germany. The fourth variety, the Jura Hound or Laufhund, comes in two types, one called the Bruno de Jura and the St Hubert type. Used to hunt the hare and to drive game to the waiting guns, there is a slight resemblance to the smooth variety of the Italian Segugio. The latter is now recognized by our Kennel Club, if not by our sportsmen.

German Hounds

Germany makes far too little of its scenthound breeds; the Romans recorded two types of hound

A Bavarian Mountain Scenthound in use as tracker.

The Steinbracke of Germany.

A Steenbrak of Holland, with her pup.

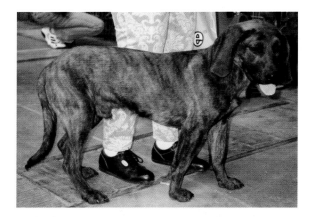

The Hanover Scenthound of Germany.

used by the Sicambri, a powerful German tribe based on the east bank of the Rhine from the Sieg to the Lippe. The smaller hound was referred to as 'petronius' or 'petrunculus', leading to speculation that these hounds were either famous for their robust feet or running capably over rocky terrain, 'petra' meaning a rock. I believe that the 'stonehound', Steinbracke in German, Steenbrak in Dutch, was named after the striking and highly individual stone-blue colour of its coat. The blue fox is similarly named *steinfuchs* in German. The FCI recognizes the Steinbracke, better known in Germany itself as the Deutsche (Sauerlander) Bracke or German (Sauerland) Hound. The Bavarian Mountain Hound is now established in Britain, a hound used to track by shooters, not as a packhound, but a very individual breed well worth the interest here. Even when living and working in

Germany I never came across a Steinbracke, a distinctive breed, again used with the gun not in a pack. The Black Forest Hound has now been claimed by Slovakia as the Slovensky Kopov.

Dutch Breeds

The Nederlandse Steenbrak or Oudhollands Steenbrakje (old Dutch small hound) is not yet fully recognized as a breed, but in many of the old German and Dutch hounds, the bone structure is lighter and flatter than most scenthound breeds, with the longer ears of the French hounds, but hanging flat, not turned, as in the Bloodhound. Steenbrakken, most unusually for a scenthound breed, can be long-haired as well as short-haired; both this breed and the Sauerland Hound have a characteristic flesh-coloured stripe up over the nose. This was I believe a feature too of the old Flemish hounds. In an increasingly urban Europe we have to be careful not to lose the ancient hound heritage in so many countries, although in the east, the rise of national spirit has awakened interest in their sporting canine legacy. The French have demonstrated how such a legacy can be reinvested after the deprivations of two World Wars.

Spanish Breeds

In Spain the Alano has only just survived the twentieth century – at one time the last two were believed to be those exhibited in Retiro Park in Madrid in 1963. But then some were discovered in Cantabria, in the western area of Vizcaya, in the Carranza and Llera valleys.

Alanos from Spain.

The breed was originally used as a hunting dog, in the classic catch-dog role of the broad-mouthed breeds. They were used as cattle-driving dogs, especially with half-wild cattle. They were used until the mid-nineteenth century in the bullring, in one of the phases of the bullfight known as the 'dogs' turn'. Not surprisingly the breed was mainly used, in the hunting field, in the 'gancho' method of hunting boar, in which the dogs 'held' the boar until it was despatched by the human hunter's knife. Around 25in at the shoulder and weighing between 77 and 100lb, the ones displaying the fawn coat, black mask and black muzzle could be mistaken for Bullmastiffs at first glance.

The Sabueso is the Spanish scenthound, coming in two sizes, the Sabueso Español de Monte or Mountain Hound, a large, heavy-boned, long-eared hound, once used by the Spanish police as a man tracker; and the Sabueso Español Lebrero or harehound, usually white and red, the size of our Harrier.

Sabueso Español, Madrid 1983.

Russian Hounds

The Russians still have their Harlequin Hound, linked by many with the Harlequin Great Dane. The Moscow Society of Hunters and Fishermen stage an annual exhibition, attracting over a thousand dogs. There you can see Russian Hounds (a breed similar to the Finnish Hound and the Estonian Hound), Russian Skewbald or Piebald Hounds and the Harlequin. I understand that the Dynamo Sport Society of Tula developed a uniform, high-quality pack of 'Harls' for use on wolf, leading to these dogs being used to upgrade stock elsewhere in Russia. As the geneticists Little and Jones

Mixed hounds used in the bear hunt; Julius Falat's Return from the Bear Hunt.

BELOW: Pack of Russian scenthounds c.1900.

Russian Bloodhounds by M. Lotz, 1886.

have shown, the harlequin white is dominant over solid colours – that is, tan, black and so on – but the factor can have a semi-lethal dimension, different again from that of the Dunker Hound's. The Russian scenthounds were used with the Borzoi in the wolf hunt.

A giant bear hound, the Mendelan, was once favoured but despite its distinct type faded from view and was lost to us. In his book *The Dog in Sport* (1938), James Wentworth Day records: '...the great Mendelans owned by the late Tsar of Russia and kept by him at the summer palace at Gatchina...were the size of a calf, and...were used for rousing bears out of thickets in summer and from their hibernating quarters in snow in winter.'

I don't believe that the rough-coated so-called Russian or Siberian Bloodhound has survived the endless upheavals of Russian society in the twentieth century. It was interesting to note that at the 1998 Moscow Dog Show as many as seventy Bloodhounds were entered, twenty-eight in the Working Class; I believe they are used to flush game.

The Spitz Breeds and the Single Trackers

Any hound capable of working successfully in sub-arctic conditions, treacherous mountain terrain and in huge expanses of largely uninhabited regions surely demands our admiration. Why then have the 'spitz-hounds' not attracted our interest? Books on hounds usually overlook the Northern breeds, which can range from the Elkhounds of Scandinavia to the bear-dogs of Karelia. Somehow the appearance of such hounds, with their prick ears, thick coats and lavishly curled tails, doesn't immediately fit our mental image of a scenthound. The Finnish Spitz is already well known here, with thirty-six newly reg-

The Schillerstovare from Sweden.

The Gotland Hound of Sweden.

Swedish Beagle or Drever.

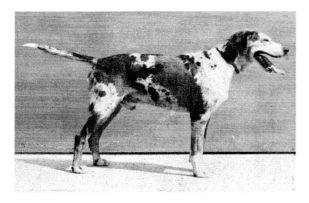

Dunker Hound of Norway.

istered with the Kennel Club in 2010, but only ten in 2011. They have been grouped with the Hounds by the KC, but as a 'bark-pointer' should perhaps be allotted to the Gundog Group. This attractive little breed is a most unusual – for us, that is – hunting dog, in a style not utilized in Western Europe. The dog is used in heavily wooded areas where it uses sight, scent and unusually good hearing to locate feathered game, upland game such as grouse or capercaillie. The location of the quarry is 'pointed' by a special stance, four-square with tail up twitching with excitement, head back and giving voice – a distinctive singsong crooning bark, which is sustained, both to mesmerize the prey and attract the hunter.

This 'point by bark' has to be audible to the hunter, who may be some distance away, and more importantly to 'freeze' the bird. The Finns claim that the tone of the bark, the agitated almost hypnotic waving of the bushy tail – and even the small white spot on the dog's chest, hold some kind of fascination for the bird, which watches intently from the relative if temporary safety of its perch. There are similarities here with the flamboyantly waving tail of the old red decoy dog of East Anglia, used to lure ducks for the hunter. The Finnish Spitz has the same rich rufous, almost red-gold coat, mobile ears and highly inquisitive nature. Just as this breed is the national dog of Finland, the Elkhound is that of Norway and the Hamiltonstovare (the word *stovare* coming from the Low German *stobern* – seeking or tracking) that of Sweden, a breed used as a single tracker, that is, used alone to follow a track not as a pack hound.

Swedish Imports

Thirty years ago, we began to show an interest in a handsome Swedish scenthound breed, the Hamiltonstovare, very similar, at first glance, to the Finnish Hound. Eight were registered in 1984, twenty-one in 1990, thirty-one in 1991, only six in 2010, then twenty-seven in 2011 but only six again in 2012. These figures are not reassuring; this is an attractive breed, but, as always, hound breeds are not ideal pets for those with no sporting facilities. Here, from the ringside, I've been impressed by an import, Santorpets Tessie at Sufayre, every inch a hunting dog. This breed was created by a devoted sportsman, bred specifically for a sporting function and one needing exercise, stimulation and above all, *scent*. This breed

Baying by bark, by G.F. Neale, 1898.

Awaiting the hunter – an elk brought to bay, 1904.

is used as a single working hound for finding, tracking and driving hare to the guns, with the hunters using horns to communicate, but relying on the baying of the hounds for information too. They just don't look at home in a suburban street.

There are over eight breeds of native hunting dog in Sweden, ranging from the better known Grey Elk Dog or Jamthund, a handsome cream-marked grey, (only recognized in 1946 but widely used in hunt-ing trials), the Swedish White Elkhound (nearly 800 registered each year), the little known Ottsjojim, an elkhound of Jamthund type, to the well established Drever, or Swedish Dachsbracke (12–16in high), the bigger black and tan Schiller and Smalands Hounds and the Hamiltonstovare. Not surprisingly, the non-spitz hounds greatly resemble their Norwegian equivalents: the Halden (only six registered in 1980, against over 600 Schillers and 290 Smalands), Hygen

A famous Swedish Elkhound, Jager, of 1903.

The Swedish Jamthund.

and Dunker (now the Norwegian) Hounds. The German influence can be seen in a number of these, with the bob-tailed Smalands looking very Rottweiler-like, even though scenthounds in Germany are not numerous, as hunting dogs, or popular as pets. As hunting dogs they are famed trackers, not hounds of the pack. Sweden also boasts a small hunting dog, the Norbottenspets, used in hunting rabbits and hares. It is not always easy to identify these breeds: the climate and the conditions have shaped them and their similarity of form is understandable.

The Norwegian Input

The best-known Spitz-hound in Britain is the Norwegian Elkhound, although its fortunes have varied. Ten years ago, 149 were newly registered with our KC; in 2010 just thirty-three, and sixty-two in 2012. Comments on the entry at championship shows in 2011 by judges of this breed give concern. These range from 'Upright shoulders and wide chests accounted for bad front movement and incorrect rear angulation prevented the correct drive from behind' and '…loose elbows and pasterns were evident in most exhibits' to 'Hind movement overall was not good, particularly in the males…they were straight in angulation in front and rear and therefore lacked both reach and drive.' The Norwegian hunters I met disapproved of too straight a stifle, arguing that such a feature made the hound 'use its back too much'

and lack endurance as a result. A 2012 show critique expressed concern about 'an ever diminishing gene pool' and the necessity to introduce new bloodlines 'to preserve the breed as we know it'.

We all know that this is a breed that relies on endurance and these judges' criticisms are worrying for the future of the breed here, famous as a working hound. I believe one has been used as a locator of people buried under snow by the Scottish Mountain Rescue Services. The Elkhounds I have seen in Norway looked stockier and shorter-coupled than those I saw in the United States, where I was saddened to see them lighter and finer-boned – and expected to 'gait' at speed in the ring, rather like Siberian Huskies. I don't think Norwegian elk-hunters would want their precious dogs to perform in such a way!

Hunting Trials

Hounds like the Norwegian Elkhound have been used for centuries to hunt bear, elk, reindeer and the wolf, but it was not until 1877 that they were recognized as a breed there. Only those that qualify in hunting trials may be awarded the full title of champion. This surely has to be the way ahead for all sporting dogs if they are to be retained as such. The Elkhound hunts mainly by scent, working silently to locate its prey, which it then holds or drives towards the hunters. As it doesn't actually 'catch and kill' its quarry, strictly speaking it shouldn't be classified as a hound.

Norwegian Elkhound of 1900.

(But under our own Hunting Act, aren't all hounds now gundogs?) Usually a shade of grey, with black tips, a black cousin is found in the Finnmark area, with a shorter coat, looking taller and lighter than the Norwegian breed. I saw some sixty years ago when exploring the Jaeggevarre ice-glacier region; the local hunters called them Sorte Dyrehund. They were leggy and thick-coated, hinting at great robustness and stamina. There is also the Halleforshund, an elkhound breed that is red-coated with a black mask, more like one of the laika breeds further east. The Russians have their own laika or point-barker hunting dog breeds, with regional differences between the West Siberian from the Northern Urals; the East Siberian, from the huge forests there; and the Russo-European varieties.

Bear Dogs

At World Dog Shows, especially the one held in Helsinki, I have been impressed by the Laika type, especially the imposing Karelian Bear Dog, a sturdy mainly black breed, used for hunting the bear, lynx and elk, but prized especially on sable. Determined, fiercely independent and immensely resolute, which is hardly surprising when you think of their bigger quarry, they have a very acute sense of smell and superb longsight, picking up movement at extreme distances. This breed originated in Karelia, a territory stretching from north of St Petersburg to Finland, with the Russian breeders adding Utchak Sheepdog blood for greater resistance to the cold. Standing 22in high and around 55lb in weight, they were originally used to hunt elk, then later to hunt bears and large game. They are related to the Russo-European Laika, often being black-coated and with a similar broad head, but easily confused with the hunting dogs from further east: the Western and Eastern Siberian Laikas. These hunting dogs have quite remarkable resistance to low temperatures and their past value to peasant hunters, especially before the arrival of firearms, must have been immense. I am told that around 70,000 hunting Laikas are in East Siberia alone, with those used on feathered game selected for air-scenting, those used on fur or hoof bred for ground-scenting skill.

The Norwegian Lundehund.

RIGHT: *The Karelian Bear Dog.*

Both the bear and the elk are formidable adversaries, with even the baying dogs being regularly killed by them. An elk, or moose in North America, is the largest living deer, about the size of a horse; the bull can have antlers of up to forty points. The use of dogs for elk-hunting in northern Europe has a long history. It took two forms: one with wide-ranging, free-hunting small packs (*loshund*) and another with dogs on a long leash (*lurhund* or *bandhund*) following a trail. The latter demanded close cooperation between dog and handler, to make full use of the wind conditions and not to startle the quarry into hasty retreat. The hound must not give tongue or the elk accelerates and can be lost. Hunting bears too was not a practice for the faint-hearted in times when only primitive weapons were available. Canada had an equivalent to the Karelian Bear Dog, the Tahltan Bear Dog, used by the Tahltan Indians of British Columbia, south of the Yukon and flanked by Alaska. It was used in packs to hunt black and grizzly bears and the lynx.

Even more specialist was the Norwegian Lundehund, used to hunt puffins on coastal cliffs. Uniquely, this breed has the ability to fold its ears shut, using cartilage around the ear-rim, and has six toes on each foot rather than four. Hunting for puffins' nests clearly demands extra features in the hound!

Now recognized by our KC, this attractive little hound is finding fanciers in the UK. Around fifteen inches high and fifteen pounds in weight, they are usually all-white underneath, with rufous, black or grey top coat.

South American Hounds

The Hound of Argentina

European breeds are behind the hunting dog of Argentina, the Dogo Argentino, unjustifiably banned from Britain under the absurd Dangerous Dogs Act (absurd because it brands four dog breeds as dangerous rather than the human social misfits who misuse such powerful dogs) and strangely not recognized as a heavy hound or running mastiff. The Argentinian breed is expected to be a hound of the chase – a running mastiff and a capture dog, when used to hunt wild pig in its native country. The Alano of Spain was probably the original form of the hunting mastiff in Argentina, taken there by colonists. Spanish explorers first reached the coastal areas in 1516 and settlers quickly followed in search of gold and silver. The second largest country in South America and the eighth largest in the world, it features the Gran Chaco, a forested region famous for its big game. Wild pig destroy crops; pumas attack cattle. The Argentinian farmer has long had a need for big game-hunting dogs. This need exemplifies the way in which hounds developed in response to function throughout history. The evolution of the Dogo Argentino, like the Rhodesian Ridgeback, described later, occurred during recorded history, unlike that of many more ancient hounds, and the process itself is worth examination; it exemplifies previous unrecorded hound evolutions.

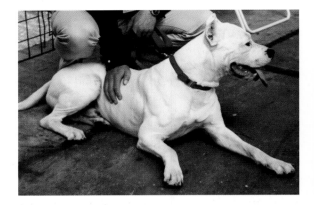

ABOVE: *The Dogo Argentino – an all-purpose hunting dog.*

RIGHT: *Strong-headed Dogo Argentino – resembling ancient Alaunt.*

The need, in this case, was met by the Alano/Perro de Presa dogs taken to Argentina by settlers. Later, the Perro de Pelea Cordobes, or Cordoba Fighting Dog, mainly white and renowned for its ferocity, became a component in the local 'boar-lurchers'. The Argentinian city of Cordoba was a base for English railway workers in the nineteenth century and some are known to have brought their pitdogs with them. Bull-fighting and cock-fighting were banned in the mid-nineteenth century but dog-fighting persisted into the 1920s. The end of dog-fighting could have led to the loss of the brave dogs misused in such a barbaric contest, but the desirable qualities in them were recognized by Dr Antonio Nores Martinez in his quest for a dog to hunt boar and puma, both enemies of the farmer.

Dr Martinez spelt out the essential qualities desired in an Argentinian big game hound at a lecture in 1974: a hound which did not give tongue until confronting its quarry; a hound able to seek air scent with a high nose, comparing this feature to that of the Pointer; a hound with scenting powers rated ahead of sheer pace; and a resolute animal, not afraid to tackle a dangerous quarry. He stressed that a hound which could not 'seize and hold' its prey was valueless, mainly because of the immense physical demands made on hunters in the terrain favoured by the quarry. It was vital to have a successful conclusion to such physically stressful hunting in the mountain forests. It is no coincidence that breeds like the Dogo Argentino, the Perro de Presa Canario,

the Cane Corso, the Perro Cimarron and the Fila de Sao Miguel, despite coming from different countries have almost identical jaws; function decided form.

It is alleged that the blood of the Pointer, the Dogue de Bordeaux and the Boxer (and some reports say Great Dane, Foxhound, Bullmastiff and Bull Terrier blood too) was blended with that of the remaining fighting dogs, but that finally Irish Wolfhound and Pyrenean Mastiff blood was introduced. This seems a strange mixture of rough-coated and smooth-coated breeds, breeds with conflicting instincts and hunting aptitudes and too little scent-hound input. It would have made more sense if a combination of Great Dane, Bull Terrier, Foxhound and the big white Bulldogs used for hog-catching in the United States had been tried. This would have produced the white, smooth-coated dog desired, with scenting powers ahead of speed and with pinning instincts well to the fore. It would be of value one day to discover the actual breed mix, for the outcome has been highly successful and a fine hunting mastiff developed.

Both Antonio Nores Martinez and his brother Agustin admitted experiencing great difficulty in eliminating dog aggression from their stock. I suspect this may have been caused by a lack of socialization when the dogs were young, perhaps inevitable when a large number of dogs are kennelled, a lack of skilful training during the dogs' development and a failure to differentiate between gameness, that is spirit, determination and courage, and undesirable aggression, exemplified by bullying, irrational bad temper and unpredictable savageness. Hounds used in the boar hunt, and to face pumas, need fearlessness, dash and boldness but not unstable temperaments.

Wild pig, whether an enraged 450lb sow or a lighter peccary with its formidable teeth, makes a terrifying adversary. A boar will face a dog without fear and is capable of ripping open a dog's flanks with its fearsome tusks. The puma that raids the herds of Argentinian cattle, concentrating on the calves, can tear a dog to shreds when fighting for its life. A running mastiff that is expected to be a catch-dog too would need the thicker skin and powerful jaws of the holding dogs, as well as the stamina, pace and scenting skills of a 'par force' hound. The specimens that I see at shows abroad have surprisingly thin skin for a dog with this function-led breeding, but they do have commendably stable temperaments.

The Brazilian Hounds

The Brazilian Tracker, or Rastreador Brasileiro, is a lighter, faster scenthound than its better known cousin, the Fila Brasileiro, and is now regarded more as a mastiff, non-sporting breed. This hound was created by Oswalde Aranha, specifically to track jaguars, using the blood of coonhounds and the American Foxhound, producing a 2ft-high, short-coated, long-eared hound, muscular and deep-chested, with a coat in most of the scenthound colours. My illustration depicts a hound much more like the American Treeing Brindle and less bloodhoundy than other specimens of this breed appear, but it may well be that this Brazilian hound has now disappeared altogether, a sad loss but perhaps an understandable one as hunting requirements change and the urban sprawl continues to reduce hunting country. The bigger, heavier sister-breed, the Fila Brasileiro, or 'holding dog of Brazil' is strangely banned from Britain, under the discredited Dangerous Dogs Act, despite being the breed most officially tested for its temperament in the world.

The Filas Brasileiro that I have seen at a number of World Dog Shows seem to vary in type: the black ones, and some of the fawns, indicating Great Dane blood, the brindle ones hinting at Mastiff ancestry and the red fawns looking decidedly bloodhoundy. But, importantly, all of them looked, as all historically correct mastiff breeds should, like heavy hounds. The British enthusiasts who made the Mastiff of England into a ponderous, cumbersome, heavy-boned, inactive yard-dog at the end of the nineteenth century have a lot to answer for. A huge dog needs soundness of physique more than a small one if it is to lead a healthy, active life. A heavy hound needs sound movement more than a lighter one if needless wear and tear is to be avoided. It is vital therefore when this breed is judged in the show ring, for it to be viewed as a sporting/working animal, possessing an anatomy that permits this. This breed is still used as a hound, on boar and jaguar, and a cattle dog, as well as an impressive guard dog.

ABOVE: *Brindle Fila Brasileiro.*

RIGHT: *The Rastreador Brasileiro – the Brazilian Tracker.*

Versatile Rhodesian Ridgeback.

BELOW: An artist's impression of Ridgebacks baying a lion.

As a tracking dog during the colonial period it was used to pursue and detain runaway slaves from the vast sugar cane plantations – the scenthound blood providing tracking skill still valued by the Brazilian Armed Forces.

African Hounds

The Hound from Rhodesia

Hunting 'at force', using par force hounds which used sight and scent in the chase has long given way in Britain to 'hunting cunning', in which the slower unravelling of scent by hounds is favoured. But in Britain we did once use 'full-mouth' hounds, heavy-headed hounds with shorter muzzles, and 'fleethounds', which went too fast even for the most speedy steeplechaser. In the colonies, however, the early settlers had a need for hound-like dogs which could hunt at speed, using sight and scent. In India, for example, local breeds were utilized, like the powerful Sindh hound, the swift Rampur hound, the Poligar, the Vaghari hound, the Pashmi hound and the strongly built Rajapalayan dog.

In southern Africa, however, the settlers blended the blood of native dogs like the I-Baku, I-Twini, I-Bansi and Sica dogs with imported breeds like the Pointer, the Bull Terrier, the Irish Wolfhound, the Foxhound and possibly Dutch breeds like the Nederlandse Steenbrak. Some of the native dogs carried a ridge of reverse hair, roughly in a fiddle shape, along their spine. The Kalahari San were seen in southeastern Angola forty years ago with ridged hunting dogs. The Khoi were recorded as far back as 1719 as owning hounds 18in at the shoulder, with a sharp muzzle, pointed ears, with a body like a jackal and a ridge or mane of hair turned forward on the spine and neck. The evolution of the Rhodesian Ridgeback is worth a close look; it exemplifies how human need led to hounds developing along definite functional lines. Unlike the evolution of much older breeds or types, it occurred during recorded history and the records demonstrate how a perceived function designed the breed.

Renowned South African hunters such as Petrous Jacobs, Fred Selous and Cornelius van Rooyen, who bought his first 'lion dogs' from the Rev. Helm, developed their 'running mastiff' in the Matabele and Mashona territories of southern Africa, using them

Prototypal Ridgeback at the Bulawayo Dog Show 1925.

as a small pack of four or five to catch pig, to pull down wounded bucks, to worry lions and to track the blood trails of wounded game. Many of these dogs were killed by crocodiles and snakes, as well as by lions. Such dogs had to have pace, power, courage, determination and remarkable agility. A type gradually developed with immense stamina and impressive robustness, severely tested by both climate and terrain.

In his *Hunting Big Game in Africa with Dogs* (1924), the American sportsman, Er M. Shelley, wrote:

Dogs are very fond of hunting them [wart-hogs], but it usually proves disastrous for the dog, for these hogs

African Bloodhounds – developed by settler-farmers as an all-round hound.

Rhodesian Ridgeback at the 1999 Hound Show.

Rhodesian Ridgeback – classic par force hound.

have two long tusks that protrude far out from the lower jaw, and they use them with deadly effect. Dogs can be maimed or killed much more readily by hunting these hogs than by hunting lions.

The early settlers in remote areas of southern Africa faced enormous dangers when hunting for food or protecting their stock. The value to them of brave, determined, powerful dogs is inestimable.

Kobben, who arrived in the Cape only half a century after the first settlers under Jan van Riebeeck (1652), noted that the Hottentots used dogs for hunting and protection and that Europeans made regular use of such dogs. Lawrence Green, in his *Lords of the Last Frontier* (1936) described the bushmen hunting dog as 'a light brown ridgeback mongrel…ready to keep a wounded leopard at bay until the master finds

an opening for his spear.' The ancient Greeks would have admired that. Forty years ago, a game warden reported bushmen's hunting dogs in southwest Africa sporting prominent ridges. It's of interest that, at the Rhodesian Ridgeback World Congress 2006, Scottie Stewart, the South African delegate, gave a presentation of the work of the contemporary breed in the Kruger Game Reserve, working with rangers to warn them of any danger from approaching 'big beasts'; not one of them fitted the modern breed standard obeyed in the show ring.

Accounts of dogs owned by early Boer farmers embrace breeds such as Bloodhounds, Greyhounds, Bulldogs, Mastiffs, Foxhounds, Pointers, Bull Terriers and Airedales. The Bloodhound was crossed with other hound breeds to make it leaner and faster. 'Steekbaards', rough-coated dogs hinting at

Deerhound, Irish Wolfhound, Airedale and continental griffon blood, were favoured by many Boer hunters. Van Rooyen had one, which was killed by a sable antelope. A writer to the *Cape Times* once gave important clues as to the make-up of these big resolute hunting dogs used by farmers in the bush. The writer stated that when he was a boy (around 1887) his father, like nearly every farmer, kept steekbaard (stiff beard) or vuilbaard (dirty beard)-honde, the size of Greyhounds. The first ridged pups he ever saw, born on his father's farm, were out of a purebred English Bulldog bitch, by a steekbaard sire. All had a distinct ridge of hair along their spines. The sire was a descendant of steekbaard dogs brought from Swellendam, when the trek to the Colesberg district took place. Steekbaards were sometimes advertised as Boerhounds (as distinct from Boerbulls or Boerboels) and occasionally as 'lion dogs'.

Pioneer farmers needed powerful, determined dogs that would stand their ground when faced by predators such as marauding lions, leopards, wild dogs, jackals, hyenas, baboons, even human rustlers; this demanded the characteristics of the holding dogs, the famed mastiff group, and led to the development of Boerboel type dogs. Farmers also needed faster but equally determined dogs to hunt, running mastiffs by inclination, leading to the development of Boerhounds or lion dogs. In that climate and terrain, against such enemies, only the most virile dogs survived. One writer described the hounds used by farmers as rough-haired Greyhounds. The hunter-writer William Baldwin, in his *African Hunting from 1852 to 1860* (1863), described the hunting dogs he preferred: 'bull and greyhound, with a dash of the pointer, the best breed possible.' A later book of his was illustrated with a drawing of a 'ridged European dog'.

Inspired by Baldwin's book, a hunter called Frederick Courteney Selous travelled extensively until the 1890s, covering most of southern Africa. Later he hunted with van Rooyen, accounts of their dogs mentioning, again and again, rough-haired Greyhounds, Pointers (prized not only for their noses but for the robustness of their feet) and mongrels between these breeds and local dogs. The *Bulawayo Chronicle* contained the following references to breeds of dog in the period 1894–1917 (source: David Helgesen,

1982): Pointer (87), Bull Terrier (25), Greyhound (20), Bulldog (19), Airedale (15), Great Dane (14), Boarhound (11) and Deerhound (10). Also mentioned were a Cuban Mastiff, a Kangaroo Hound and a 'Ridgeback'.

Selous is forever mentioned by Ridgeback historians but I remain to be convinced about his standing as a hunter *with dogs*. His book, *A Hunter's Wanderings in Africa* of 1881, is made up of over 450 pages, more or less his hunting diary of the previous few years. In it he hardly mentions hunting with dogs. He refers to being a guest of the Rev. C.D. Helm (from whom van Rooyen bought his dogs), without mentioning his dogs. In his hunting exploits of 1876, he records: '...our mongrel pack. At the mere scent of the lion all but two rushed precipitately past us, not forwards, but backwards, with their tails between their legs, some of them yelping with fright; nor did they put in an appearance again until the hunt was over.' He doesn't come across as a dogman at all.

The first printed use of the word ridgeback for a breed was in a newspaper advertisement of 1912, offering 'Well bred "Ridgeback" hunting pups for sale.' An English vet working in Bulawayo, Charles Edmonds, took an interest in these 'ridged lion hunters', as he called them, and suggested classes for them at dog shows, based on a description of: height 24in, weight 60lb, colour tawny, fawn or brindle, coat short and hard, head rather broad, cheek muscles well developed, in the shape of the old Bull Terrier. That is a fair summary of the phenotype of any prototypal running mastiff. It is interesting to note that in *Hunting Big Game in Africa with Dogs*, Shelley observes on jackal hunting: 'There was a smooth-coated red dog in the bunch named 'Red' that did most of the catching. He was faster than the others and had a good nose.'

Another Englishman, Francis Barnes, settled in Salisbury in 1875 and became interested in the breed. He wrote to the national kennel club in 1925, stating that a breed club had been formed for the Rhodesian Ridgeback (Lion Dog) Club. Another Salisbury resident, B.W. Durham, a Bulldog exhibitor, helped Barnes to produce a breed standard and get the new breed recognized. In 1926, the South African Kennel Union recognized the breed. The Rhodesian Ridgeback is now recognized across the globe, gaining championship status in Britain in 1954 and admission to the American Kennel Club registry in 1955. The British KC correctly places the breed in its Hound Group, something it denies to the Great Dane.

I have long been impressed by Swedish hound breeders and that includes the Ridgebacks of Sonja Nilsson, who produces hounds like field tracking champion Roseridge Rusticana, the dam of several other tracking champions. It was interesting to listen to Lorraine Hulbert, a very successful American breeder from the mid-1950s up to her death in 1976, talk about her hounds; she called them 'brown Dalmatians', seeing many similarities between the two breeds. She pointed out that the original standard for the Ridgeback was based, almost word for word, on the Dalmatian standard, an indication to me of the hound identity of the latter. Their past function would have led to their design in words.

When working briefly in Kenya forty years ago, I was impressed by two Ridgebacks used by a local European farmer as par force hunting dogs on small deer; one was deep red, the other light wheaten, a coat colour I've never seen in the show ring. At the very first Ridgeback shows in South Africa and Rhodesia the prevalent coat colour was a smudgy beige, with yellow and near-white also featuring. There was mention too of black ones and brindles, never seen now, perhaps because the reds were usually the outstanding specimens both in the hunt and in the ring.

Comparable ridges on the backs of dogs have manifested themselves in Weimaraners and a pure-bred Labrador. Many fawn dogs of mastiff type, as well as Bulldogs and Boxers with red in their coats, have been known to display spinal markings of darker colouration and on hair with a different texture. A few years ago, in New Zealand, two pure-bred Mastiffs went through quarantine there, each featur-

An Ibex hunt in the Sudan, 1902, with local hounds.

ing a ridge of reverse hair along their spines.

This distinctive feature is, however, the hallmark of the African and Thailand breeds, with Rhodesian Ridgebacks respected all over the world for their hardiness and character. They may not be used as running mastiffs in the classic manner any more but their service to the early settlers, especially the hunter-farmers, was invaluable. A medieval master huntsman like Gaston de Foix would have admired them; they evolved in a tough environment and developed in a tougher school. We must now perpetuate them as famous African hunters designed them to be: hugely capable par force hounds, true running mastiffs. In America, the breed has now been allowed to compete in AKC Sighthound field trials; this could lead to a leggier, lighter-boned hound prized for its speed at the gallop ahead of its stamina and UK breeders need to aware of this change of use.

Basenjis

Just as the Finnish Spitz is difficult to identify as a gundog – a 'bark-pointer', or as a hound, working to the gun – the Basenji is similarly difficult to catego-

rize as either a scenthound or a sighthound. They are used in their homeland in small packs, hunting by sight, scent and their remarkable hearing. Valued as flushing dogs, they use their wide variety of hunting skills to find and drive game to the net or the spears of waiting hunters. This echoes the use of hounds in early medieval times in Europe. Known as a type from Sudan right across to the Congo, explorers and travellers from Europe were fascinated by them.

In 1897, Paul Schebesta, whilst exploring the Ituri Forest in the depths of the Belgian Congo (where they were called Saba Dogs, after the Queen of Sheba legend), wrote in his *My Pygmy and Negro Hosts*:

> The hunting dog, with wooden bell around its neck, is the faithful companion of the Bachwa and Bambuti pygmies. The marriage dowry varies in different localities, in one village it may be a matter of ten spears, with a hunting dog thrown in, in another village it is only five spears and a hunting dog…

The value of these small hunting dogs to these primitive people is made clear. The brindle coat colour

Superb Basenji.

has been traced to a Whippet owned by a missionary, with the black coat alleged to come from a Dobermann cross in Liberia. The Bongo tribe's dogs featured the bushy tail, the Dinka tribe's dogs being smooth-tailed. Some of the recent imports into the United States came from Zaire.

It was depressing to read the 2011 Crufts judge of the breed express concern at the loss of hound type in the entry. Those wishing to see them developed as *hounds*, rather than just another show dog, look for substance as well as clean-limbed elegance in their Basenjis. Some despair over obsessions with coat colour and facial wrinkle, often relegating soundness in favour of breed type. Last year I was told of one registering 32.6 seconds on a 400-yard track, a quite remarkable turn of speed. In 2011, twenty-eight were newly registered with our KC, forty-six in 2012; in 1979, 121 were registered. This is a breed that could disappear from our lists in the next half-century. From the ringside in 2012, I was impressed by Ch./Am. Ch. Klassics Million Dollar Baby at Tokaji – for me, a hound straight from the words of the breed standard.

Asian Breeds

Distinct Type

We know very little about the hounds of China, apart from artefacts and illustrations from ancient books, and these are often of hawking expeditions featuring sighthounds. But the Jindo of Korea and the Balinese Mountain Hound have become known, with some

The 'Oriental Hound' of 1840.

Hound in China, c.1750 by Giuseppe Castiglione (a court painter there).

of the former featuring in the Discover Dogs area at Crufts, after their importation in 2002. The Thai Ridgeback is exhibited at World Dog Shows but the Japanese breeds are the ones from this region of the world best known to us. The Jindo, from the island of that name in Korea, the Balinese breed and the Kishu of Japan are remarkably similar in type, all used as hounds and almost entirely in mountainous areas. Also from Korea comes another in this mould, the Cheju or Temla, introduced onto Cheju Island off the Korean coast from Cholkang Province in China, and used to hunt boar and deer, as well as indicate pheasant. The Jindos at Crufts attracted a great deal of attention, as many exotic breeds do initially in Britain; related to the rarer Poon-san and the shaggy-haired Sapsal, and all three now protected breeds in South Korea. The Jindo is renowned for its acute hearing and strong scenting powers, being used widely as a service dog.

The Hounds of Japan

Any mention of hounds in the Western world conjures up immediate images of elegant smooth-haired sighthounds, strongly built tricolour drop-eared scenthounds or rough-haired Griffons out of France. A prick-eared dog with a bushy tail curled over its back doesn't quite fit the bill, but the hounds of Japan are highly individual and deserve recognition. Two of their hunting dog breeds, the Akita and the Shiba, have become established here but as show dogs not sporting ones, and neither classified as hounds or sporting dogs by our Kennel Club. There were 226 Shibas registered here in 2011 and over a thousand Akitas, of both types, mainly the 'American' type, with only fifty of the *Japanese* Akita variety featuring – for me, a regrettable differentiation. The heavier, more powerful Akitas may have come down from the mixed breed dogs used for fighting and possess a different temperament from the Japanese type. The KC breed standard for the Akita mentions its role as a hunting dog on black bear, wild boar and deer, and for the Shiba describes its role as a hunting dog, mainly of ground game, but used to track larger game such as boar and deer; then classifies both, with remarkable perversity, not as hounds, but in its Utility Group.

I have long been intrigued by the native breeds of Japan, sparked initially by learning that genetically Japanese dog breeds, with one exception, originated

from a common ancestral type, in which both A and B haemoglobin alleles were present, whilst the European breeds originated from a different ancestral group in which the A allele was absent. My interest in one of their breeds, the Akita, was heightened on reading that the late Joe Braddon, arguably the greatest show judge of the late twentieth century here, rated a Japanese Akita he judged in Norway the best dog he ever saw. In a thirty-year career as an international judge, he must have gone over hundreds of thousands of dogs in the ring. By our definition a hound, the Akita is an impressive breed, having a tangible presence, an imposing self-assurance, almost a natural grandeur about it. The Japanese Akita weighs around 70–80lb but now there is a variation in America that weighs well over 100lb.

The international kennel club, the FCI, recognizes a number of Japanese hunting dogs: the Akita, the Ainu, the Kai, the Kishu and the Shiba, often named after the localities where they developed, with the Akita also called the Akita Matagi Inu or dog that hunts bears. The Ainu is also called the Hokkaido Dog, as it was favoured in the mountainous regions of Hokkaido Island. The black brindle Kai Dog was also called the Tiger Dog, because of its coat colour. The usually white Kishu was used as a hunting dog on the large island of Kyushu, with the Shiba Inu (or small dog) developed on Honshu Island, and now very popular in Britain. With over 200 a year being newly registered, the Shiba Inu seems well established but I know of no one using one as a hunting dog here. (There is a similar but slightly taller breed called the Shikoku, used to hunt deer, but not I believe known in Europe.)

The Shiba is an enchanting fox-like little dog with a hard, thick coat, sparkling eyes, an alert posture, attentive manner and inquisitive nature, so valuable in a hunting dog. They are used extensively on rabbit in Japan but are great ratters too, being determined, quick and extremely agile. Local varieties were named after the locality that favoured them, rather like our terriers of old. You hear of Mino Shiba, Shinshu Shiba, Sekishu Inu and so on; they were used to hunt small game, such as hare, racoon dog (tanuki), fox, weasel and birds. I have been very impressed by their soundness when viewing them both at English and overseas dog shows. This may be because to judge the breed in its native country you need demand-

The Akita of Japan – used on big game.

The Shiba Inu of Japan – used on small game.

ing training and extensive experience. It was good to read a show judge's critique in 2010 stating: 'Always remember the purpose and origin of the Shiba. A small hunting dog, very nimble, agile and able to leap from rock to rock, in its pursuit to hunt small game in the mountains of Japan.' It would be good to hear of their use hunting rabbits here. The ones I see in our show rings seem to have heavier bone and straighter stifles with higher hocks – a feature sometimes criticized through a misunderstanding of the phrase 'well let down at hock', originally intended to produce long cannon bones, not low-set hocks.

The strong brindle colours of the Kai Ken, its versatility in the hunting field and its sheer charm as a breed have made it an immediate favourite outside its home country. There are two bloodlines in the breed that determine their physical characteristics: Dairo and Kaikuro; the first being lighter and used on deer, the other stocky and used in the boar hunt. It has been claimed that three Kai Ken can bring down a full-grown boar. They are very much mountain hunting dogs, agile, sure-footed and very determined. Increasingly popular in the United States and Canada, they are valued as companion dogs more than hunting dogs.

Far better known here is the Akita, although the division in the breed causes much confusion away from the show rings. At a championship show in Germany a few years ago, one of Japan's leading experts on their native breeds, Kosuke Kawakita, gave this advice on breeding them: do not overdo the white markings, especially on the face. Make use of brindle dogs to lessen the pale colours that occur prevalently in this breed. Conserve the characteristic facial expression of the breed that mainly relies on correct ear placement. Breed for a strong lower jaw, look for a rounded appearance when viewing the jaw from the front. He stated that the original breed standard was based on hunting dogs, not ornamental ones.

Some of the show dogs are strikingly imposing; I admire particularly the two-tone, black over silver or fawn undercoat or Kuro-goma type, a really eye-catching variety. I have seen some impressive Akitas in Britain but others have displayed temperamental flaws, probably from being owned by the wrong people – they did become 'status dogs' for a while. I was impressed by one: Ch. Redwitch Prince Consort at Stecal, of great type, attractive coat colour and the

right size. In 2012, from the ringside, I was very taken with Kabu Shine Thru Shyllar, full of breed type and soundness. In Japan, just after World War II, three types of the breed emerged: the Matagi Akita or bear-hound; the Fighting Akita or Kong-go dogs with

The Thai Ridgeback – an impressive hound.

mastiff blood; and the Shepherd Akita, used as a flock protector. The first type is the true one, the second one is to be avoided. The Akita was always intended to be a hound.

The Thai Ridgeback (Mah Thai)

Another ridged breed, the Thai Ridgeback Dog is gaining popularity; a light chestnut red, pure black and silver blue (acknowledged mastiff colours), it is 24in at the shoulder, weighing 60–75lb, very similar to the African dog. Claims have been made that the African dog descends from a ridged dog, the Phu Quoc dog, found in the Gulf of Siam, with some suggesting a westward movement of such dogs. My view is that it is more likely for the African ridged dogs to have been taken to Asia with black slaves, that is, an eastward movement. The Arabs were trading slaves to Canton and Siam as long ago as AD900 (Jeffreys, 1953). I have been quite impressed by the quality of the dogs of this breed entered for World Dog Show classes, mainly from one American kennel. I do hope that 'breeding for the ridge' doesn't blind show breeders to the soundness required in a breed with a small

gene pool outside its native country. The ridge in this breed is less 'fiddle-shaped' and more a straight raised spinal ridge than in the African dog. I see some that are too facially wrinkled for their future well-being and I do hope this tendency is not bred for by those fanciers who view this as a 'unique breed feature'; it is not, and the exaggerators need curbing, as in any breed. There is a danger too that such a breed can become desired because of its exoticness, rather than its innate qualities. This is an imposing, very individual breed, deserving to be perpetuated as a hound.

Throughout more than 99 per cent of human history, hunting has been an unchallenged tap root of life, as well as a cornerstone of culture. Often, the success of hunters has meant the difference between feast or famine, and their exploits and service to the community have been celebrated in song and story, setting standards as positive role models. In fact, throughout nearly all of human history, hunters have been unchallenged cultural heroes.

James A. Swan, *The Sacred Art of Hunting: Myths, Legends and Modern Mythos* (1999)

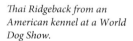

Thai Ridgeback from an American kennel at a World Dog Show.

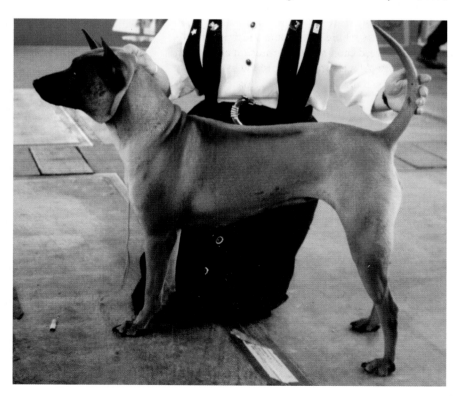

CHAPTER 4

THE FUTURE

Breeding Healthier Hounds

Our rich hunting heritage has left us with an impressive array of native hound breeds, with the Foxhound a leading figure. Less well known outside their own circles are the even longer established Harrier, the loyally supported Trail Hound and the relatively recently introduced English Basset. Distinct types like the Welsh Hound, the Fell Hound and the Staghound are little known beyond the hunting fraternity. Sadly we have lost the most distinctive, arguably best-bred, pack of Dumfriesshire Foxhounds, with their gleaming black and tan jackets and superlative field performance. Introduced into the show rings here in the last half century are any number of foreign hounds, ranging from the Hamiltonstovare from Sweden, the Segugio from Italy, the Basset Fauve de Bretagne and the Grand Bleu de Gascogne from France to the Bavarian Mountain Hound from Germany and the Shiba Inu from Japan. Pure-breeding, or rather, the misguided mindsets of modern breeders, means, however, that their blood cannot be used to widen the gene pool of either our native breeds or each other; even though informed outcrossing created all these breeds in the first place.

Breeding Within

The traditional breeding technique in the twentieth century and just before was to restrict breeding to within a breed and often within the pack. In *The Book of Foxhunting* (1977), J.N.P. Watson quotes the Earl Bathurst, Master of the Vale of the White Horse, on the latter:

> I do not object to breeding rather closely occasionally if I am sure that the dog or bitch is absolutely right and a particularly good one. There are instances of this that have turned out extraordinarily well. As a rule the fourth generation is near enough, and, if one can arrange for what I call a double cross, that is when two separate hounds' names occur in the fourth generation of both sire and dam, it is most advantageous, again, that is, that they are both sterling good hounds in their work…

Healthy-looking hunting Bassets.

Diane Cooke with her fine Tedandi couple and a half of Hamiltonstovares.

Watson also quotes the legendary breeder, 'Ikey' Bell as advising:

> If your hounds are a well-bred lot, with a history sheet of constitution and stamina and no hereditary faults, such hounds can be bred closer to than those of a less excellent strain. It would be playing for safety if no name repeats itself prior to the fourth line, and then only once. On the other hand, if the hounds spring from different strains, it is necessary to breed closer, so as to form a uniform type…

It is the pursuit of a uniform type in breeds that can lead to unwise inbreeding by breeders with less knowledge and experience than those quoted. It is unskilled, unknowing breeders that breed too closely, producing offspring lacking constitution and virility and all too often with genetic flaws. Breeding outside breed gene pools is rarely permitted by national kennel clubs, even when inherited defects are appearing. When appearance is all, this is a predictable outcome.

Blind Pursuit of Purity

I have given space to hound breeds little known here: the well-established Swiss harehounds like the Lucernois, the many varieties of French, those of the Balkans and the Baltic, as well as those of Eastern Europe. Some of these are very similar to breeds well known here, as function decided type, and they represent a reservoir of untapped genes, increasingly valuable as small gene pools reveal their limitations. Foxhound breeders have long resorted to outcrosses to retain virility and maintain performance. Lurchermen pride themselves on the prowess obtained from the judicious use of mixed blood. For the show ring however the pursuit of breed purity is all, despite the loss of robustness and litter-size, as well as the veterinary costs resulting from such irrational and unjustifiable recalcitrance.

A sound Bavarian Mountain Hound.

A top-class Italian Segugio – the smooth-coated variety.

Outcrosses have been made in KC-registered pedigree breeds, *and authorized*: Greyhound blood in the Deerhound and English Springer blood in the Field Spaniel, for example. The Irish Wolfhound was recreated using Deerhound blood, with an outcross to the Tibetan Mastiff too. The Mastiff has been recast, sadly not in its traditional form, using foreign blood like the Great Dane, the smooth St Bernard and the Tibetan Mastiff. In working terriers the Plummer, the Sporting Lucas and the Lucas came from deliberate blends of other terrier breeds. As writers like 'Idstone' and 'Stonehenge' testify, our sporting ancestors often used

Old blue-mottled Foxhound Roamer, depicted by Robert Polhill Bevan in 1890.

mixed blood. The KC once recognized cross-bred re-trievers and registered them as such. French hound breeders prize the blended product, as the very names of their packs demonstrate: Anglo-Français Tricolore, Grand Gascon-Saintongeois, and so on. It's worth noting that an influential Foxhound, Carmarthen Nimrod '24, had no less than four breeds in the first three generations of his pedigree. They were: the old Devonshire Harrier of blue-mottled Southern blood, Kerry Beagle, Bloodhound and a dog hound from the Badminton kennel.

Inbreeding Concerns

If the coefficient of inbreeding is a source of worry in some imported and native pedigree hound breeds, as it is, there is ample breeding stock from outside Brit-ain to blend with breeds based on a limited number of original imports. If, say, the Hamiltonstovare is be-coming inbred, then the blood of the Finnish Hound or the Schillerstovare would be an ideal reinforce-ment. If the show Bloodhound is becoming too closely bred or too exaggerated for its own comfort, then just as the blood of the Dumfriesshire Foxhound was once utilized in the packs, that of the Gonczy Polski or Polish Hound, or the Jura Hound of Switzerland could be introduced. Why is mixed blood prized in the creation of breeds but scorned when an infusion of unrelated blood would benefit today's hounds? Is it breed-blindness, breeder-ignorance or fear of losing type? The coefficients of inbreeding (COIs) can be ascertained for each pedigree scenthound breed rec-ognized by the KC by consulting their helpful website for this. Some breed COIs are worryingly high.

Geneticist Bruce Cattanach crossed the Boxer with the Corgi to obtain a tail-less Boxer; after three gen-erations no one could tell the resultant Boxers from the long-pure-bred ones. I see Mastiffs at Crufts that are more like Alpine Mastiffs (as the ancestor blood comes through) than the Mastiff of England – and no Mastiff fancier seems to care! If you dared to suggest

Outstanding hounds – Kerry Beagles, depicted by Arthur Wardle in 1899.

to them that true type has been lost, they would just shrug. So much for the importance of true type! As a boarhound, the Great Dane, more aptly named the German (Hunting) Mastiff, was never as huge as it is now. More hounds died in the boar hunt than boars; to survive they had to be superbly agile, immensely athletic and physically superlatively coordinated. Today's type could not hunt the boar; pedigree breeders prefer the show type to the real thing in any number of breeds. The Plott Hound in America typifies the real big game hound, true to type and wholly unexaggerated. The KC's slogan of 'Fit for Function' needs to be rigorously applied to the scenthound breeds recognized by them.

Informed Outcrossing

Uninformed outcrossing is *not* the answer; there has to be research as well as vision. In the wake of the revealing BBC TV programme *Pedigree Dogs Exposed* of 2006, leading geneticist Steve Jones wrote and was quoted in several newspapers, that for pedigree breeds of dog 'a universe of suffering' is ahead with continued inbreeding. Fellow geneticist Bruce Cattanach was similarly quoted as stating: '…inbreeding has been ingrained in dog breeder psyche from the beginning and is hard to break, even when it is possible to show that it is not the most successful way to breed…'. He went on to state that some pedigree breeds may well become extinct in our lifetimes without intervention, advising outcrossing to other

related breeds. But who will listen to him; dogma will prevail and not just lurchermen will wonder at such folly – and such damage to long-established breeds. I did, however, see a Beagle-Basset cross at a show at the Heythrop kennels a few years ago, an unexaggerated, sound, symmetrical hound. In the world of the pedigree hound there is so much untapped breeding material – and so many closed minds!

In her *Bridleways through History* (1936), Lady Apsley includes an Appendix giving an account of a visit by the distinguished sporting artist and sportsman, Lionel Edwards, to the kennels of David Davies' Welsh Foxhounds at Llandinam:

A mixed lot. Cross bred: Welsh-English, English-Fell. Fell-Welsh-English, Welsh (pure bred). The purebred Welsh mostly white, rough-coated, with high occipital crest, as No.2.

No.1. Rough-coated, red-tan in colour with white nose, collar, pads and tip of stern… Mr David Davies himself prefers the rough white-coated and breeds for them… Many were smooth-coated and typical Fell Hounds, from which they were bred – being only first and second crosses – these, of course, not eligible for Welsh stud book… There seemed to be some difference of opinion on type, as one rough-coated looked a very small bitch, had a ruff and the general appearance of a collie, yet took a prize at Welshpool.

Beagle × Basset Hound; a strong symmetrical hound.

The Llandeilo Farmers' Hound Show 2012. A hound trail followed this show.

Whatever their looks, hounds have to function; breeding for type and a level pack is a refinement.

Crufts Material

The claim by the KC that Crufts is a show for the 'Best of the Very Best' is in conflict with the critiques produced by the judges they appoint to officiate there. In 2011, the Beagle judge found too many incorrect bites; the 2012 Beagle judge complained of far too many poor fronts; the 2012 Bloodhound judge was disappointed by the bite and the amount of haw in the eyes of the entry; the 2012 judge of Grand Bassets Griffon Vendeen found a lot left to be desired in the hindquarters – high hocks, cow hocks and narrow thighs – and in the movement of the entry; the 2012 Rhodesian Ridgeback judge wasn't pleased with the jaw shape in far too many of the entry; the 2012 Basset Hound judge found the ears still far too long – a persistent fault in this breed.

In the championship shows in recent years, even more worrying faults have been reported. Beagles have been shown with short rib cages, distressing movement and poor bites. Bassets and Bloodhounds were found to have incorrect movement and worrying anatomical flaws. Rhodesian Ridgebacks displayed poor feet and a lack of drive from behind. Hamiltonstovares were found to be lacking substance and quality of bone. Norwegian Elkhounds seem to have poor rear angulation as a persistent fault. I would be surprised if these pedigree dogs were not bred from; you do not get healthier hounds from flawed stock.

KC Action

The KC lists both the Bloodhound and the Basset Hound on their 'High Profile Breeds' or 'vulnerable breeds' register, that is, those pedigree breeds, registered with them, with visible exaggerations, potentially harmful. Many prominent show breeders, but not prolific breeders, have striven to reduce the likelihood of this but of course, as always, it's the puppy farmers, not the leading show kennels, that

A KC show Basset Hound 2012.

A KC show Foxhound, sound but lacking hard muscle.

stand to benefit from what, sadly, some members of the public see as 'appealing' in pups with soulful eyes, an abundance of loose skin and a cartoon-like appearance. Writing on the Basset Hound in *Dog World* in November 2012, Sandra Thexton gave the view that:

> Very few "show breeders" register puppies. Most who do are unknown to us and some advertise puppies as having extra long ears, droopy skin, and droopy eyes – something we have been trying to avoid for many years. These 'breeders' are hard to track down and influence. We are easy meat…

And in the same issue, the distinguished Bloodhound breeder Sue Emrys-Jones, wrote: 'The majority of breeders will always try to breed with care and forethought. After all, it is not to their advantage to churn out Bloodhounds that have poor eyes, are unsound and are generally over-exaggerated.' Such hound breeders have my sympathy; until the KC actually examines specimen litters from *prolific* breeders, the perennial difficulty of ensuring that only the soundest of hounds are bred will persist. That is bad news for any breed.

KC Progress
After a century of neglecting the health aspects of pedigree dog breeds, and perhaps shamed by the hard-hitting BBC TV documentary of 2006, *Pedigree Dogs Exposed*, the KC has, to their credit, now embarked on wide-ranging activity to examine and oversee the production of healthier pedigree breeds. Their Dog Health Group supervises the 'Fit for Function' campaign, from which the hound breeds especially should benefit. Their Assured Breeder Scheme Sub-Group puts into operation those health screening requirements agreed by the Dog Health Group in close cooperation with breed clubs and councils. Their Breed Standards and Conformation Sub-Group now works with breed clubs on specific conformation-related health issues.

Two particular hound breeds certainly need such work. In 2012, officially appointed observers and expert judges raised these specific issues: on the Basset Hound – eyes, excessive haw, incorrect bite, inadequate ground clearance, teeth, eyelid conformation, unsound movement, short in upper arm and upright in shoulder, obesity, excessive wrinkle and, worryingly, temperament; and on the Bloodhound – incorrect bite, eyes, unsound movement and, just as worrying, temperament. This relates to a relatively small number in each breed, not the breed itself, but these two breeds still deserve close scrutiny, after well over a century of wholly unsupervised breed-led indifference to the gross exaggeration in some show specimens. I give the KC great credit for facing up to their responsibilities in such a serious matter.

Breed Involvement

The main area for future action however may well lie with breed clubs ahead of national schemes. If you take the breed of Otterhound, for example, there is an urgent requirement for all those breeding Otterhounds to look hard at the highly unsatisfactory situation regarding hip scores in the breed. Over the last fifteen years some 230 Otterhounds have been hip-scored, providing a breed mean score of 46.7 – with over 50 as the mean score for the last five years. The next worst is the Bulldog! There is clearly a giant task ahead of Otterhound breeders to improve these disturbing statistics. As far as elbow scores go in this breed, 120 hounds have been scored, giving a summary of 41 per cent at zero, 38 per cent at 1, 25 per cent at 2 and nearly 6 per cent at 3. Hounds scoring 2 or 3 should not be bred from; of the 120 scored this would mean that thirty-seven should not be used in breeding programmes – but it may well be that they are! Breed clubs cannot just react to edicts from above, they are the guardians of the breed and without a conscientious commitment from within a breed, the work of the KC is not likely to succeed.

Colour Prejudice

Breeding sound but still typical hounds has long been a challenge. But it has never been wise to reduce breeding stock by favouring a colour, to the neglect of good dogs in an unfavoured colour. Commenting on the widespread desire at one time for the 'Belvoir' tan in hounds, hound expert Earl Bathurst, in his *The Breeding of Foxhounds* (1926), wrote:

> This fashion, for it is nothing more than a fashion, is really quite a modern invention, and rather an unfortunate one, for some breeders of hounds it is almost carried to excess, with more thought of breeding for colour than work… I believe this fashion for the tan colour has done an immense amount of harm. It has caused the destruction of hundreds, perhaps thousands of whelps…

This could be said of any number of pedigree hound breeds on the show circuit. As described in an earlier chapter, a century ago the distinguished vet and sportsman Frank Townend Barton destroyed a white pup born to a Bloodhound dam, sired by another Bloodhound, later greatly regretting the loss of this genetically valuable offspring. I can remember George Leake, when Joint Master of the Shropshire Beagles in the 1980s, telling me of the rare coat colour known as 'Berkeley Blue' cropping up in Beagle

A top-quality show Bloodhound – Maplemead Melodean from Marksbury.

Ridge-less Rhodesian Ridgeback.

litters; he found it often came along with light-coloured eyes, which he didn't favour, but he mourned the loss of the old blue-mottled coat colour. Coat colours and coat features, like texture, don't 'make' the hound. I recently saw an outstanding Rhodesian Ridgeback that had been neutered – just because it didn't feature the expected fiddle-shaped spinal ridge; what a loss of quality material to valueless prejudice. If you want healthier hound breeds, get rid of such a mindset!

Health Surveys

How I wish that all pedigree hound breeders would match the work of the Petit Basset Griffon Vendeen and Griffon Vendeen clubs worldwide, whose health survey resulted in 524 owners providing details on 1,148 hounds for subsequent analysis. This gives a base line for future study: scientists need *data*! A large international survey like this one is, for any breed, a major step forward and all other hound breed clubs must aim to match this valuable study.

Show Bloodhound with excessively loose skin.

Basset Hound at Crufts, 1991; over-long ears and loose eyelids punish the hound.

There is work to be done, for example, in the Basset Fauve de Bretagne breed, where, admittedly in a small survey, chronic kidney problems were cited as common a cause of death as cancer or heart disease. The work on dog health in countries like Finland and Sweden shames us but if the example of the 'GV' fraternity can be matched by the other pedigree hound breed clubs and associations, the hounds would in time greatly benefit. The introduction, in 2013, of the Karlton Index Health Awards, pioneered by Philippa Robinson, which recognize the time and effort invested in breed health by *breeders and breed clubs*, is a most praiseworthy advance in the promotion of health surveys and should make a really positive contribution to the future health of the dog. I do hope that every hound breed club steps forward and strongly supports this admirable initiative.

Breed-Specific Instructions

The Swedish KC has a routine programme, the Breed Specific Instruction (BSI), regarding exaggerations in pedigree dogs, which is a complement to the breed standards in forty-six high-profile breeds. These breeds have been accepted by them as being at risk in their health and soundness due to the exaggerations in breed points preferred by show ring judges – and therefore selected as breeding stock. The BSI is made up of recommendations, not imposed rules, so that the integrity and independence of judges is respected. These BSI routines have been applied to all official Swedish KC shows since 2009; it is widely accepted by Swedish breed clubs that this system will be, in the long term, beneficial to their breeds.

A watered-down scheme has been introduced by our KC but has been greeted with aggressive resentment amounting to rebellion. This situation does not reflect well on our clubs. Would the show Basset Hound not benefit from shorter ears, a shorter spine and less crooked legs? Would the show Bloodhound not be healthier with shorter ears and less skin abundance on its head and throat? The good breeders in these breeds are quite capable of breeding out harmful exaggerations; who is going to force those actually favouring such excesses to change their ways? The KC controls the registry and is therefore in a strong position to insist on cooperation – or decline registration. As I point out above, the KC *is* improving its guardianship over breed health; now it must become even more demanding in the name of healthier dogs. If its newish slogan 'Making a difference for dogs' is not to be mere words, the KC simply *has* to place healthy dogs ahead of handsome ones. Breeding healthier dogs takes sustained effort and great determination, backed by informed enlightened judges, and this I cover in the next section.

My justification for out-crossing hounds is connected to two sound fundamentals that were drummed into me by Bill Goodson, a man renowned for success in breeding many varieties of stock: First, never be satisfied by what you have achieved in breeding, and, second, the importance of injecting hybrid vigour into long-established lines, whether human or canine! These were two maxims he had already proven over 40 years of practice, over many generations of hounds, before I appeared on the scene.

Martin Letts, *Memories of My Life at the College Valley* (2012)

Looking At Hounds – Making A Judgement

In 1911, there were nearly four hundred packs in Great Britain and Ireland, not counting foot harriers, beagles, and otter hounds. The first hound show was held at Redcar, in 1859, and since then exhibitions have, little by little, augmented interest in the show points of hounds, regardless of their working ability, until the show type English foxhound has become marvelously uniform in a certain standard of conformation most pleasing to the eye that is accustomed to such a standard. However, whilst this 'perfection to please the eye' has gone on, certain qualities have been neglected, notably, nose and cry. Its cry is now deficient, and its nose is regarded by many as the most inefficient in any breed of scenting hound.

Joseph B. Thomas, *Hounds and Hunting through the Ages* (1937)

Do you have 'an eye for a dog'? According to old timers, if you have this 'eye' you could be placed in a ring with a large class of a breed you've never seen before and not only come up with the best four dogs in order of merit, but also be able to declare in detail how each of the others depart from basic canine balance… Having an 'eye for a dog' combines both science and art. Knowledge of the science of the dog and the ability to develop an appreciation for the art involved are required for the successful judge and exhibitor. On the science side, you must know the purpose a breed serves. This provides the clues as to how the dog should be structured and move. The art involves the ability to recognize beauty, form, symmetry and style – in other words the dog's aesthetic appeal. One category complements the other. Without the application of science, judging would be poor, and the same can be said for art.

Robert W. Cole, *An Eye for a Dog* (2004)

Looking at hounds will always be a source of joy to me, the condition of the hounds alone giving so much pleasure. A hound show, especially one as well-conducted as the annual Honiton or Dunster Lawns events, is for me a celebration of all the pleasures provided by these canine athletes. The sheer style and restrained pageantry of judging at a hound show adds to this celebration, a welcome contrast to the urban atmosphere of most KC-licensed dog shows. Thirty years ago I was standing at the ringside of a KC championship dog show when I overheard the following conversation. Younger man: 'Why does the judge need to put his hands on the dogs?' Older man: 'Because you don't become an architect by staring at walls!' I was reminded of this snatch of conversation when at-

Foxhounds on the flags at Belvoir.

The Puppy Show at Wynnstay by Terence Cuneo.

Tiverton Foxhounds on parade.

Hounds get ready for judging at Dunster, 2010.

tending the 1999 hound show at Honiton and one a decade later on Dunster Lawns. The judges were immaculately attired; the hounds beautifully presented; their handlers colourful and impressive; the sun shone, all was right with the world; but was it?

Hounds on Parade

The splendid Honiton show, with its dazzling array of hounds – Beagles, Harriers, Foxhounds, Staghounds and Minkhounds – is always rewarding to visit but this time I felt disappointed. First of all, only the Minkhound judge examined the mouths of exhibits; does dentition, 'bite' and jaw construction not matter in animals designed to hunt? Secondly, the hounds were never touched by the judges, to verify muscle tone, bone and the construction of key joints. Thirdly, the hounds could only be animated in the ring by being urged to chase a constant shower of small biscuits. To me this totally degrades canine athletes bred to near perfection and shown in superb condition. Here were magnificent hounds from distinguished packs being treated like village curs. Could they really not show off their movement without such demeaning public bribery?

Writing on this in *Hounds* magazine in December 1994, 'Mariner' contributed to a debate on Beagle judging at a hound show by giving the view:

This summer, as I walked out my own hounds... I pondered more and more on...how we judge our beagle hounds... In the show ring, we 'stand' our

hounds – and 'move them'. This entails getting them, by judicious dispensing of biscuit, to gallop continually from one end of the ring to the other. This is an important 'exercise', because it helps to judge 'stride' and 'balance'. But at the gallop it is very difficult to see how straight a hound moves... In the horse world or at championship dog shows, no judge would want to put up any entry that he had not seen fully at the slow paces as well as the fast... Finally, why do hound judges never look at a hound's mouth?

I share his concerns; it is not just the knowledge the judges possess but the technique they use to ensure their knowledge is precisely applied that matters.

Hands-on Examination

After several months of watching all too many overweight, under-muscled dogs parading, sometimes waddling, around the rings at KC conformation shows, it was a delight at Honiton to see the rippling muscles, effortless movement and sheer athleticism of these well-bred functional animals. These were surely the best of the best, this was their day, rosettes awaited. But then came a further disappointment as I studied one or two hounds quite closely and was allowed to run my hands over them. Behind the muscular suppleness, graceful outlines and noble bearing were some of the long-acknowledged anatomical scenthound faults: fleshy feet, toeing-in, over-boned pasterns and ramrod-straight forelegs when viewed from the side. This was disappointing,

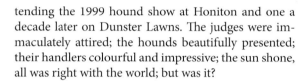

because although none of these flaws were present to an alarming degree, these were the very best hounds of their packs, carefully selected representatives.

I suppose it could be argued that if hounds can hunt successfully over a long day in difficult country, then that is the best possible test for them. But a hound show is a competition to find the best-made hounds, often with breeding programmes in mind. If judges are not going to bother to look at mouths, examine the feet or feel the shoulders and loins of the exhibits, faults can so easily be overlooked. If hounds can be entered, not only to represent their pack but also to strive for the honours, whilst carrying noticeable physical flaws, then, behind all the admirable glamour of such a prestigious show, is there *real* credibility?

That may sound over-critical and as though arguing a case for fault-judging, with the latter of course something to be discouraged. But I don't want our precious hounds to be judged on the bloom of their coats, their showiness when 'stacked' or their flashy markings but on their *soundness*. In any sporting dog, and especially in a hound used to hunt live quarry, feet and legs, shoulders and loins, the position of the elbow and jaw construction are vitally important. If the hounds taken to a hound show to be judged on the flags by the experts of the day have worrying faults, what are the hounds like that are left in kennels?

The Importance of Respecting Function

I have written earlier on how, in the second half of the nineteenth century, the Foxhound fraternity lost its collective head and actually favoured massive leg bone, over-knuckled feet, bunched toes and woefully pin-toed fronts. The redoubtable 'Ikey' Bell and his followers fought hard against such folly and the penalty to a hound of being over-timbered or unsound afoot was eventually conceded. Quite why any lover of hounds would want them to resemble carthorses has never been satisfactorily explained. What is frightening about what Daphne Moore, the greatly respected writer on hounds, has called the 'shorthorn' era is that so many highly experienced MFHs and huntsmen went along with the foolishness of the day. Consensual foolishness is still foolishness!

That is why it is worth the risk of being accused of being hypercritical and of suggesting judging on faults. At a time when there are serious external threats to our native hounds we can do without internal ones. When I have judged working terriers, I have assessed their physical soundness, the ability of their anatomy to allow them to perform in the field. When I judged working tests for gundogs, I assessed them on their working skills as displayed at the time. When I have judged, say, American Bulldogs, a breed without, today, a discernible role or defined functional purpose, I have looked for the construction of a 'catch-dog' or 'holding dog', as once needed by primitive hunters to 'grip' their quarry after the scenthounds had hunted and 'bayed' it. Sporting dogs, whatever their cosmetic appeal, have to relate to their function. Their original function will have shaped them the most.

Breeding Hounds for Show

Major Maurice Barclay, in *Hounds & Dogs* (Lonsdale Library, 1932), makes a point for me when he states: '...it is with the working capabilities of a foxhound in view that judges at Hound Shows look for certain points. These points are not just for show purposes to please the eye and fashion only, as so many unthinking sportsmen seem to imagine.' I would like to see hound show judges, and 'not just for show purposes', examine mouths. Buchanan-Jardine, in his well-known *Hounds of the World* (1937), wrote that: 'In judging hounds, little or no attention is paid, as a rule, to their heads...' Whatever the precedent, that cannot be good sense; heads, especially jaws, really do matter.

Buchanan-Jardine also wrote: '...that exaggerated straightness which causes a hound to turn his toes right in, is a mistake.' At Honiton there were several hounds with pin-toed fronts. There were several hounds there that were far too straight in the foreleg when viewed from the side. In *Foxes, Foxhounds and Fox-hunting* (1928), Richard Clapham noted that: 'It will be easily understood that the shorter and straighter the pastern, the more jar will there be, and the quicker will it be carried to the knee, and so upwards. Also, the heavier the bone, the greater the concussion...' There were several hounds at this show that were too straight in the pastern in profile and over-boned at the knee.

In her informative *Foxhounds* of 1981, Daphne

ABOVE: *The Llandeilo Farmers' Hound Show at Llangadog, 2012.*
RIGHT: *The Welsh Beagle Club's Championship Show, 2012.*

Moore wrote: 'Good clean flat bone, similar to that of a greyhound, is the type required, not the rounded vulgar variety…' Why would anyone want a hound with thick ankles? When the esteemed Beckford wrote in his *Thoughts on Hunting* (1781) on the Foxhound 'Let his legs be straight as arrows…', he meant when seen from the front, not the side. Most of the hounds in the ring at Honiton in 1999 were excellent. Some, however, displayed too much weight on the forehand, standing on the outside of each foot, pin-toed fronts, out at elbow, knuckling over at the knee and bunched-up toes. Some may have had defective mouths but this would have gone undiscovered. But feet and knees are even more important.

Show-Ring Follies
I have seen some quite magnificent scenthounds on parade in show rings, from Honiton to Hungary; I have also seen, both in kennel club conformation shows around Europe and in shows for hounds from the packs in England, some disappointingly mediocre ones. At Crufts you expect to see 'the Best of the Very Best', as the KC promises. But I do see Beagles there with too much flesh, far heavier bone than in say, a top-quality hunting pack like the Dummer, and with front feet that toe-in. The Basset Hounds there are to me woeful exaggerations of hounds originally bred for the hunting field. The Bassets Fauve de Bretagne, however, usually impress. The Otterhounds seem to

be heading away from the waterproof coats of their ancestors and the Bloodhounds are too loose-lipped, over-dewlapped and too throaty. I have seen a couple of sound Foxhounds, but their breeding was closer to the packs. I like the look of the Bavarian Mountain Hounds and the Vendeen Bassets. The Hamilton-stovares are a handsome breed but how good it would be to see a parade of Harriers, Fell Hounds, Trail Hounds, Welsh Hounds and Staghounds from the packs.

The total separation of the three sports, showing, trailing and hunting, does not benefit the hounds. The show breeders could learn a great deal from the hunting field, and mutual understanding in times when opportunities for using hounds are so curtailed has to be for the better. It would be good to see the KC encourage the packs to attend their open-air shows – and have the very best long-term interests of the hound breeds at the front of their minds. In the last half-century I have enjoyed learning from attendance at seven different World Dog Shows, held from Helsinki to Lisbon, innumerable KC-approved dog shows and many Hound Shows for hounds of the packs; the sadness for me has been the realization that there would be enormous benefit to the hounds, especially the KC-registered ones, for there to be cross-attendance, that is, the huntsmen meeting the showmen. It should start with the judges! When the Otterhound first came across from the packs, it was the practice to invite judges from their former packs to act as show judges, so retaining the focus on function. The current rules on show judge qualifications may now preclude this – a great pity and not in the best interests of hounds.

In his informative book *The Dog: Structure and Movement*, published in 1970, R.H. Smythe, a vet and exhibitor, wrote:

> …many of the people who keep, breed and exhibit dogs, have little knowledge of their basic anatomy or of the structural features underlying the physical formation insisted upon in the standards laid down for any particular breed. Nor do many of them – and this includes some of the accepted judges – know, when they handle a dog in or outside the show ring, the nature of the structures which give rise to the varying contours of the body, or why certain types of conformation are desirable and others harmful.

There are many misconceptions amongst show breeders and exhibitors, as I have set out in Chapter 1; some concern the angulation of the hindquarters, some affect the thinking behind short legs in breeds like the Basset Hound and, more generally, the shoulder placement in scenthounds that rely on pace, sustained pace.

Show-Ring Faults

When I first went to KC-approved championship dog shows over fifty years ago, the judges of hounds were often from the hunting field, men who knew the demands of the chase on scenthounds. In the twenty-first century this is rare and in time, as the Hunting Act restricts experience, hounds at such shows are going to be judged by people with no knowledge of the field use of the hounds before them. This could be disastrous for the breeding of functional hounds. You only have to look at judges' critiques in the last few years to see the falling away of standards in this Group of show dogs. The judge at the Basset Hound Club's 2011 June show stated that, as in most places around the world, the front assembly in the breed is not correct, with short upper and forearms, leading to short-stepping. Such a fault is serious in a hunting dog relying on stamina to succeed. The judge at the Bloodhound Club's show in that same month, and an ex-working trial owner, lamented the loss of true

head shape in the breed, faulting the narrow muzzles on view at the show. I have written of the Richmond Show judge's scathing remarks in the section on the Bloodhound in Chapter 2. It was alarming to read of several Rhodesian Ridgeback judges reporting weak pasterns and even flat feet in the entry, not good news in a hound breed. The Crufts judge of Rhodesian Ridgebacks in 2009 reported that:

> Fronts and front movement were disappointing in a lot of cases… Some dogs had rather short ribcages combined with long loins, which is a poor combination in this breed which should excel in endurance and strength of movement. Some had weak pasterns, combined with poor feet, another severe fault in a hound breed.

How could such exhibits *qualify* for Crufts with these faults?

Soundness before Beauty

For any hound carrying such disadvantages to be even taken to a KC show for hounds is disturbing. For the exhibitors to be seemingly unaware of such basic flaws is even more disturbing. Judges at such events have to ask themselves 'Could the hound in front of me succeed in the hunting field?' A KC judge knows that the entry before him will be bred from. The late Sir Newton Rycroft wrote in *Hounds* magazine (winter, 1987): '…if a *truly great breeder* wins prizes at a big hound show in front of two good judges, all credit to him, he will never let it affect his breeding plans…' Wise words; hound shows have a role but there needs to be a concentration not on canine beauty but on structural soundness. The judges have immense influence too – their mistakes or misconceptions affect breeding plans and therefore the future of a breed.

In his valuable book *Hounds and Hunting* (1937), Joseph B. Thomas, a respected American MFH, wrote:

> The British are the greatest breeders of livestock the world has ever seen or probably will see. They breed their mares to the winner of the Derby; they breed their greyhound bitches to the Winner of the Waterloo Cup; and yet they often breed their foxhound bitches to the Winner of the Peterborough Show, which winner is judged…without regard to what

this same animal can do in accounting for foxes, or whether he has cry or nose.

Hound show judges can hardly be expected to judge cry or nose, but they are perfectly capable of spotting anatomical flaws that handicap a hunting dog and should be penalized, not rewarded. The immaculate turnout of judges and hounds is very much part of the cosmetic appeal of such a show, but a rosette won after a wholly *visual* examination of noble hounds, mostly whilst there is an unseemly and rather degrading scrabbling for bits of biscuit, is not going to earn real respect. We must be careful lest we pass on these precious hounds to future generations with inbred faults; judges at hound shows can shape the future by settling on designs, rather like architects – who didn't become qualified by only 'staring at walls'!

Peterborough Foxhound Show, July 1901.

Value of Hound Shows

The basic value of the show ring surely is the identification of quality, if only to influence breeding plans. This is not always straightforward; the excellent Bloodhound Ch. Marksbury Wistful won twenty-nine challenge certificates but was never able to produce one pup to perpetuate those qualities. The significance and the value of hound shows like Honiton, Rydal and Peterborough have long caused debate in the hunting world. A pack like the Berkeley elected not to show hounds. One Master in France is alleged to have bred two packs, one for showing and one for hunting, after finding disappointment when showing the hunting hounds. Some state that the racehorse has triumphed without the need for conformation shows, whilst others want to breed a *pack* rather than the odd outstanding hound. It has been pointed out to Hunts that the economy obtained from *not* showing does not lead to the sport suffering. The great hound expert Sir Newton Rycroft, in his *Rycroft on Hounds, Hunting and Country* (2001), wrote that:

Peterborough Hound Show, 1905.

If a successful and experienced Master arranges his matings without even thinking of Peterborough, he will, because he realizes how important foxhound conformation is for the essential virtues of pace, stamina and long hunting life, breed good-looking hounds. If such hounds are shown, it seems much more likely they will do good rather than harm, because they will have been bred for work only.

Hounds of the pack are tested for soundness, hounds shown at KC shows rarely are.

Let us never forget that although shows are wonderfully happy occasions in the summer, as regards conformation they probably do more harm than good. Shows of sheep, pigs and cattle may well be helpful for the butcher and the breeder can see in the animals the qualities he wants. Not so with hounds; all the most desirable qualities – nose, constitution, voice and brain – are totally invisible.

Philip Burrows in *Hounds* magazine (December 1989). He went on to state that he had tried to show only his very best working hounds, but (because the hound shows had become purely 'beauty shows'), he had been 'laughed out of court and had to give up'.

A perfect foxhound is like a great picture – its wondrous beauty grows upon you by degrees, and the more you look the more you admire…

Otho Paget, *Hunting* (1900)

Hounds should combine strength with beauty, and steadiness with high mettle. Perfection of shape consists in short backs, open bosoms, straight legs, and compact feet. The first qualities of hounds are fine noses, docile tempers, steadiness to their game and stoutness in chase.

Nimrod, *The Life of a Sportsman* (1903)

The two things it is impossible to judge in the show ring are nose and voice. Are there any more important qualities in a hound (apart from drive)? So when I am told of Masters going to the kennels of Peterborough dog champions and asking if they can use them on their bitches, without first at least asking how they perform in the field, my heart sinks. Even worse, I have heard stories of such people being told that the dog's brother is better in his work, but then still insisting on using the champ. If you breed enough litters on this basis, the chances are you will get something half decent enough to show – breed a few more litters and you might get a hunting pack as well.

Al Lonsir, in *Hounds* magazine (November 2012)

Foxhound judging at an agricultural show, Lincoln; these shows for judging dogs pre-date KC-dog shows.

Foxhound puppies being judged, from a picture by G.D. Giles; such shows were a major social event in the rural counties.

Recasting Hounds – Appreciating Differences

…men who fancy hounds are frequently less concerned with purity of breeding, registration, and appearance than they are with results. Over the years they have shown no hesitancy to cross a good individual of one breed, strain, or variety on another good hound of another persuasion. The resultant progeny are unmistakably hounds, but the pure breed fancier may tab them cross-breeds or possibly grade hounds, and the genealogical researcher will have trouble sorting out his bloodlines.

David Michael Duffey, *Hunting Hounds* (1972)

From the very earliest times in the history of civilized man, we find two rough divisions of dogs – those that hunt by scent, and the others that hunt by sight. It may be that the ancestral wolf, from which, in all probability, dogs have descended, exhibited both of these qualities, and we can understand how important they were in the eyes of primitive peoples scarcely emerged from the savage state. They wanted an animal that would help them to supply the larder. It was only after civilization had reached such a stage as to dispense with the bare necessity for living that men began to use dogs in their sports.

A. Croxton Smith, *Sporting Dogs* (1938)

Hunting by Sense

Time and time again, writers of books on the hound breeds, as illustrated in the above quote, inform their readers that hounds hunt either by scent or by sight and that hound breeds fall into just two categories: scenthounds or sighthounds. In previous chapters I refer to the inadequacies of this categorization. Such an arbitrary division is not only misleadingly superficial but does scant justice to many distinguished hound breeds or to those hounds, such as the podencos of the Mediterranean littoral, which pursue their quarry using sight and scent (as well as their remarkable hearing). If you elect too to divide sporting dogs into hounds, terriers and gundogs, how do you then allocate hounds that hunt for the gun (*chasse a tir*), bark-pointers or, say, Airedale Terriers used in hunting trials in the USA? The classification of quarry hounds, especially by kennel clubs, has often been conducted in a lazy, ill-informed manner, unsupported by research or insight and badly needs rectifying.

In *Dogs and I* (1928), Harding Cox, sportsman, exhibitor and judge, wrote:

It is a pity that the term 'hound' has been tacked on to certain of the 'Sight' dogs; for such are the very antithesis of the true hound. This careless nomenclature has, in many instances, led show committees and others responsible for the drafting of schedules, into the error of including Greyhounds and Deerhounds in the same section as Harriers, Bassets, Dachshunds, Bloodhounds and others of the ilk.

This 'careless nomenclature' even when applied today, means that in one European country some hound breeds can be judged by those more familiar with Working or Utility Group breeds, whilst in others, the reverse can apply, as in the case of the Dalmatian. Show winners get bred from and if selected on the wrong criteria can harm a breed's ability to be 'fit for function'.

Hunting by Speed and Stamina

All hounds hunt by sight and scent. Some hunt making best use of their *speed*; they succeed principally because of their speed *not* their sight. Some are prized because of their scenting skill; they succeed mainly because of their *stamina* ahead of their scenting prowess. If either type cannot keep up with their quarry they don't succeed, even if they continue to see it or scent it. The phenotype of the so-called sighthounds is epitomized by that of the Greyhound, that of the so-called scenthounds perhaps by the Bloodhound. But what about the 'par force' hounds, which hunted at pace using their sheer power, utilizing sight and scent in equal measure? Should they be lost to the Hound Group, as they have been? They are a key element in the development of the hound family.

In medieval hunting, the par force hunt was more like a steeplechase, with drive valued more in hounds than their music. In time this style became less favoured than two other methods: hunting in enclosed parks, really an unregulated form of coursing, and 'hunting cunning' in which slow hounds were prized for their skill in unravelling scent. But hunting with 'fleethounds' continued in the north of England despite changes in style further south. Par force hounds, fleethounds or 'running mastiffs' are perpetuated today in breeds like the Great Dane, the Dogo Argentino, the Rhodesian Ridgeback and, in the United States, by the Black Mouth Cur, whatever their classification by kennel clubs.

As explained earlier in this book, a further type of hound was the 'hunting mastiff', used to close with and either seize or pull down big game such as boar, wild bull, aurochs and stag. The 'bandogge' was the mastiff-like catch-dog. Many were killed by their

Par force hounds in medieval Germany: Johann Ridinger's Der Windhetzer, *1780.*

Par force hunting c.1790, depicting hounds using scent and sight.

quarry. They were often ferocious and therefore held on leashes in the hunt, for release only when the baying hounds had done their job. This is why they were called bandogges (band + dog). It was *not* because they were tethered guard dogs or tied-up yard dogs as some writers have claimed. Undoubtedly some bandogges found employment as guard dogs on chains in yards. But there is an old English ballad of around 1610 that includes these lines: 'Half a hundred good band-dogs, Came running over the lee.' There is little indication of solitary, tied-up yard dogs in these words. Sadly, far too many of the hounds used at the final stages of the medieval hunt, the 'holding and seizing' dogs, are regarded today as guarding breeds and their hunting instincts and capabilities not prized or even acknowledged.

Bandogges being released at the final stages of the stag hunt.

Fernando IV of Naples, hunting boar at Cassano by Philip Hackert, late eighteenth century; the held bandogges are in the foreground.

More 'Careless Nomenclature'

Further confusion has arisen through the misuse of the word 'gazehound'. So many writers seem to see the word as a synonym for sighthound; it is not. Dr Johannes Caius, in his classic treatise *Of English Dogs* (1576), made quite separate mention of the Greyhound and the Gazehound; he did not regard the former as embraced by the latter. His words on the gazehound are worthy of study.

> Our countrymen call this dog Agasoeum, a Gazehound: because the beams of his sight are so steadfastly settled and unmovably fastened… Horsemen use them more than footmen, in the intent that they might provoke their horses to a swift gallop… and that they might accustom their horse to leap over hedges and ditches…

That is a clear description of par force hunting, a steeplechase with a pack of fast-hunting hounds. It is

hardly a description of hunting with a brace of sighthounds.

Nicholas Cox, in *The Gentleman's Recreation* of 1674 (predictably using other peoples' material, in this case Caius), mentions gazehounds as 'used for catching the fox and hare, hunting chiefly by sight in open country, employed by people riding.' He too lists the Greyhound quite separately. Thomas Bewick, in *A History of Quadrupeds* (1790), stated that the gazehound 'was somewhat similar to the greyhound… It was formerly in great repute, but is now unknown to us.' Bewick was not an authority on dogs and had little knowledge of hunting. His full text is a lift from Caius. 'Stonehenge', in his *The Dog* of 1867, stated that Bewick 'does not appear to have any authority for what he writes on this particular.' But he himself wrote: 'This breed is now lost, and it is very difficult to ascertain in what respects it differed from the greyhound' – words not markedly different from Bewick's.

The Gazehound Function

The word gazehound never, of course, referred to a breed but to a function, rather as the word sighthound does. Hounds in the Middle Ages were used on all sorts of game, without specialization. In 1318, Philippe VI authorized all noblemen to hunt big game 'by force and cunning' to distinguish it from stealth and ambush hunting, using nets and spears. This hunting at pace using the strength of the hounds led, not surprisingly, to the breeding of faster, stronger hounds, hunting in packs. In his *Hounds in Old Days* (1913), Sir Walter Gilbey wrote:

> The old plan, advocated by Cockaine in 1591, of breeding a pack that should hunt any and every quarry, had so completely gone out of use in Beckford's time [late eighteenth century] that the practice of a friend of that authority who possessed a pack of large fleet hounds, which at times had hunted all game – red and fallow deer, fox and hare – was regarded as 'very extraordinary'.

Specalization, of course, brought our surviving breeds of hound to us; although today Staghounds are really only Foxhounds with a different purpose and minkhounds can be 'recycled Foxhounds' or re-employed Otterhounds. In many ways each Foxhound pack constitutes a separate breed of Foxhound. It would be an enormous pity if we were to lose the varying pack idiosyncrasies as well as the constructional subtleties of the different packs. With hunting using dogs under threat, we need to give thought to the conservation of our hounds of the pack; they are very much part of our sporting, and canine, heritage.

Recognizing Role

Any move towards the recognition of hounds in Groups as: those which hunted by speed, those which hunted by stamina, those which hunted 'at force' and those which seized big game, that is, the mastiff breeds, would be resisted by kennel clubs. They prefer the status quo in most matters. Show breeders too seem to fear innovation. But the recognition of the Mastiff, the English breed, as a heavy hound, would undoubtedly do it some good. I do wish the Mastiff fraternity could shed the mistaken Victorian concept of their breed as a massive, slothful, inactive yard dog and rekindle the long sporting heritage behind this type of dog. No real dog man would ever prize his dog because of its weight and size, as quite a number of Mastiff breeders have. A group of Mastiff lovers in the United States have now lost confidence in their fellow Mastiff breeders and decided to outcross to the Anatolian Shepherd Dog in the pursuit of a sounder dog, naming the emergent breed the American Mastiff. I applaud their work.

As I have set out in Chapter 2, there is ample evidence in selected quotes there to demonstrate the hound role of the English Mastiff: 'A mastiff is a manner of hound,' wrote the second Duke of York in *The Master of Game* (1406). 'Mastiffs were still kept as guard-dogs, but their value in hunting disappeared with the wild boar' wrote Roger Longrigg in *The English Squire and his Sport*. 'The mastiff is a huge, stubborn, ugly and impetuous hound,' wrote William Harrison in his *Description of England* (1586). 'Those of the mastiff type – the massive dogs – which attack the larger animals in the hunt' wrote the Fiennes in *The Natural History of the Dog*. 'In the very specialized circumstances of the Tudor animal fight, the mastiff was really very much at a disadvantage. It had never been bred, originally, as an animal-fighting dog at all. It was a hunting dog,' wrote Carson Ritchie in *The British Dog*. In the light of these quotations, why is our Mastiff breed so miscast? What other breed of hound was ever raised like beef?

A Mastiff by Ben Marshall, 1799; the Mastiff was originally a hound.

If we continue to miscast the Mastiff (and the Great Dane, still languishing in the KC's Working Group, despite its boarhound ancestry), and fail to acknowledge that there were hound functions beyond purely

The Englische Dogge or hunting mastiff; famous all over northern Europe as an accomplished hound.

sight and scenthounds, then we undermine the rich heritage of our distinguished breeds of dog. Running mastiffs/fleethounds/gazehounds like the Rhodesian Ridgeback hunted with their heads up, seeking air scent. Hunting mastiffs/holding dogs/seizers like the Dogue de Bordeaux carried their heavier heads lower, ready to close with their quarry. Stamina hounds like the Basset moved with their noses to the ground, pursuing the scent of their prey. The speedsters, like the Greyhound and the Saluki, eyed the middle distance, striving to spot animal movement. These functions should affect how we allow our hounds to move in the ring, how we judge their anatomies and how we must strive to meet their spiritual needs. We bred them for a *function*. When hound breeds are allocated to non-hound Groups by misguided kennel clubs around the world, some just copying the older clubs, it is rather like insisting that an Olympic runner can only enter the field events, where running skills are not tested, or indeed required, and is actually banned from the track events. Would this be acceptable or appropriate? Why should canine athletes be treated like this?

Recognizing Houndwork

I look forward to the day when, at a hound show or at the Game Fair, a parade of hounds is accompanied by this commentary: 'And now, Ladies and Gentle-

Great Dane being judged at a KC championship show – but not as a hound by a judge familiar with hounds and their function.

men, we welcome into the ring the precious hound breeds. First come those that hunted by speed: the Whippet, the Greyhound, the Saluki, the Borzoi and the Deerhound. Then those that hunted by stamina: the Basset, the Beagle, the Foxhound and the Harrier. Next come those that hunted 'at force': the Mastiff of England – once famous as the 'Englische Dogge' in the Central European hunt, the German Boarhound

Dogo Argentino in the ring at the World Dog Show 2003 – not being judged as a hound.

The Cane Corso from Italy, never assessed by hound *judges.*

Poor-quality Mastiffs being judged, not as hounds, at a World Dog Show; once a breed's function is not bred for, deterioration sets in.

– the Great Dane, the Rhodesian Ridgeback, the Dogo Argentino and the recently introduced Black Mouth Cur from America. Finally, the holding dogs, the hunting mastiffs: the Dogue de Bordeaux, the Alano of Spain, the Cane Corso of Italy, and, last but hardly least, the British Bulldog!'

Our British Bulldog in a parade of hounds, there's a thought! They'd have to be leggier, longer-muzzled and more active to complete the circuit and wouldn't that be a good thing? We may no longer wish our Mastiff and Bulldog to pull down big game but that is what they were designed to do, and if we went back to the physique that allowed them to do so they would be healthier breeds for it. Redundancy should not mean slow decline; it should represent a time to honour past service and respect true heritage. Surely the great joy in owning a hound is to allow it to take part in *houndwork*. And before that comes the need to know what our hounds were for. If we lazily divide our hound breeds into sighthounds and scenthounds only, we ignore centuries of hound activity across a wide spectrum. It's time we respected the hound heritage and stopped lumping types together for administrative ease; that's hardly sporting!

Stable Companions: Hounds and Horses

Men are generally more careful of the breed of their horses and dogs than of their children.

William Penn (1644–1718)

Remarkable Harmony

The close association between horse, hound and man is a long and varied one. All over the world, through-

out recorded history, mounted hunters and sporting dogs have worked together in remarkable harmony. There always seems to have been a special affinity between hounds and horses. Neither seems to have any preoccupation with themselves, quite unlike man. Both the horse and the dog are more interested in external stimuli rather than self-interested introspection.

A triple alliance.

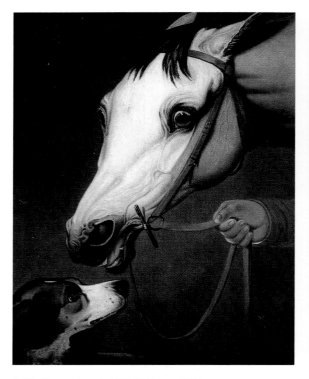

Stable Companions *by W.R. Robinson, 1836.*

Friends *by Arthur Wardle, 1902.*

Man, horse and hounds – straight-legged Bassets; by John Emms (1843–1912).

This makes both of them loyal and selfless, ideal companions for each other and valuable servants to, and sometimes victims of, man.

Breeds like the Dalmatian and the harlequin Great Dane have been traditionally used as carriage dogs, lending a distinct elegance to coach travel, as well as having the functional value of keeping village curs from alarming the horses. Bull Terriers and small mastiffs were often used to guard valuable horses in stables. Rat-catching breeds like the Manchester Terrier were widely used to keep vermin down in stables. As a direct result of such an association is the fondness for horses which many breeds of dog retain to this day. But the classic sporting trinity is that of man, horse and hound. Many artists have captured this relationship very skilfully.

Down the centuries, man the hunter has needed the mobility of the horse and the catching and killing ability of the hound. Xenophon described three varieties of the Cretan hound: the Cnossians, famous as trackers; the Workers, so keen they hunted by day and night; and the Outrunners, which ran free under the huntsman's voice control only. According to Aristotle, the latter variety ran instinctively beside the horses during a hunt, never preceding them and not lagging behind. Unlike many of the other hounds used by the Greeks in the chase, the Outrunners were neither dewlapped nor flewed. They were used by the Cretans to hunt a four-horned antelope, as Aelian has recorded.

Mutual Consideration

These Outrunners were too valuable for use on boar hunts, where some hounds were killed. They were considered too special for use in hare hunting. Sufficiently biddable to be used as 'braches' or free-running hounds, as opposed to 'lymmers' or leashed hounds, they hunted using sight and scent, rather as our own fleethounds used to. In this way, the Cretans' use of horse and hound was exceptional and showed the advanced state of their training and breeding skills. In any hunt involving hounds and horses, the latter have to show consideration for the former or injuries would be frequent.

In The Lonsdale Library's *Fox-Hunting*, Lt Col. Brooke wrote:

The main advantage of such a trial [in the hunting field] is, that in addition to trying your mount over fences, you can ascertain whether he is temperate with hounds, an important item from the point of view of enjoyment…one must take into consideration the fact that every horse is keener with hounds and is much more easily controlled when ridden in a field than he would be in a hunt… Remember that we depend upon the hounds to give us our sport. The modern child understands the necessity of tuning a wireless to the correct wavelength. It is somewhat a similar problem with hounds, but in their case, it is the question of 'nose', the receiver and 'scent' the wave-length.

It is quite remarkable that, in the excitement of the chase, horse and hound manage to run together with such ease: horse, hound and human rider in harmony.

Substance and Stamina

A hunter is around 67in at the withers, a Foxhound only 25in; the all-round vision of a galloping horse is not limitless yet accidents in which hooves

damage hounds are almost unheard of. Just as the hound is a pack animal, so the horse is a herd animal. Each has an instinctive awareness of the other. In the hunting field, down many centuries, horse and hound have run together in mutual support and remarkable empathy. In such an activity, horse and hound need speed, stamina, drive and spirit, with the hound also needing nose, cry, pack sense and discipline in a group. Both need sound feet; the old hunting man's expression 'No hoof, no horse' has relevance for hounds too. Both need hard exercise, the right nutrition and good breeding.

In his valuable book *Hunting* (1900), from the Haddon Hall Library, Otho Paget wrote almost a summary of such needs:

A few seconds' respite on the turnip-ground gave your horse an opportunity of getting his second wind, and he now seems as fresh as ever, but you feel very thankful that most of his forebears are recorded in the stud-book… Hounds are driving along now at a tremendous pace over the old turf, and there is not a sign of one tailing off. You are delighted with the result of your kennel management, with summer

Waiting to go out *by Colin Graeme, 1904; unspoken affinity.*

Stable Mates *by Colin Graeme, 1883; stable companions.*

Favourite Companions *by John Emms, 1901; hounds and horse share a moment.*

conditioning and autumn education. This is the moment when you reap the fruits of all your care and labour. In spite of the severity of the pace, neither old nor young show the slightest symptoms of flagging.

Breeders of hunters in the last century usually went for the thoroughbred horse on the half-bred mare. But some favoured the reverse, going for size and strength in the sire and quality and stamina in the dam. Some of the best hunters a hundred years ago were by half-bred stallions out of thoroughbred mares. Clearly, performance ruled with the horse then just as it did with the hound. In his *Hounds of Britain* (1973), Jack Ivester Lloyd wrote that:

…genuine hunting folk have displayed considerable elasticity of mind by introducing out-crosses when these would benefit the breed in which their interests repose. This is the reason that all hounds now hunting in Britain possess stamina, health and intelligence, virtues which could not be claimed for all the canine breeds kept as pets or for display on the show bench.

The domestic dog is the most complete, the most singular, and the most useful conquest that man has gained in the animal world… The swiftness, the strength, the sharp scent of the dog, have rendered him a powerful ally to man against the lower tribes; and were, perhaps, necessary for the establishment of the dominion of mankind over the whole animal creation. The dog is the only animal which has followed man over the whole earth.

Baron Georges Cuvier, the naturalist

These comments strangely overlook the value of horse to man and ignore the remarkable contribution of horse and dog together, not just to man's hunting and sporting activities, but to exploration and farming across many centuries. Dog and horse have literally accompanied man 'over the whole earth', with dog having the size advantage when it comes to sharing the hearth.

Valuable Combination

Cuvier would have been on surer ground if he had stressed the sheer versatility of dog in its usefulness

Horse being stabled, hounds being kennelled; a scene once valued.

Mounted herdsmen using hard-eyed herding dogs have benefited from this combined value for centuries, from the puszta of Hungary to the outback of Australia. Genghis Khan used the hunting field to train his cavalry, accompanied by huge hounds. In South America, mounted huntsmen still pursue wild pig using big hounds like the Dogo Argentino. In Russia, horsemen used the handsome Borzoi to run down wolves, accompanied by scenthounds, in unusual combination, for their ultimate sport. Whilst in the Arab world, horsemen with hawk and Salukis, continue the age-old skill of gazelle hunting.

In each case, in each part of the world, man utilizes horse and hound or herding dog to achieve his end, with all three working in harmony to one purpose. It is a unique combination in the animal kingdom and in man's use of subject creatures. Long may it continue, whatever the pressures of man's demand on land and the threat from his recently developed moral vanity. Perhaps the complete lack of vanity in both horse and hound makes them especially attractive to man, certainly as companions. Such a mutually beneficial, stable relationship is one to be treasured and well worth preserving in times when 'town-mindedness' threatens to blind our traditional affections. May twenty-first-century man have the wisdom to appreciate and then respect such a precious partnership.

to man. This versatility, allied to the facility given to man by the horse and man's own unique adaptability, makes an extraordinarily valuable combination.

The York and Ainsty hounds on the ferry at Newby by Thomas Blinks, 1898; man, horse and hounds all at ease with each other.

CONSERVING OUR HOUNDS

> The most careless observer of the course of world affairs must be aware that – as has been the case in all ages – in proportion as a country has arrived at the highest pitch of wealth and refinement, the taste for the humble, but nearly unalloyed pleasures of a country life, has more or less declined.
>
> Nimrod, *The Life of a Sportsman* (1903)

Unprecedented Challenges

The faithful service, infectious enthusiasm and immense appeal of hounds thoroughly merits man's compassionate concern about their long-term future. In the preceding chapters I have striven to argue for stronger support for the hound breeds and packs. Both face unprecedented challenges in the twenty-first century. Without a test of function every sporting animal is much more likely to be bred to a mistaken design. In the show ring the exaggerators will strive to defend the harmful work of their predecessors, often arguing that 'traditional type' and breed integrity is threatened when overdone physical features that handicap the dog are questioned.

History is not on their side – our more distant sporting ancestors never sought excess in the anatomies of their charges. There is ample evidence, in paintings, sketches and early photographs to demonstrate the imposition of fairly modern exaggerations currently afflicting a number of hound breeds. The

Resting Hounds *by John Emms, c.1890; if animals have rights – do these hounds not have the right to hunt naturally?*

show ring is about canine beauty not canine soundness, and this has to stop. But before the hunt followers get smug, harm too has been done in the hunting packs, in the past by the absurd desire for 'great bone' and in more recent times by ill-informed breeding to hound show winners, not to proven field performers. We all love a handsome hound but an incompetent one is an embarrassment.

Each native breed of scenthound, whether in the packs or on the show bench, has problems to be faced, whether threats to its health and virility or to its existence at all. A century ago this was not the case. Imported hound breeds too have difficulties over their future here and in the form they are being cast in. It is pointless to moan about the loss of our sporting heritage when hound breeds are under threat; what is needed is vision, an ability to look ahead and plan their survival in challenging times. Just as so many of these long-established breeds were shaped by knowledgeable sportsmen and bred for a function by skilful informed breeders, we now need inspired patronage from a new generation, able to live in changing times, adapt to contemporary attitudes, yet manage to conserve country sports albeit in a reshaped form. Hounds are much more adaptable than we imagine; when the 'quarry' changes they can change too. The pursuit of scent is their whole life and, as the trail hound fraternity have demonstrated, nose, pace and scenting skill can still be tested in our eager hounds. I admire the work of the Bloodhound community in running their special stakes annually; their Brough Cup, Milvery, Bracken and Kelperland Trophies provide a great test to find working champions amongst the show hounds in their kennels – and what spiritual exercise for both hounds and humans!

Conventional Disadvantages

Orthodoxy and convention so often rule in contemporary society and the days of sporting 'eccentrics' may have passed. In 1912, this was hardly the case: Major Walter Russell-Johnson, when Master of the West Kent Harriers, a pack of eighteen couples of 'dwarf Foxhounds', also ran his own private pack of Beagles, the Riverside, consisting of thirteen and a half couples of 14in, which were termed 'pure old-fashioned Kerry blue-mottled Beagles' *and* two small packs of what were termed 'badger' and Otterhounds. Where are today's super-rich when we need them! Conservation should embrace our sporting heritage as well as our wildlife; once they were inter-dependent. However hunting with dogs is legally conducted, hounds, especially our time-honoured hounds of the pack, need to express themselves.

Field Test

In this connection, it's good to read of the Basset Hound Club of America holding a number of trials every year to stimulate interest in the function of the breed. These trials are of two kinds, each quite different from the other. One is hunting in couples, the other hunting in packs. The couples trial is run on cottontail rabbits – similar to the rabbit here – with the pack trial being conducted on hare. It is a strict rule of the American Club that the heats of the couples' trials are 'conducted in the manner best calculated to give the competing hounds ample opportunity to display true hunting ability or a lack of this'. In the pack trials, the hounds experience a more orthodox hare-hunt, but in the couples' events the trials have to last at least one and a half hours, with an endurance test of not less than three hours being imposed in the all-age stakes. To become a champion at such an event is a much-coveted distinction. It would be of value to breeders here who value function in their stock to have such a trial season; the Basset is a sporting dog, despite the attempts to turn it into a caricature of itself by some show breeders.

Loss of Role

Those involved in the world of hounds used for hunting need support if our precious packs of hounds are to be conserved. We have already lost a number, including the distinctive and highly efficient Dumfriesshire pack of black and tan Foxhounds, and way before that, the mainly white Curre and the distinctively blue mottled or 'marbled' Hailsham Harriers. This alone represents a considerable loss of unique irreplaceable genes from the packhound pool. We need to give thought to the long-term future of our

Harriers, Staghounds, English Bassets and that valuable breeding source, the Welsh Hound. With the new emphasis on 'Britishness' perhaps the hunting dogs of Britain will receive some much-needed interest from the public. The public try to care about conservation but have long been badly informed by the popular press about hunting with hounds. When once managing a country estate, I was horrified at the slaughter of wildfowl there by wilfully released mink from a nearby fur farm. There is a continuing need for minkhounds!

Anatomy to Succeed

The Otterhound has reached the KC rings, one form of conservation. From their long and mixed ancestry, it would be a tragedy if their appearance became increasingly exaggerated, as so often happens with longer-coated and longer-eared breeds. The show-ring Basset Hound indicates all too clearly what can happen to a breed when its distinctive features become distinctively exaggerated, the ear and back length in the show hounds not being fair on the dog. The Bloodhounds of the show ring too often display an ear length and head wrinkle not present in their distant ancestors. This is a human indulgence, not a canine requirement.

The standard of mouths, dentition especially, can deteriorate away from the packs; strong teeth, even teeth, and a scissor bite are all important in a hound. Variation in shoulder height is not a bad fault in scenthounds, where packs are bred to suit country, as long as the hound is balanced, free-moving, vigorous in action and not clumsily cumbersome through being too rangy. A fault to be penalized in any scenthound is when depth of rib does not reach back the whole length of the ribcage; lung room is vital.

The fate of many foothound breeds now rests with show-ring breeders. It is a challenge and a considerable responsibility. Otters no longer pose a threat to our larders and are rightly conserved. So too must be the hounds that once hunted them, they are an important part of our sporting heritage. If we do not respect their sporting past and only breed them for their coats, the 'uniqueness' of their ears, a 'very loose and shambling' gait and 'exceptional' stride, as their breed standard demands, then we will be betraying the work of past breeders like Captain Bell-Irving with his renowned Dumfriesshire Otterhounds. May such hounds, whether in minkhound packs or in the show ring, go from strength to strength, a distinctive hound well worth saving. But so too are the other packhounds.

Resting minkhound.

Beagles from the Dummer pack.

BELOW MIDDLE: Beagle at Crufts, 1991.

BELOW RIGHT: Head study of Basset Fauve de Bretagne.

The contrast between, say, the Beagles in the Dummer or Claro packs and the show-ring specimens, as far as type and size is concerned, is stark. I see show-ring Beagles that are handsome enough, but barrel-chested, over-boned and straight-shouldered. There is no benefit to a harehound in such limitations to pace and stamina. I see Bloodhounds in the show ring that seem to be prized for their excessive facial wrinkle, sunken eyes (giving a strangely desired 'sad' look) and the looseness of their lips. What would a tracking hound, let alone a pack hound, gain from such unnatural features? The pack Bloodhounds resemble their ancient ancestors. For me, the best-bred hounds in the show ring are the less well known Bassets Fauve de Bretagne; the entry I have seen, at the Bath Dog Show in particular, over several years has been quite excellent, yet never been selected for Group or Best in Show honours. They appear to have the anatomy to succeed in the hunting field. We have no equivalent native breed but we do have our overlooked hunting Bassets and elegant, well-bred Harriers.

Fluctuating Fortunes

A glance at the registrations of hounds with the KC reveals the fluctuating fortunes of most breeds. In 1908, scenthound breed registrations were: Basset Hounds 15; Beagles 4; Bloodhounds 113; Elkhounds

5, with no KC registrations of Otterhounds, Harriers (recognized then) and Foxhounds. No other scenthound breeds were recognized then. A century later (2012), the scene is very different for these breeds: Basset Hounds 766 (up from 25 in 1950); Beagles 2,728 (up from 64 in 1950); Bloodhounds 50 (up from 39 in 1950); Norwegian Elkhounds 62 (down from 300 in 1950); Otterhounds 37 (up from zero in 1950), with no registrations of Harriers (still unrecognized, or Foxhounds, despite being recognized). But in 2012, 1,070 Rhodesian Ridgebacks, after only 56 in 1954, 318 in 1980 and 643 in 1992, were registered; a remarkable increase. By contrast, in Hamiltonstovares, after 31 in 1999, only 6 were registered in 2012. Bassets Fauve de Bretagne went from 40 a year in the 1990s to 103 in 2012. Into the lists came Bavarian Mountain Hounds with 73 in 2010, but only 10 in 2012.

Otterhound from the packs.

BELOW: *Griffon Vendeen.*

Grand Bleu de Gascogne.

Staghound.

It is difficult to make rational conclusions from such fluctuations beyond human whim, combined with our fondness for novelty. The success of the Rhodesian Ridgeback as a breed is well deserved – there is responsible breed stewardship here and impressive hounds in the ring; in a previous chapter I set out its evolution, which, like that of the Dogo Argentino, is, unusually in hound breeds, a matter of recorded history. We are denied the latter breed by the ill-conceived Dangerous Dogs Act, but the African hound has truly and deservedly made its mark here.

Buy British!

Why favour a scenthound from Sweden, like the Hamiltonstovare, when we have superlative and very similar hounds here like the Studbook and West Country Harriers? Why import a Grand Griffon Vendeen when we have our endearing Otterhound available, of comparable type? Why, if you fancy the Basset Hound, not go for the delightful little scenthounds developed as the English or Hunting Basset? What are the advantages of the Grand Bleu de

Gascogne over our steadfast and long-proven Staghound? And have those now bringing in the Segugio Italiano ever seen a Trail Hound in Cumbria – they really are something special. They race rather than hunt, they run freely rather than as a pack, but their genes are so valuable. They have Pointer and Harrier blood in them; their breeders sought performance from superb hounds, not pure-blooded fading stock, losing virility yet still bred in a closed gene pool for 'old times' sake' or salient breed points unconnected with performance. We lost the famed Dumfriesshire Foxhounds and now import the similar-looking Bavarian Mountain Hound, much as I admire the latter, already committed to tracking trials that should 'keep it honest'. The KC's Schweisshund tests are open to all KC-registered dogs, not just the 'professionals' – like the Bavarian hounds.

Preserving Bloodlines

Perhaps the best way of ensuring that there is a future for our distinguished varieties of packhound is a sustained cooperation between MFHs and the breed clubs for the show hounds, rather as Beagles

Hound racing. (Photo: Nigel Bloom)

and the Albany Bassets were once run. Judges in both 'sports', for hunting hounds and for purely KC-show hounds, could learn much from each other. It would be good to see too, from the show-ring fraternity, sustained moral support for the packs, financial support for the Countryside Alliance, allied with indefatigable campaigning for the misguided Hunting Act to be removed from the statute book. Those who breed hounds need an incentive. Those who breed superlative hounds anywhere need motivation.

Perhaps a revival of hunting-hound trials, held in the early days of Foxhunting, would be of value. In 1829, for example, 600 riders watched seven couples from local packs in the north Midlands compete against each other in a match. At a subsequent contest in Yorkshire, eighteen couples competed, with each hound able to score up to ten points, with marks deducted for babbling, rioting, overshooting the hunted line, and so on. We shouldn't leave it to the French to perpetuate such hunting field fun. Let's keep the activities going. Let's keep the bloodlines going – and the campaigning. For all scenthound pet owners too, I have a plea: afford them spiritual release, give then nose-work, let them go tracking, provide them with sensory stimulation. These dogs were specifically developed over centuries to exercise their incredible powers of scenting; respect their instinctive needs and see the happier hound you have empowered. It should not take a foreseeable but unpredicted, sizeable asteroid to hit Mother Earth, and make man become a hunter-gatherer once more, to demonstrate the unique value of hunting dogs to us all!

Vale of the White Horse Foxhounds – not going hunting today!

Hunting has become a freemasonry of countrymen who recognize the lamentable truth that the population of Britain now constitutes two nations. One, through no choice of its own, is town-based and, also through no fault of its own, cannot know the facts of life in the fields and woods and farmsteads which lie beyond the points where the pavements end. Ignorance is generally the breeding ground of disapproval and intolerance.

Wilson Stephens, *The Farmer's Book of Field Sports* (1961)

Trail hound waiting to race.

Obselete dogs of the chase.

THE ANATOMY OF THE HOUND

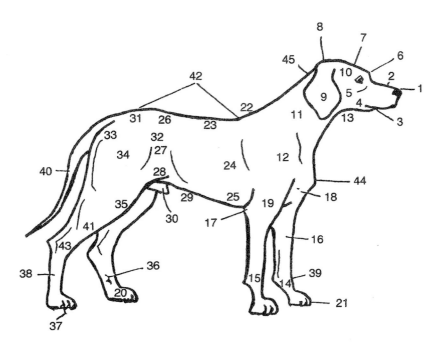

1. Nose
2. Muzzle
3. Lips
4. Flews
5. Cheek
6. Stop
7. Foreface
8. Peak or occiput
9. Ear
10. Brow
11. Neck
12. Shoulder
13. Dewlap
14. Pastern or metacarpus
15. Wrist or carpus
16. Forearm
17. Elbow
18. Brisket
19. Upper arm
20. Foot
21. Toes or digits
22. Withers
23. Back

24. Ribs
25. Chest
26. Loin
27. Flank
28. Groin
29. Belly or abdomen
30. Sheath
31. Croup
32. Hip
33. Rump
34. Thigh (upper) (first)
35. Stifle or Knee
36. Dewclaw
37. Toenail
38. Metatarsus or hind pastern
39. Knee or manus
40. Tail or stern
41. Thigh (lower) (second)
42. Topline
43. Hock
44. Sternum or breast bone
43. Crest

GLOSSARY OF TERMS

Action Movement; the way a dog moves.

Angulation The degree of slope or angle of the shoulder blade in the forequarters and in the sharp angles of the inter-related bones in the hindquarters – thigh, hock and metatarsus.

Babbler Noisy hound; one giving tongue when not on the line.

Back Area of the dog between the withers and the root of tail.

Balanced Symmetrically proportioned.

Barrel-hocks Hocks turned outwards, resulting in feet with inward-pointing toes (similar to bandy-legs).

Barrel-ribbed Well-rounded rib cage.

Blanket The coat-colour on the back from the withers to the rump.

Blaze A white patch of hair in the centre of the face, usually between the eyes.

Bloom The sheen of a coat in prime condition.

Bodied up Well developed in maturity.

Bony or boney Strongly-boned or well-timbered.

Brace A pair (often reserved for sighthounds), a couple.

Breed points Characteristic physical features of a breed, often exaggerated by breed fanciers.

Brisket The part of the body in front of the chest.

Button ear The ear flap folding forward, usually towards the eye.

Cannon Bone (shank) Bone uniting knee and pastern bone in front, hock and pastern bone in hindquarters; the desire for a long cannon bone in the hindquarters must not be confused with the mistaken pursuit of a low hock (*see* well let-down at hock).

Carry a good head To run and keep together on a good scent.

Cast To spread out in search of scent.

Cat-foot The rounded, shorter-toed, compact type of foot.

Champion A dog achieving this level of merit under KC-approved judges.

Chest The area from the brisket up to the belly, underneath the dog.

Chestnut Coat colour, lighter than bay, darker than tan; *'fauve'* in French, as in the Basset Fauve de Bretagne.

Chiselled Clean cut, especially in the head.

Chopping Exaggerated forward movement through abbreviated reach.

Clean boot Trail left by human quarry.

Close-coupled Comparatively short from the last rib to the leading edge of the thigh.

Coarse Lacking refinement.

Cobby Short-bodied but not close-coupled; compact in torso.

Conformation The relationship between the physical appearance of a dog and the imagined perfect mould for that breed or type.

Couple A pair of hounds other than sighthounds (a pair of the latter forming a brace).

Couples Connection of hindquarters to torso.

Couplings The length between the tops of the shoulder blades and the tops of the hip joint.

Cow-hocks Hocks turned towards each other (similar to knock-knees).

Cross-bred Having parents from two different breeds.

Croup (rump) Region of the pelvic girdle formed by the sacrum and the surrounding tissue.

Dewlaps Loose, pendulous skin under the throat.

Dewclaw Rudimentary toe or claw, corresponding to the thumb in humans, above the feet and inside the lower leg, less usual on the hindleg and often removed on sporting dogs to avoid their being torn.

Dog hound The male hound.

Down at pastern Weak or faulty metacarpus set at an angle to the vertical.

Draft To remove hounds from a kennel or pack.

Drag An artificial line; the scent left by the quarry when returning to its lair.

Draw To search for quarry.

Drive A solid thrust from the hindquarters, denoting strength of locomotion.

Elbows out Elbows positioned away from the body.

Enter To introduce a hound to its future role.

Even bite Meeting of both sets of front teeth at edges with no overlap.

Feathering Distinctly longer hair on rear line of legs, back of ears and along underside of tail.
Fetlock Pastern bone (strictly speaking the lock of hair at the pastern).
Flank The side of the body between the last rib and the hip.
Flat-sided A noticeable lack of roundness in the ribcage.
Flews The overhanging lips of the upper jaw.
Forearm Part of foreleg extending from elbow to pastern.
Forequarters Front part of dog excluding head and neck.
Front Forepart of body viewed from the head-on position.
Furnishings Long hair on ears, trailing edge of legs and under part of tail.

Gait Pattern or rhythm of footsteps.
Gallop The fastest gait, with a four-beat rhythm, propelling the dog at great speed, with all four feet off the ground seeking of sheer pace.
Grizzle Bluish-grey or steel-grey in coat colour.

Hackney action High-stepping action in the front legs (named after the carriage horse).
Harbourer Hunting staff used to track a deer to its resting place.
Hare-foot A longer, narrower foot, usually with an elongated third digit.
Haunch Rump or buttock; fleshy part of junction of body and hips; bones of that area.
Haw Sagging inside eyelid.
Height Distance or measurement from the withers to ground contact in the standing dog.
Hock Joint on the hindleg between the knee and the fetlock; the heel in humans.
Hound-marked Coat colouring involving a mixture of classic Foxhound coat colours, white, black and tan, in varying proportions, usually mainly white, especially underneath.
Hound-tail Tail carried on high, up above the rump.

Irish spotting White markings on solid coat, usually on the blaze, throat and toes.

Knee The joint attaching fore-pastern and forearm.

Layback The angle of the shoulder compared to the vertical.
Lay of shoulder Angled position of the shoulder.
Leather The flap of the ear.

Level back The line of the back horizontal to the ground.
Level bite (pincer bite) The front teeth of both jaws meeting exactly.
Line The track taken by quarry and revealed to the hounds by scent.
Loaded shoulders When the shoulder blades are pushed outwards by over-muscled development (often confused in the show ring with well-muscled shoulders on a supremely fit dog).
Lumber Superfluous flesh and/or cumbersome movement arising from lack of condition or faulty construction.

Mask Dark shading on the foreface, most usually on a tan or red-tan dog.
Moving close When the hindlimbs move too near each other.

Occiput The peak of the skull.
Out at elbow *See* elbows out.
Over-reaching Faulty gait in which the hindfeet pass the forefeet on the outside due to hyper-angulation in the hindquarters.
Overshot jaw The front upper set of teeth overlapping the lower set.
Oversprung ribs Exaggerated curvature of ribcage.

Pace Rate of movement, usually speed.
Padding A Hackney action due to lack of angulation in fore-quarters.
Paddling A heavy, clumsy threshing action in the forelegs with the feet too wide of the body on the move.
Pastern Lowest section of the leg, below the knee or hock.
Pedigree The dog's record of past breeding; sometimes used as shorthand for pure-breeding.
Pile Dense undercoat of softer hair.
Pincer bite *See* level bite.
Plaiting (or weaving or crossing) The movement of one front leg across the path of the other front leg on the move.

Racy Lightly built and leggier than normal in the breed.
Ribbed-up Long last rib.
Roach- or carp-backed Back arched convexly along the spine, especially in the hindmost section.
Roan Coat colour, usually red or blue, flecked closely with grey hair; favoured in Gascony hounds and the old Hailsham Harriers.
Root of the tail Where the tail joins the dog's back.
Rounding Trimming the extremities of the hound's ears to reduce the risk of tearing.

Saddle A solid area of colour extending over the shoulders and back.

Saddle-backed A sagging back from extreme length or weak musculature.

Scissor bite When the outer side of the lower incisors touches the inner side of the upper incisors.

Second thigh The (calf) muscle between the stifle and the hock in the hindquarters.

Self-coloured A solid or single-coloured coat.

Set on Where the root of the tail is positioned in the hindquarters.

Shelly Weedy and narrow-boned, lacking substance.

Short-coupled *See* close-coupled.

Shoulder layback *See* layback.

Sickle-hocked Lack of extension in the hock on the rear drive.

Skirter A hound that runs wide of the pack.

Slab-sided Flat ribs, with too little spring from the spinal column.

Snipiness Condition in which the muzzle is too pointed, weak and lacking strength right to the nose end.

Soundness Correct physical conformation and movement.

Splay feet Flat, open-toed, widely spread feet.

Spring of rib The extent to which the ribs are well-rounded.

Stance Standing position, usually when formally presented.

Standard The written word picture of a breed.

Stern The tail of a hound.

Stifle The joint in the hindleg between the upper and lower thigh, equating to the knee in man, sadly weak in some breeds.

Stop The depression at the junction of the nasal bone and the skull between the eyes.

Straight-hocked Lacking in angulation of the hock joint.

Straight-shouldered Straight up and down shoulder blades, lacking angulation or lay-back.

Strain A family of related dogs throwing offspring of a set type.

Symmetry Balance and correct proportions of anatomy.

Tan Rich light-brown coat colour; in hue, between bay and buckskin; a richer sorrel.

Throaty/throatiness An excess of loose skin at the front of the neck.

Tied at the elbows When the elbows are set too close under the body, thereby restricting freedom of movement.

Topline The dog's outline from just behind the withers to the rump.

Trot A rhythmical two-beat gait, with hind and forequarters working in unison.

Tuck-up Concave underline of torso, between last rib and hindquarters, lack of discernible belly.

Tufter Specialist hound used to locate and then rouse a stag from covert; *limier* in France.

Type Characteristic attributes distinguishing a breed or strain of a breed.

Undershot Malformation of the jaw projecting the lower jaw and incisors beyond the upper (puppies with this condition appear to be grinning).

Upper arm The foreleg bone between the shoulder blade and the elbow.

Upright shoulders Too straight an angle in the shoulder joint, also called steep in shoulders, usually giving a shortened front stride and a short-necked appearance.

Variety Subdivision of a breed.

Well-angulated Well-defined angle in the thigh-hock-metatarsus area.

Well-coupled Well made in the area from the withers to the hip bones.

Well-knit Neat and compactly constructed and connected.

Well-laid Soundly placed and correctly angled.

Well laid-back shoulders Oblique shoulders ideally slanting at 45 degrees to the ground.

Well let-down at hock Hocks close to the ground; having low hocks as a result of long muscles in what in humans is the calf. (This is an often misunderstood term; in both racehorses and sporting dogs, the seeking of long cannon bones led to the use of this expression. It was never intended to promote short rear pasterns).

Well ribbed-up Ribs neither too long nor too wide apart; compact; ribs reaching well back into flanks, with noticeable rounding.

Well-sprung With noticeably rounded ribs.

Well tucked-up Absence of visible abdomen.

Wheel back Excessive roaching; marked arching over the loins.

Wire-haired A coat of bristly crispness to the touch, hard in texture.

Withers The highest point on the body of a standing dog, immediately behind the neck, above the shoulders.

Yawing (crabbing) Body moving at an angle to the legs' line of movement.

BIBLIOGRAPHY

Acton, C.R., *The Foxhound of the Future* (Baylis & Sons, 1953)

Adams, E. (ed.), *Deer, Hare & Otter Hunting*, Lonsdale Library Vol. XXII (Seeley, Service & Co., 1936)

Alderton, D., *Hounds of the World* (Swan Hill, 2000)

de Almeida, A., *Jaguar Hunting in the Mato Grosso and Bolivia* (1976)

Almond, R., *Medieval Hunting* (Sutton, 2003)

Anderson, J.K., *Hunting in the Ancient World* (Univ. of California, 1985)

Appleton, Douglas H., *The Bloodhound Handbook* (Nicholson & Watson, 1960)

Apsley, Lady, *Bridleways through History* (Hutchinson, 1936)

The Badminton Magazine of Sports and Pastimes, 1902

Baldwin, W., *African Hunting and Adventure from Natal to the Zambesi from 1852 to 1860* (Richard Bentley, 1863)

Barton, Frank Townend, MRCVS, *Hounds* (Long, 1913)

Bathurst, Earl, *The Breeding of Foxhounds* (1926)

Beckford, P., *Thoughts on Hunting* (1781)

Berkeley, G., *A Month in the Forests of France* (1857)

Beaufort, Duke of, and Morris, M., *Hunting* (Longmans, Green & Co., 1894)

Billett, M., *A History of English Country Sports* (Hale, 1994)

Bingham-Hull, D., *Hounds and Hunting in Ancient Greece* (1964)

Blaine, D.B., *The Encyclopaedia of Rural Sports* (1870)

Bradley, C., *Fox-Hunting from Shire to Shire* (Routledge, 1912)

Brander, M., *Hunting and Shooting* (Weidenfeld & Nicolson, 1971)

Brander, M., *The Hunting Instinct* (Oliver & Boyd, 1964)

Brewer, D., Clark, T. & Phillips, A., *Dogs in Antiquity, Anubis to Cerberus* (Aris & Phillips Ltd, 2001)

Bryden, H.A., *Hare Hunting and Harriers* (Grant Richards, 1903)

Buchanan-Jardine, Sir J., *Hounds of the World* (Grayling Books, 1937)

Budgett, H.M., *Hunting by Scent* (1933)

Butler, A.J., *Sport in Classic Times* (Ernest Benn, 1931)

van Bylandt, H., *Dogs of all Nations* (1904)

Caius, Dr, *Of English Dogs* (1576)

Carr, R., *English Fox Hunting – A History* (Weidenfeld & Nicolson, 1976)

Chalmers, P., *The History of Hunting* (Seeley, Service & Co., 1936)

Clapham, R., *The Book of the Otter* (1928)

Clapham, R., *Foxes, Foxhounds and Fox-hunting* (Heath Cranton Ltd, 1928)

Clark, T. and Derhalli, M., *On Hunting (Al-Mansur's book)* (Aris & Phillips Ltd, 2001)

Clark, D. and Stainer, J., *Medical and Genetic Aspects of Purebred Dogs* (Forum, 1994)

Cole Robert W., *An Eye for a Dog* (Dogwise Publishing, USA, 2004)

Cone, Carl B., (ed.), *Hounds in the Morning* (Univ. Press of Kentucky, 1981)

Courtney Williams, A., *Beagles, their History & Breeding* (Grayling Books, 1974)

Coughlan, J., *Hound Trailing – A History of the Sport in Cumbria* (Coughlan, 1980)

Couteulx de Canteleu, Comte le, *La Venerie Française* (1858)

Cox, Major H., *Dogs and I* (1924)

Croxton Smith, A., *British Dogs* (Collins, 1945)

Croxton Smith, A., *Hounds & Dogs*, Lonsdale Library Vol. XIII (Seeley, Service & Co.,1932)

Croxton Smith, A., *Sporting Dogs* (Country Life, 1938)

Cummins, J., *The Hawk and the Hound: The Art of Medieval Hunting* (Weidenfeld & Nicolson, 1988)

Dalby, David, *Lexicon of the Medieval German Hunt* (Gruyter, 1965)

Dalziel, H., *British Dogs* (1881)

Daniel, Rev. W.B., *Rural Sports* (Bunny & Gold, 1801)

Davies, C.J., *The Theory and Practice of Breeding to Type* (Our Dogs, 1952)

Delme Radcliffe, E.P., *The Noble Science – A Few General Ideas on Fox-Hunting* (Routledge, 1911)

Dixon, W.S., *Hunting in the Olden Days* (Constable, 1912)

Dogs in Canada, Nov 1996

Dog World, Nov 2012

Drury W.D., *British Dogs* (Upcott Gill, 1903)

Drury, W.D., *The Twentieth Century Dog* (1904)

Dubois, Rene, *So Human an Animal: How we are Shaped by Surrounding and Events* (Scribner & Sons, New York, 1968)

Duffey, D.M., *Hunting Hounds* (Winchester Press, New York, 1972)

Edwards, L., *Famous Foxhunters* (Eyre & Spottiswoode, 1932)

The Foxhound magazine, 1910, 1911

Fiennes, R. and A., *The Natural History of the Dog* (Weidenfeld & Nicolson, 1968)

Frederick, C. (ed.), *Fox-hunting*, Lonsdale Library Vol. VII (Seeley, Service and Co., 1930)

Free, Roger, *Beagle and Terrier* (1946)

Friedman, Mira M., *Hunting Scenes in the Art of the Middle Ages and the Renaissance*, Vol. 2 (Tel Aviv Univ., 1978)

Gilbert, J.M, *Hunting and Hunting Reserves in Medieval Scotland* (John Donald, 1979)

Gilbey, Sir Walter, *Hounds in Old Days* (1913; SPC reprint 1979)

Goss, F., *Memories of a Stag Harbourer* (Witherby, 1931)

Graham, Joseph A., *The Sporting Dog* (Macmillan, and Norwood Press, USA, 1904)

Griffin, *Blood Sport – Hunting in Britain since 1066* (Yale, 2007)

Harrison, W., *Description of England* (1586)

Hartig, G.L., *Lexikon für Jäger und Jagdfreunde (Lexicon for Hunters and Friends of the Hunt)* (1836)

Hartley, O., *Hunting Dogs* (Harding, Ohio, 1909)

Hindle, D., *The Hunting Basset* (Hindle & Hounds Magazine, 2009)

Higginson, A. Henry, *Foxhunting – Theory and Practice* (Collins, 1948)

Hore, J.P., *The History of the Royal Buckhounds* (Remington & Co., 1893)

Horner, Tom, *All About the Bull Terrier* (Pelham Books, 1973)

Hounds magazine, Dec 1987, Dec 1989, 1991, Dec 1994, Dec 1995, 2004, Nov 2012

Hutchinson, W.N., *Dog Breaking* (1909)

Ivester Lloyd, J., *Hounds of Britain* (A&C Black, 1973)

Ivester Lloyd, T., *Hounds* (Hutchinson & Co., 1934)

Jardine, Sir W., *The Naturalist's Library*, Vol. X (1840)

Jesse, G., *Researches into the History of the British Dog* (Robert Hardwicke, 1866)

Jobson-Scott, Dr D., OBE, MC, MD, Ch. B, *Beagling for Beginners* (Hutchinson, 1933)

Johnson, T.B., *The Sportsman's Cyclopedia* (1831)

Johnston, G., *The Basset Hound* (Popular Dogs, 1968)

Johnston, G. and Ericson, M., *Hounds of France* (Spur Publications, 1979)

Kaleski, R., *Australian Barkers and Biters* (1914)

Kennel Gazette, Mar 1888

Lee, R.B., *Modern Dogs*, Sporting Division Vol. I (1897)

Leighton, R., *Dogs and All About Them* (1914)

Leighton, R., *New Book of the Dog* (Cassell, 1912)

Letts, M., *Memories of My Life at the College Valley* (Trafford, 2012)

Link, V. and and Skerritt, L., *Petit Basset Griffon Vendeen – a definitive study* (Doral, USA, 1999)

Longrigg, R., *The English Squire and his Sport* (Michael Joseph, 1977)

Lovell Hewitt, W., *Beagling* (Faber & Faber, 1960)

Lowe, B., *Hunting the Clean Boot* (Blandford, 1981)

MacKenzie, M., *Great Danes – Past and Present* (Our Dogs, 1928)

Marples, T., *Show Dogs* (c.1920)

Mason, J., *The Eskdale and Ennerdale Foxhounds: The History of a Lakeland Pack*, (Merlin Unwin, 2005)

Miller, W.H., *The American Hunting Dog* (George Doran, New York, 1919)

Moore, D., *Foxhounds* (Batsford, 1981)

Moore, D., *In Nimrod's Footsteps* (1974)

Nimrod, *The Life of a Sportsman* (Methuen & Co., 1903)

Noakes, A., *Sportsmen in a Landscape* (The Bodley Head, 1954)

Onstott, K., *The Art of Breeding Better Dogs* (Denlinger, 1947)

Paget, J.O., *Hunting* (J.M. Dent & Co., 1900)

Phillips, A.A., and Willcock, M.M., *On Hunting with Hounds, Xenophon & Arrian*, (Aris & Phillips Ltd, 1999)

Phoebus, G., Comte de Foix, *Livre de Chasse (The Hunting Book)* (1387)

Recum von, A.F., *Hunting with Hounds in North America* (Pelican, 2002)

Ribblesdale, Lord, *The Queen's Hounds and Stag-Hunting Recollections* (Longman, Green & Co., 1897)

Ritchie, C.I.A., *The British Dog* (Robert Hale, 1981)

Rycroft, Sir N., *Rycroft on Hounds, Hunting and Country*, edited by J.F. Scharnberg (The Derrydale Press, USA, 2001)

'Sabretache', *Monarchy and the Chase* (Eyre, 1944)

Salisbury, N., *The History of the Coniston Foxhounds 1825–1925* (Ryelands, 2008)

Schebesta, P., *My Pygmy and Negro Hosts* (1897)

'Scrutator', *Recollections of a Foxhunter* (Hurst & Blackett, 1861)

Serrell, A., *With Hound and Terrier* (Blackwood, 1904)

Shaw, V., *The Illustrated Book of the Dog* (1879)

Shelley, E.M., *Hunting Big Game with Dogs in Africa* (1924)

Simpson, Charles, *The Harboro' Country* (The Bodley Head, 1927)

Smythe, R.H., *The Anatomy of Dog Breeding* (Popular Dogs, 1962)

Smythe, R.H., *The Conformation of the Dog* (Popular Dogs, 1957)

Smythe, R.H., *The Dog: Structure and Movement* (Foulsham & Co., 1970)

Smythe, R.H., *The Mind of the Dog* (1958)

Somervile, W., *The Chase* (1735)

Soman, W.V., *The Indian Dog* (Popular Prakashan, 1963)

The Sportsman's Cabinet or a correct delineation of the Canine Race (Cundee, 1803)

Stables, Gordon, *Our Friend the Dog* (Dean & Son, 1907)

Stephens, W., *Gundog Sense and Sensibility* (Pelham Books, 1982)

Stephens, W., *The Farmer's Book of Field Sports* (Vista Books, 1961)

'Stonehenge', *The Dog* (1867)

'Stonehenge', *Dogs of the British Isles* (1878)

Suffolk, Earl of, *The Encyclopaedia of Sport* (Lawrence & Bullen Ltd, 1897)

Swan, J.A., *The Sacred Art of Hunting: Myths, Legends and Modern Mythos* (Willow Creek Press, 1999)

Thomas, J.B., *Hounds and Hunting through the Ages* (Garden City, New York, 1937)

Tongue, C., *The Foxhound Studbook* (1866)

Turbervile, *Book of Hunting* (1576)

Turner, J. Sidney (ed.), *The Kennel Encyclopaedia* (1907)

Vezins, Comte Elie de, *Hounds for a Pack* (1882; translated by J.A. Allen, 1974)

Wallace, R., *A Manual of Foxhunting*, edited by Michael Clayton (Swan Hill Press, 2003)

Walton, I., *The Compleat Angler* (1653)

Watson, J., *The Dog Book* (1906)

Watson, J.N.P., *The Book of Foxhunting* (Batsford, 1977)

Webb, H. (ed.), *Dogs, their Whims, Instincts and Peculiarities* (1883)

Whitney, L.F., *How to Breed Dogs* (Orange Judd, 1947)

Whitney, L. and Underwood, A., *The Coon Hunter's Handbook* (Field & Stream, Holt, New York, 1952)

Wentworth Day, J., *The Dog in Sport* (Harrap, 1938)

Willis, M. *Practical Genetics for Dog Breeders* (Witherby, 1992)

Wimhurst, C.G.E., *The Book of the Hound* (Muller, 1964).

Wilson, Dr B., *A Bother of Bassets – A History of the Working Basset* (Denny Publishing, 2004)

Wynn, M.B., *The History of the Mastiff* (1886)

'Yoi-Over', *Hold Hard! Hounds, Please!* (Witherby, 1924)

York, Edward Duke of, *The Master of Game* (1406), edited by W.A. and F. Baillie-Grohman (Chatto & Windus, 1909)

Mutual affection.

INDEX